# awakened hearts

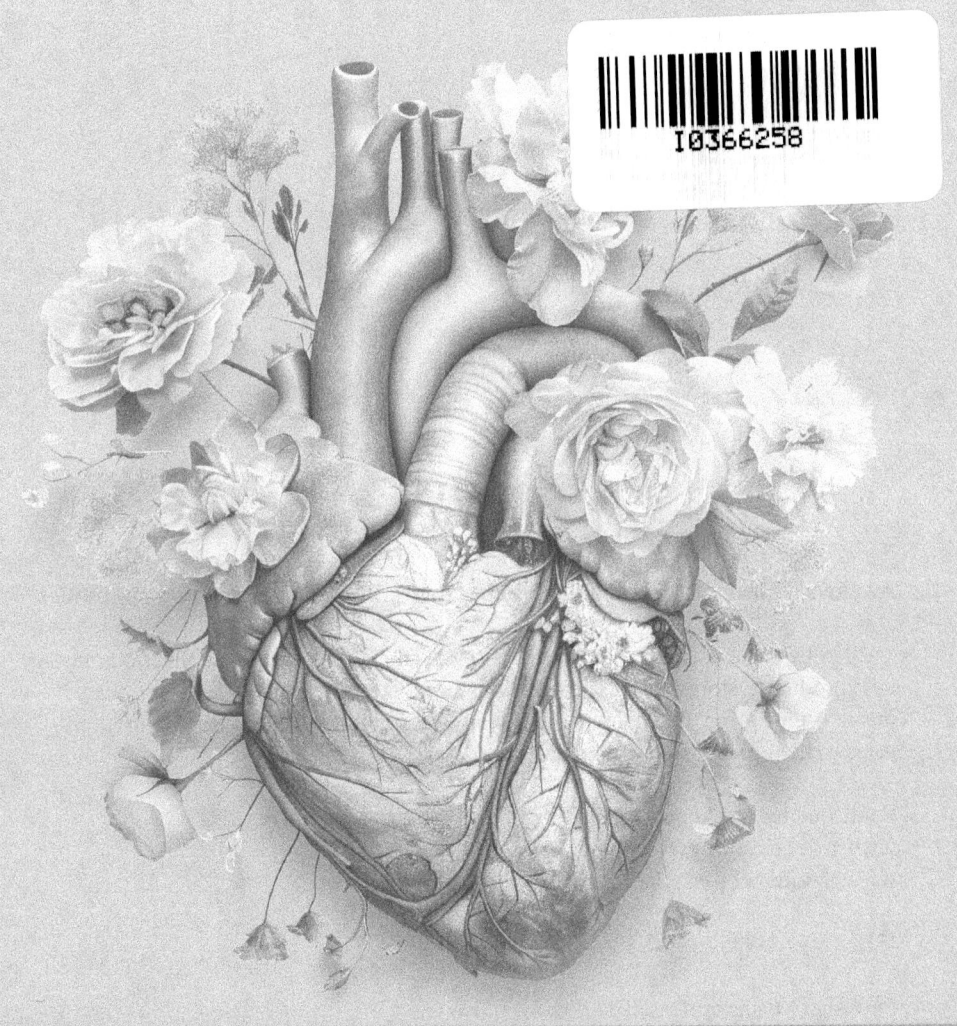

STORIES OF EMBRACING LIGHT,
LOVE, AND LIMITLESS POSSIBILITIES

**Awakened Hearts: Stories of Embracing Light, Love, and Limitless Possibilities**

© 2025 by Awakened Media. All rights reserved. No part of this publication may be reproduced, stored in a retrieval system, or transmitted in any form or by any means—electronic, mechanical, photocopy, recording, or otherwise—without the prior written permission of the publisher.

Published by Awakened Media
www.awakenedmagazine.com
www.awakened.lifestyle

ISBN: 978-1-935798-23-1

Publisher / Curator: David Trotter
Cover design: Julia Burtseva and Andrew O. Malbas
Cover image: Berit Kessler. Licensed via Adobe Stock
Interior design and layout: Julia Burtseva
Editors: Tracey Regan and Chelsea Wilcox

For permissions or bulk orders, contact: hello@awakenedmagazine.com

*To you — the seekers, the dreamers, and the brave hearts:*
*May you always remember who you truly are...*
*Light, love, and limitless possibility.*

# awakened magazine

**Awakened Magazine** is a leading resource for soulful storytelling, conscious living, and transformative wisdom from today's most inspiring healers, coaches, and spiritual leaders.

Subscribe for free:
www.awakenedmagazine.com

**Awakened Lifestyle** is your go-to directory to discover conscious events, healers, and podcast opportunities—locally and globally.

Explore listings or add your own:
www.awakened.lifestyle

**Awakened Hearts** is a series of heart-opening anthology books featuring real stories of spiritual awakening, healing, and transformation.

Share your story:
www.awakenedheartsbook.com

*We're here to support you on your awakening journey!*

# Section I: The Awakening Begins

| | |
|---|---|
| 01. Happy for No Reason – Marci Shimoff | 10 |
| 02. Awaken the Purpose Within – Karen Weaver | 20 |
| 03. Remember Who You Are – Dixie Willis | 26 |
| 04. The Quiet Return to Myself – Dinah Simpson | 36 |
| 05. The Sacred Alchemy of Purpose: Awakening to My Soul Mission – Lauren Dickinson | 46 |
| 06. Reclaiming This Body and Becoming HER – Michele Marie Neyers | 56 |
| 07. The Six Heart Illuminations: How Divine Love Transformed My Life's Path – Jennifer R Dickens | 68 |
| 08. One Spark, Collective Flame – From Inner Power to Uplifting Humanity – Tiffani Churchill | 78 |

# Section II: From Shadows to Healing

| | |
|---|---|
| 09. The Courage to Feel – Natasha Davidson | 90 |
| 10. The Choice That Changed Everything – Michelle Hays | 100 |
| 11. The Unseen Hand: Whispered Prayers and the Power of Belief – Ida Ra Nalbandian | 110 |
| 12. Whispers of the Heart: A Ten-Year-Old's Path to Healing – Deborah Kane | 120 |
| 13. Off the Roller-Coaster of Pain and Into the Light – Ragan Thomson | 130 |
| 14. The Journey to My Heart – Laura Muirhead | 140 |
| 15. No Hair. No Mask. Just Me. A Radical Reclamation of Self-Worth and Truth – Sara Hunter | 150 |
| 16. Anchored in Earth, Ascending in Spirit: The Tightrope Between Two Worlds – John Klug | 160 |

## Section III: Breaking Open, Breaking Free

| | |
|---|---|
| 17. **Shattered Innocence: A Child of War** – Toni Ghazi | 172 |
| 18. **Streetwise and Soul-led: From Surviving to Rewiring**<br>– Shannon Shade | 180 |
| 19. **Finding Heaven on Earth After Living Through Hell** – Martin Lewis | 190 |
| 20. **Don't Fall Asleep Now: The Dream That Changed Everything**<br>– Marlu Harris | 200 |
| 21. **Journey in Becoming an African Violet** – Gretta Chamberlain | 212 |
| 22. **Connecting the Spiritual Dots** – Sandi Duverneuil | 222 |
| 23. **A Rainbow Rises Beyond the Darkest Wave of Grief**<br>– Ellie Epstein-White | 232 |
| 24. **Divine Whispers** – Julie Wasmer | 242 |

## Section IV: Embodying the Light

| | |
|---|---|
| 25. **A Visitor Among Us! – Journal of an ET Being** – Viviane Chauvet | 254 |
| 26. **Called Upon by Heaven: My 'Miraculous Awakening Experience'**<br>– Oracle Maureen | 262 |
| 27. **Bahamas: A Journey of Healing and Awakening**<br>– Cristina Valle-Parke | 274 |
| 28. **Death: A Doorway to Love** – Nina Palmieri | 284 |
| 29. **Hotel Bedouin** – Guru Matthew John | 294 |
| 30. **Invited to Remember** – Christina L. Woods | 306 |
| 31. **Inner Rebirth: How I Rediscovered My Strength and Life's Purpose**<br>– Victoria Basil | 318 |
| 32. **Rising From Hell and the Infinite Power in Our Bodies**<br>– Desi Dimitrova | 328 |

# We are living in a time of great awakening.

The veil between the ordinary and the extraordinary is thinner than ever, and more people are remembering who they truly are...spiritual beings having a human experience.

After launching *Awakened Magazine*, I started hearing hundreds of stories of awakening, and I began to dream about putting these extraordinary narratives in your hands so that you could be inspired to keep awakening as well.

For most of us, awakening is rarely a single, life-altering moment. It often unfolds through a series of experiences that awaken our hearts...each one arriving at just the perfect time.

In our first *Awakened Hearts* anthology, 32 courageous souls share deeply personal stories of transformation, healing, and awakening. These aren't just stories. They are mirrors for our soul, reflecting back to you the light and love that has always lived within you. Some authors broke free from religious boxes. Others navigated grief, trauma, or spiritual disconnection. All emerged with a new understanding of who they are and why they're here.

We envision a world where everyone is awakened to Love. We believe...

You come from Love.
You are healed by Love.
You express yourself most fully when you Love yourself and others.

Most simply...you are Love.

**David Trotter**
Curator / Publisher - Awakened Hearts
Co-founder / Publisher - Awakened Magazine

*P.S., If you are impacted by a particular story, please reach out to the contributor to share your thoughts or seek their support on your journey.*

# Section I:
# The Awakening Begins

- Can you remember a time when your soul whispered, "There's more than this"?

- What experience first invited you to question the life you were told to live?

- What does it mean to "awaken"?

## chapter 01

# Happy For No Reason

*by Marci Shimoff*

By June of 1998, I had achieved the major things I'd set out to accomplish in life!

Almost two decades earlier, when I was in my early twenties, I had set five goals for myself, figuring that once I'd achieved those goals, I'd finally have the happiness that I'd deeply longed for as a child:

- ✓ A successful career helping people.
- ✓ A wonderful husband/life partner.
- ✓ Fabulous friends.
- ✓ A comfortable home.
- ✗ The equivalent of Halle Berry's body.

*(While I didn't have a body like Halle Berry's, I'd grown to love and appreciate the healthy body I had!)*

After years of hard work to fulfill these goals, I should have been on top of the world!

Three of the *Chicken Soup for the Woman's Soul* books that I co-authored were in the top five on the *New York Times* bestseller list... at the same time! I'd just given a speech to an enthusiastic audience of eight thousand people, gotten a rousing standing ovation, and signed 5,432 copies of my books. My client had even hired a massage therapist to massage my hand every fifteen minutes so I could keep autographing.

I felt like an author "rock star."

But after autographing that last book, I rode back to my hotel in the limo my client had hired and went up to the penthouse suite my client had gotten for me. I immediately walked over to the huge window overlooking Lake Michigan, took in the magnificent view, then collapsed on the bed and burst into tears.

Despite what I'd achieved, I still felt the deep emptiness in my heart that I'd felt as a child. I realized that I could no longer fool myself into thinking that just one more success would bring me the lasting happiness I so yearned for.

I made a commitment to myself, right there and then: I was going to finally figure out what it took to be truly, deeply happy.

## Discovering Meditation, Manifestation and My Life Vision

You see, I was born depressed. I came out of the womb with existential angst and it stayed with me throughout my childhood. (I've since come to believe that the angst was either based in ancestral trauma or past-life PTSD.)

I was a spiritual seeker from the get-go, always asking my parents about the meaning of life. "Tell me about God," I would often say, and though they did their best to give me answers, I never felt satisfied.

One day, in the eighth grade, I did something I'd never done before – I asked my mom if I could stay home from school. "Are you sick?" she asked. I wasn't sick, but for some odd reason, I felt compelled to stay home. Because it was so out of character, she agreed.

I sat on my parents' bed to watch TV, as theirs was the only bedroom that had a TV in it. (It was 1971.) I turned on the TV to a channel we had never gotten before, and on the air was *The Phil Donahue Show*, a popular talk show at that time. Phil's guest that day was a small Indian man in a white robe sitting cross-legged on a couch – his name was Maharishi Mahesh Yogi, the founder of Transcendental Meditation.

As soon as Maharishi began speaking, I was captivated. Before long, he had answered many of the existential questions I'd been asking. *I'm not alone. There are answers.* I knew why I'd been compelled to stay home from school that day. After the show ended, I wrote down the name of his book: *The Science of Being and Art of Living,* and I called every bookstore and library in my hometown of San Mateo,

California, to get a copy. Nobody had it, so I stuffed away that little piece of paper into my desk drawer and soon forgot about it.

A few years later, when I was a junior in high school, I was walking through downtown San Mateo and saw a poster with Maharishi's picture and a quote of his, *"Life is here to enjoy."* I certainly loved that idea and remembered how much I had appreciated all he'd said on TV years earlier, so the next day, I went to the introductory lecture that was advertised on the poster. I learned how to meditate that weekend, and it was the first thing that truly changed my life – and one of many synchronicities I'd encounter that would shape my life's direction.

Around that same time, a friend's mother took us to see the motivational speaker, Zig Ziglar. As Zig walked back and forth across the stage, inspiring the whole crowd, I knew what I wanted to do with my life – I saw myself traveling around the world, speaking on big stages, and inspiring people to see what was possible in their lives. It was a clear vision of my future! When I got home, I told my parents, "I'm going to be an inspirational speaker." It was a shock for them. My father was a dentist and they wanted me to be a dental hygienist – because that's what *girls* did back then! In true *Mom style* though, she quickly added, "Well, honey, you sure love talking – you might as well get paid for it."

I later went on to college at Maharishi International University, where *everyone* – the staff, faculty and students – meditated twice a day. Meditating regularly profoundly impacted me then and continues to this day, fifty years later.

To bring my vision of being a speaker to life, I followed one breadcrumb after another. I immersed myself in both spiritual teachings and success practices. I got my MBA from UCLA and found a job where I was responsible for training and inspiring employees – and even got to share with them the success attitudes and actions I was so passionate about. I went on to work as a corporate trainer, delivering communication skills and stress management programs to Fortune 500 companies.

To continue honing my skills, I hired a coach to help me with my career. He introduced me to his three-part formula for manifesting, which was:

*Intention – Attention – No Tension*

*Intention:* Be clear about what you want.

*Attention:* Put your thoughts, words, feelings and actions behind your intentions.

*No Tension:* Relax, trust and let go.

I've successfully used this formula many times and have also taught it to others. I've found that most people are really good at one of the steps, okay at another and not very good at the third. I was always good at having a clear intention and putting my attention on my dreams with my thoughts, words, feelings and a LOT of action. The step I struggled with was *No Tension*, which is all about letting go.

My work as a trainer continued to grow, and soon I was speaking all over the country, which I loved – but I really wanted to start teaching self-esteem courses for women. (It's said that we teach what we most want to learn.) Jack Canfield, who was then a top self-esteem expert, became my mentor. (This was years before he came up with the idea of *Chicken Soup for the Soul*.)

Day after day, city after city, I would teach for eight hours to rooms of fifty to one hundred women at a time before getting in the car to drive another three to four hours to my next day's engagement. I was a road warrior. And, I was burning myself out!

One day, a dear friend of mine came to me with concern. She said I looked awful and that I needed to take a break, so she invited me to go with her on a seven-day silent meditation retreat. I joked that I hadn't been silent for more than two hours in my life and that would be impossible! But she was very persuasive and a few weeks later, off I went with her into silence.

Spending the retreat without the distraction of conversation and meditating for many hours a day finally allowed me to move into that state of *no tension* I'd always struggled with.

And then, on the fourth day of the retreat, during one of my meditations, a light bulb went off and I saw the words flash in my mind, *Chicken Soup for the Woman's Soul*. At the time, only the first *Chicken Soup for the Soul* book had been released – and nobody had thought of any specialty books. I knew in my heart that this was exactly what I was meant to do and what would propel me onto the world stages I had seen in my vision as a teenager. Although I was thrilled by the idea, I had to keep it to myself for the next three days of the retreat. As soon as the silence was over, I ran to the closest pay phone and called Jack with my idea. "Oh my God, I can't believe nobody's thought of it," he said. He called the publisher who said those exact same words.

We worked together to create the book that I'd envisioned and it soared straight to number one on the *New York Times* bestseller list the week it was released. I went on to co-write six more *Chicken Soup for the Soul* books. But by 2003, after the seventh book, I was done! While there was still money to be made, I couldn't bring myself to write another *Chicken Soup* book, and my inner voice shouted at me to move on.

**From Chicken Soup to Happiness**

A seed had been planted in me back in 1998 when I'd made the commitment to discover what it takes to be *unconditionally happy*. So I began speaking with every researcher I knew on the subject of happiness. I tracked down and interviewed one hundred happy people. I started doing what they did, noticing some very dramatic shifts in my own experience of happiness. I had to share what I was learning! It was in meditation, again, that I came up with the name for my book: *Happy for No Reason.*

*Happy for No Reason,* which I co-authored with my best friend since college, was published in 2008 in thirty-three languages and has met with wonderful success. I'm so grateful that it's helped people all over the world experience deep and lasting happiness.

*So,* what does it mean to be "unconditionally happy"?

In my research, I found that there's a "continuum of happiness." On one end of the continuum is NO happiness or unhappiness. We know what that is all too well. Sadly, there's an epidemic of unhappiness in our society these days, with one in four women in America being treated for depression.

The next stop on the continuum is being happy for BAD reason – which means trying to find happiness through unhealthy means: *I feel bad and I want to feel better, so I'm going to use addictions/overeating/drugs to get "there."* And these self-destructive behaviors lead to anything but true happiness.

Next is being happy for GOOD reason. This type of happiness is based on specific positive outcomes: *I'll be happy when... I have a good job, I have money, I have good friends and a nice house.* The only problem wrong with this kind of happiness is that it's unstable and dependent on circumstances.

So what's the other option?... You can be *Happy for NO Reason.*

This is unconditional happiness: *an inner state of peace and wellbeing that doesn't depend on circumstances.*

When you're happy for no reason, you *bring* happiness to your outer experiences rather than trying to *extract* happiness from them. You don't need to control the world around you to try to make yourself happy. You live *from* happiness, rather than *for* happiness.

In my research, I also discovered that we each have a *happiness set point* – like the setting on a thermostat. When good things happen to you, you feel happy, and when setbacks happen, you feel unhappy, but soon your happiness level returns to your original happiness set point. The good news is that you can raise your happiness set point by cultivating *Happiness Habits* – the twenty-one habits I discovered in my research that unconditionally happy people have in common.

When I share the expression *happy for no reason* with people around the world, it seems to strike a deep chord. We know intuitively that our innermost essence is happiness. You don't have to create it – it's who you are. Through practicing the happiness habits, you can return to that state.

It took what felt like a lifetime for me to find my own Happiness for No Reason, but there was more in store... in the most recent years, I've found myself living in what I've come to call "the Miracle Zone."

**Living in the Miracle Zone**

Around 2013, I noticed I was waking up every morning with a rush of gratitude; a feeling that I was *in the flow* – almost impossible to describe. Opportunities were coming out of the blue. I was lunching with amazing people I never imagined meeting. Synchronicities were happening every day. I was in that place I call the Miracle Zone, and since then, I've been helping people move into the Miracle Zone too.

Most of us are in a very deep and habitual pattern of creating and living from our fear-based egos. But, miracles, love and all possibilities are in the realm of the soul. To live in the Miracle Zone, we need to allow ourselves to dream from the soul (without knowing "how" our miracles will come to be).

When you're taking action on an ego-based intention, the journey can be full of struggle. When you're operating from a soul-based intention, you get in the flow of universal energy. You still take action, following one breadcrumb after another, and you're open to a greater force that allows things to happen with ease. The path is paved with grace, and miracles begin to reveal themselves... over and over.

I look back on my journey and see now that I've been following my soul intentions at every turn. I didn't know it, but my soul has been guiding me to the Miracle Zone all along.

Ultimately, I think we're all here to learn how to move from living in the vibration of fear to living in the vibration of love.

I'm often asked if it's selfish to focus on living a happy and miraculous life... but honestly, it is the least selfish thing we can do, because when we shift into living in the vibration of love, we impact the people around us, too.

So, if you've ever felt that it's selfish to live the life of your dreams, I'd like to leave you with this beautiful Chinese proverb:

*"When there is light in the soul, there will be beauty in the person. When there is beauty in the person, there will be harmony in the house. When there is harmony in the house, there will be order in the nation And when there is order in the nation, there will be peace in the world."*

May we each experience the light in our souls, the love in our hearts, and through that, may we, together, bring greater peace to our world!

# Marci Shimoff

Marci Shimoff is a #1 *New York Times* bestselling author, world-renowned transformational teacher, and expert on happiness, success, and unconditional love. Her international bestsellers include *Happy for No Reason* and *Love for No Reason*, and she co-authored six books in the *Chicken Soup for the Woman's Soul* series. With over 16 million books sold in 33 languages, she is among the bestselling female nonfiction authors of all time.

A featured teacher in *The Secret*, host of the PBS show *Happy for No Reason*, and narrator of the award-winning film *Happy*, Marci shares her wisdom worldwide through keynotes, seminars, and her mentoring program *Your Year of Miracles*. Her opening seminar has reached more than 200,000 people.

She holds an MBA from UCLA and a certification in stress management, and is a founding board member of the Transformational Leadership Council. Through her books and teaching, Marci continues to inspire millions to live empowered, joyful lives.

🌐 www.happyfornoreason.com
🌐 www.youryearofmiracles.com
Scan QR code to learn more about Marci Shimoff.

chapter

# 02

# Awaken the Purpose Within

*by Karen Weaver*

I distinctly remember my awakening journey. It happened when I moved to Australia from Ireland. Wisdoms started to flow through me, and I felt a call to write. My perspective changed, and I began to see things wider and deeper. I was being called to do things and started to see signs. This was really interesting for me as a mum of four, one just a new baby.

But the real catalyst to my awakening was an epiphany I had that led to me writing my first novel in thirty days. What really stood out to me were the signs I just couldn't ignore; the inspired thoughts were so profoundly intense.

They called for me to give them a voice... so I did and I *showed up*. And in November 2010, I wrote my first novel, *The Visitor*. The irony of it all was that I was not good at English in school; it certainly wasn't my favourite subject. I never imagined I would ever be a writer, though I did go on to study it later in my humanities degree. When the call happened, I wrote a fifty-thousand-word novel... and it changed my life.

But more important than that was the awakening I experienced. I was writing articles for a website called *Building Beautiful Bonds,* before Facebook really kicked off, and they had a platform with a chat environment, where I would share my *mindful* musings with the people in there. Although it was a bit of a surprise to me, they just loved them so much, they asked for more. It totally lit me up to share the wisdoms that would just come through me – I don't think I could write like that now! But I honored the calling and poured these musings and articles out into the world, that were mostly between five to seven hundred words long.

And as I was submitting them, the person who owned the website acknowledged how they were filled with such profound insights. When I read them today, it just blows my socks off, the things that were coming through. I believe this sort of thing happens in an awakening process, whenever we start to see wider and deeper. It's a very special time that shifts us and lifts us, raising our energy.

When I was asked to become part of the team and write "official" articles for the website, I was so honored to do it. Then the articles started to get picked up by other sources, like *Universal Mind* magazine and an organisation in the Czech republic, asking for permission to share them.

This at-home-mum of four (at the time) was having her thoughts picked up and shared across the world. I could hardly believe it... *wow, I'm resonating with people.* This was what gave me the confidence to step into what I now know is my purpose, writing from my heart and soul to reach the heart and minds of those destined to read it. Because when we share our stories, when we share our wisdoms, we awaken the best in people.

It's just the most beautiful gift we can ever give to the world. So I honored it, I showed up for it and, in turn, I have been rewarded for it. I went on to have two more children (I have six), and I continued to write, now being the author of over forty books. I've also been in forty-six anthologies, just like this one. I am continually amazed at how the power of story can reach, connect and heal.

With that in mind, I want to go back and share another powerful story that happened during my awakening. I had been having heart palpitations and thought there was something very wrong with my body. I went to the doctor and they put me on a heart monitor for two days to discover more about the palpitations I was having. I was getting a big rush of energy along with the palpitations and of course, being human, I went to the worst-case scenario; that's one of the things that humans do, right?

When the test results came back, everything was fine. But the "rushes" would come and go, and I was concerned. Looking back, I think my heart was just so *activated*. I was invited to go to a meditation with a friend, which was a big deal at the time, as I never let myself do anything other than take care of my family, being the primary caregiver, and as we'd just immigrated to a new country, I had never really left them.

So this was a big deal for me to go to this meditation, but I wondered if it might help my palpitations. There were just four of us and we were in someone's home... it felt really weird and uncomfortable – though I've never been a great meditator; writing is my meditation.

I remember sitting there, trying to get comfortable when they put on a CD of an oriental guy, which I found hard to understand, but I just went with it and allowed it to happen. During that meditation, he brought us through ourselves; from our mind, on down into our body and toes and then back up, landing in our heart. And my heart started to do the palpitations. Importantly, what he was talking about was love – deep, profound love – and how it activates within us and how that energy field is so powerful. What kept coming through was how love is a super fuel... for everything... and how you can use that energy.

My heart was truly reverberating and I could feel the energy just beaming and pulsating from me. I was completely in awe, (and a little afraid) but I stuck with it and stayed in my chair, exuding love energy.

After the meditation, I opened up my eyes and everyone was just staring at me. *And I was like,* "What?" *And they were like*, "What happened to you?" They could feel the energy radiating from me. They wanted me to tell them what happened, but I had no idea. I still thought I had something wrong with my heart.

But after another few days on the heart monitor, I realised it was just *love...* and love was beaming from me. I had somehow activated my love core and it just vibrated. I realised that whenever we use love as a super fuel, we can make amazing things happen.

That was when I realised that the answer is LOVE... and I wrote from that place. Since then, (amazingly) I have been able to access that love as a sacred field for success in all of the things I do and put into life.

Later, in that meditation, everyone was sitting around and we had to take a piece of each other's jewellery and hold it in our hands to see what came through. As I held the jewellery, my ear began to ache really badly. There was pain inside, as if my eardrum was about to burst. I didn't know the person whose jewellery I had, but she asked, "What came through, Karen?"

I told her, "I have the worst pain in my ear. I actually have to put this bracelet down because it's stabbing my eardrum. It feels as if it's about to explode."

The pain was horrendous. The woman said, "Oh, my goodness. My grandson, who is staying with me, has been complaining about a sore ear. He's only young, and today we discovered that he has a bad ear infection." I had just been reading Louise Hay's *You Can Heal Your Life* so I suggested she look at the spiritual reasoning behind the eardrum and to say an affirmation for him, along with the medicine he'd been given.

It was just such a profound experience. And these things have continued happening throughout my life since because I began to see wider and deeper into everything. I feel into it before I react. I love and project onto my children how *love will conquer all*, and it helps us to get through the hardest times. So, my awakening has now led me to huge experiences. It's led me to experience the best of life and to continue to show up for it.

So here's to an awakened life, joining others on their journey, so they can feel supported. Because *awakening* can unsteady the ground beneath you. It can make you feel like you're going insane, as it goes against the expected *norms* of humanity. Do you feel it too? But never forget, in this great awakening we are having and the shift in consciousness that the world is going through right now, *we can choose*.

We can choose to positively show up for ourselves and take control of our thoughts and our actions. Or we can choose to stay behind and stay in the negative. I know what I choose... but it does take effort.

But if we show up every day and awaken our minds, pouring positive thoughts into life, positive things will happen. I'm so excited for you as you step forward on your awakening journey.

 # Karen Weaver

K.P. Weaver is a visionary author, accomplished publisher, TEDx speaker, and motivational coach whose work centers on mindfulness, intention, love, gratitude, forgiveness, and belief. With over 40 books published across multiple genres—from motivational and spiritual literature to novels, children's books, and journals—she has inspired a global audience through the power of storytelling.

Karen is also the founder of a successful publishing company, where she helps nurture new voices while continuing to grow her own brand. Her teachings are grounded in the transformative power of "Knowing," a core concept that helps individuals align with their purpose and manifest their dreams.

Through her signature Seven life principles, Karen encourages personal growth and spiritual awakening. Her philosophy reminds us that when awareness, love, and intention come together, true magic unfolds. Her mission is to awaken those who are "asleep"—to help people remember their own power and live with clarity and purpose.

🌐 www.kpwofficial.com
Scan QR code to learn more about Karen Weaver.

chapter

# 03

# Remember Who You Are

*by Dixie Willis*

For most of my life, I've struggled to understand who I am, why I'm here and what I want to be when I grow up. I spent years earning degrees, licenses and certifications. I attended workshops, training sessions and amazing retreats. In my search for meaning and purpose in my life, I worked with a variety of people, including counselors, spiritual teachers, preachers, ministers, shamans, spiritual mediums, psychics, tarot readers, mentors and coaches.

It wasn't until much later that I realized the answers had been within me all along. For some reason, I felt someone else knew what I was supposed to do with my life and who I was supposed to be. I desperately searched outside myself, seeking answers everywhere I could, to better understand my life and purpose, everywhere except going deeply within.

As I sat in my windowless office, feeling like an exhausted caged bird, I didn't have the drive to continue working as usual after my last client that day. My routine was to jump on my laptop and write down the notes from the day's sessions, even though I had already had a full day of clients back-to-back. I worked through lunch, eating at my desk while writing notes and even ignored the need to use the restroom. I constantly pushed myself to do just a few more notes, so I wouldn't spend another weekend working. I would usually continue to push through without having the time or thought of what I needed. I wondered how I had gotten here.

I'd worked hard for many years to become a clinical counselor. As I was staring at the screen on my laptop and hoping that the notes would magically write themselves, something came over me. It's as if my soul took over and paused my drained, burned-out body. I sat back in my chair, got still and listened.

At that moment, I had a deep knowing, an awakening. I've heard of awakenings and have had experiences where I listened to my soul's guidance, and it was always the right choice. This time, it was a very clear message I could have chosen to ignore, but I didn't, and because I didn't, my life changed for the better.

It felt like time stood still, like you see in the movies. My spirit gently reminded me that I am here to continue helping people on a much larger scale, not just in Colorado, but worldwide. The focus was to inspire higher consciousness, guiding people to remember who they truly are and continue to help the planet heal. Even though it was a tall order and a broad statement, it felt right; something within me knew. I lit up, and my tired body started to feel excited! It was a knowing, the kind that goes beyond the bones and can be felt deeply in the soul. It all made so much sense, but my logical mind quickly chimed in, thinking it needed to protect me from ruining my life and career. My ego kicked in as the questions began to swirl in my head. It wanted to know how I was going to do this. *Don't I remember how hard I worked, how many years I spent writing APA papers for countless hours into the morning during grad school while going through a divorce, and let's throw in a worldwide pandemic while earning my master's degree?* It continued, *What would my clients and others think? What would this even look like? Have I lost my mind?*

I had no idea what to do next. I just knew I had to free myself and trust in the unknown. At that moment, I had a choice; I could continue to live in fear or take a leap of faith and follow the guidance I had received from my heart. The idea of being my authentic self without constraints, while continuing to help others and the planet globally, felt right, but I had to have the courage to free myself first.

I recalled attending a meditation retreat one weekend while trying to decide whether staying or leaving my profession was the right choice. My soul's guidance was to reach out to a coach I had seen speak, years ago, about letting go of fear. As it turned out, I would work with her to let go of fear of the unknown.

As a clinician, I worked with clients who shared what I was experiencing. I've heard from doctors, lawyers, therapists, engineers, preachers and military women and men, just to name a handful of the people who dreaded each day because they were either so burned out, felt trapped or simply dreaded their work or daily life. Many shared that they were doing the work of at least two, maybe even three people. They felt shame because they spent their own or their parents' money to earn a degree, only to live a life they never wanted or thought they wanted.

I could completely relate. I truly cared about my clients, but was continuously exhausted, not having the time to care for myself, no time to talk to family or friends, just work. My life became all work with no end in sight. I would stay up late doing notes, wake up early, deal with traffic, go to work, maybe run to the restroom between clients if I was lucky, work through lunch, go home and work some more, and continue working on the weekends. This was not the life I intended or wanted. After all, I was a therapist who encouraged self-care, so I had to do the same and care for myself.

With a lot of courage and fear of the unknown, I chose to leave the profession I had worked so hard for and had spent years working towards. I didn't know my next step at that moment; I just knew it was the right choice for me: to free myself and listen to the guidance from my heart and soul.

I'm not encouraging anyone to up and leave their job or career. I chose to do this and had to spend several months preparing to go. I also had some savings to help with this transition. I had no idea what I would do; all I knew was that I had to trust something that did – my soul that guided me to free myself. After I gave my notice, transferred my clients and left my cage, I reached out to the coach who had spoken years earlier about letting go of fear, who guided me to rest and take care of myself due to complete burnout.

I'd seen the incredible Dr. Wayne Dyer, Eckhart Tolle and Dr. Deepak Chopra collaborate on stage to discuss higher consciousness years ago. I didn't realize then that I would be guided to do something similar with my life. As I figured out my next steps, I was guided to listen to Wayne's book, *Inspiration: Your Ultimate Calling,* and Eckhart Tolle's book, *A New Earth: Awakening to Your Life's Purpose*. Both resonated deeply. They got it, they got me! This is similar to what my soul guided me to be in the world. Again, it was a knowing from my heart and soul. I still didn't know the "how"; I just knew it felt right.

I meditated on my next steps and received no insights for a while. At first, I was trying so hard to know the "how" and get on with it, but I learned that we can't force an answer; it comes when the time is right, in divine timing, not my own. I then decided to journal and remembered that I loved writing, even as a teenager. I made a list of all the careers, jobs and volunteer work I had done throughout my life. Although I enjoyed many careers, the one I truly loved was founding my spiritual business, which started with writing inspirational blogs and quotes. It felt natural and free. I would lose myself in the moment. I wrote from my heart and thought it was worth it if I helped just one person.

I love writing and expressing myself creatively by using my voice and words to inspire higher consciousness. Writing is how I feel like my most authentic self. When I wrote inspirational blogs in the past, I received responses from people I'd never met, who let me know they'd read a blog I'd created or a quote I shared that had helped and inspired them. This also encouraged me to keep writing from my heart.

I wrote inspirational blogs and offered healing modalities, including reiki, spiritual mediumship, angel intuitive readings and shamanic journeys through my spiritual business. I did this for five years. I loved my work; it felt natural. Unfortunately, I stopped writing and doing the other healing modalities that I loved because I started to worry about having a "real job", societal expectations, cultural norms, and being seen as "too woo-woo." Instead of staying with the life I loved, I went into fear and looked into a grad program. Although I had always been interested in being a counselor and loved helping people, I thought I needed "real" credentials and a "real" job to be taken seriously. I applied to grad school, was accepted and started the journey to become a licensed professional counselor. I continued to write for my spiritual business for a while, but my creative writing was put on hold as I started writing way too many APA papers in grad school. I earned my master's degree and worked as a counselor for several years before my awakening. I'm not saying that being a counselor is a wrong career choice for some; I know the importance of mental health and have friends and colleagues who are amazing counselors. I enjoyed working with clients when I had my private practice, but it was when I worked for a mental health company, with the expectation of seeing too many clients in a week, along with the constant paperwork, that I burned out. I truly cared for and missed my clients, but I had to take care of myself to continue to help others again, eventually, but in a different way.

As I sat on my meditation pillow and went into a deep meditation, I placed my hands over my heart. I asked if I made the right decision to leave my clinical career, and my heart and soul answered quietly yet powerfully, knowing this was the right decision for me. I already knew the answer, but this was different; I felt free and lighter, as if a heavy weight had lifted. As I cried with gratitude, released the fear of the unknown, and let go of what I thought my life should be, I embraced the unknown even more. It took me eight months to deactivate my license as a licensed professional counselor. I had spent those months earning another certification and contemplating how to follow the guidance from my soul to inspire higher consciousness into the world and help the planet heal.

Some will stay in the work they are doing if they feel there is no other way; no way out of their current life situation, job or career they find themselves in. It may be the right choice to stay for a little while if you're safe and able to save financially, consider moonlighting, volunteering or creating a tentative plan and taking a step toward your goal. Some clients who spoke about unhappiness in their careers or lives said they didn't have time to explore alternatives or try something different. What I've seen happen and what happened to me is that burnout and low mood can occur when you're overworked and may be suppressing who you are. You may not feel you have the time, money or even the right to change your life to create the life you love. So I ask you, *do you see yourself living the life you are living for another day, month or year?*

Change can be scary, but what's more frightening is not living the life you're meant to live and later looking back on your life with regret for not taking the chance. Life happens in the moment. No one knows how much time they have, so *why not start today?*

You can start with one step at a time, for example, getting up or staying up fifteen to thirty minutes more each day to start freestyle writing or making a list of anything that has brought you joy. It doesn't have to be a career or job; it can be something you love, like spending more time with like-minded people, journaling and being out in nature more. Your purpose is not just one big thing you do, and that's what you do for the rest of your life, although it can be. It's discovering what brings you joy in the moment. *What do you want? What do you love that brings you joy?*

We are spirits having a human experience, and we are here to experience life, love, joy, challenges, release fear, live from love, love ourselves, each other and the Earth, and to create the life we love. We are not alone, and our lives are meant to be joyful, with a sense of freedom to explore and experience life to the fullest. We are not meant to be robots or zombies waiting for the day or years to finally receive the award, check or retirement plan (although these are great if that's what you want). Life is meant for us to take chances; if it doesn't work out, maybe it's not meant to. Try something that lights you up.

*What lights you up? Is it a hobby you put to the side for a day, and that day becomes months, and you've never returned to it?* Think of a time in your life when you felt joy. *What were you doing or being?* Life is meant to be fun. Instead of taking life so seriously, start with one thing that brings you joy.

Many people may feel that they'll be happy once they get their degree, find the "perfect career", get married and have kids, and that life will be what it's meant to be when these things happen. Although that is culturally acceptable and ingrained in many of us, I'm here to ask you, *are you happy? Are you living the life you truly want? Do you look forward to getting up in the morning to start your day?* If you're living the life you love, keep going! If you're not, *what can you do today that excites you?* If you're telling yourself, *one day,* that day is today! Take a step to change your life.

*Do you find yourself dreading each day, getting through it, and then spending weekends catching up on the work that wasn't finished?* Many jobs, careers and family lives demand a lot from one person, leaving us exhausted and in a low mood. Our hearts and souls know the way. We get caught up in our heads and forget that our hearts and souls will guide and help us. Sometimes, the universe may be louder in getting your attention if you ignore your true feelings, passions, talents, values and interests.

Take a moment to ask yourself if you're happy with what you're doing right now. *Do you see yourself doing whatever you do for the rest of your life?* If you're happy and content, awesome! However, like many people worldwide, you may not know you're unhappy because it's become routine. I want you to consider this: *Would you be doing what you're doing now if you had only a week left to live in this world?* If the answer is no, consider freeing yourself to find what lights you up, brings you joy, or sets you on fire. Discover where your passions lie and create the life you love. It may be scary to take this leap, but what's more frightening is dying with the music still in you.

Remember, you are not alone; your soul will guide you if you listen. Most of us have become caught up in worldly views of what we should and shouldn't do with our lives. You, and only you, know (maybe not yet), but give yourself the permission and freedom to consider what you want in your life, discover your purpose and create the life you love. Start with one step today. I believe in you, and I hope you do, too.

## Dixie Willis

Dixie Willis, MA, is a certified life coach and meditation facilitator trained through Mindvalley. She is a former licensed professional counselor who left her clinical profession to return to her spiritual practice, guiding seekers in discovering who they truly are and creating the life they love. Additionally, Dixie is a spiritual medium, reiki master, shamanic practitioner and published inspirational author. She holds a master's degree in clinical mental health. With over twenty years of experience in teaching, counseling and coaching, Dixie utilizes a diverse range of healing modalities to support her clients on their spiritual journeys. She is the author of *You Are in This World, Not of It: Remember Who You Are and Create the Life You Love* and writes for *Awakened Magazine*.

Her passion is helping humanity remember their light and encourage higher consciousness, love, unity, equality, peace and environmental sustainability. If you are feeling lost, alone, uncertain or want to create a life you love, reach out to Dixie.

🌐 www.dixiewillis.com
in www.linkedin.com/in/dixie-willis-spirituallifecoach
Scan QR code to learn more about Dixie Willis.

chapter

# 04

# The Quiet Return to Myself

*by Dinah Simpson*

I remember the rush, the never-ending cycle of working, giving and producing. My job in corporate finance was demanding with long hours, tight deadlines and the pressure to perform at all costs. It was the picture of a "great job" – prestigious, well-paying, respected – but the stress was mounting, and I couldn't see it at the time.

There were days when I'd stay at my desk long past everyone else, my mind buzzing with tasks I hadn't yet finished, my body screaming for rest that never came. I'd drown in the to-do list, too afraid to step back, too focused on keeping up the pace. It wasn't until the panic hit that I realized just how far I had pushed myself.

It started with vertigo, a sudden, spinning sensation that knocked me off balance. I'd find myself clutching the edge of my desk, eyes closed, trying to steady my mind, thinking it would pass. But it didn't. It only got worse. The panic followed, gripping my chest like a vice. My heart would race, and no matter how many deep breaths I took, the room kept spinning.

One evening, I was driving the kids to their activities when it hit again. I couldn't focus. The world seemed to tilt, and I could barely keep my hands steady on the wheel.

I rushed to the hospital, convinced I was having a heart attack. It turned out to be exhaustion and burnout. The physical sensations that knocked me completely off, compelling me to go to the ER, was my body sounding the alarm – *hear me, I'm not okay.* I was at my breaking point, everything I had worked for had led me here, to the emergency room.

For months, I felt disconnected from my body. I knew something had to change, but I couldn't seem to slow down. By then, I had left corporate and started my own business, but the patterns were the same. I was overproducing again, caught in the cycle of doing more, achieving more, until my body screamed for relief.

*Inhale for a count of five. Hold the breath for a count of five. Exhale for a count of five.*

I felt the call to go deeper into myself and strengthen my connection to my inner self. Going inward takes a lot of strength, requiring us to witness our vulnerabilities; the suffering, the cycles and patterns that keep you in the emotions of fear or mistrust. Seeing the ego mind doing what it naturally does to protect you and keep you safe. Through the stillness, through meditation, through spirit, I awakened to self-compassion, realizing that the narrative is the mind, trying to keep me safe because it is what it knows, even if it is in a pattern of suffering. Changing anything is a risk in the mind, but once you become aware that stepping into the unknown is a step toward growth, that risk brings healing and trust in the self, which is what your soul is calling for in this journey of life. You only live once... it's time to free your soul.

The first spark of awakening came in meditation. A familiar feeling actually, in stillness. I felt an energy fill my body and my mind. I could see stars of light behind my closed eyes. I was in a different field of life yet it also felt the same. But I saw things like stars and pools of light. I realized that those pools of light are us. We are energetic beings. In that meditation, I saw myself as love and other entities were there too. I could not only see these entities of light, I could feel them. I could feel it in my heart. We are all energetic beings of purity. And I felt I was in a parallel universe but with only love; no suffering, no pain, no divide, no anger, no him against her or her against him. It was only love in an energetic essence. I didn't want to leave, as it felt like home. *This was home.* When I came back to the present moment, I was sad but also happy to have felt that experience.

Another obstacle that made me question my path was when I started receiving messages from spirit during reiki sessions or in meditation. I would receive visions; my clairvoyance was awakening, remembering. I doubted myself so many times because I didn't know if they were real or valid, my mind perhaps recalling something I saw somewhere at some point in time.

In the beginning, when I received whispers or images from spirit during my reiki sessions, it would be so clear and vivid. An example would be, I had a client who was working through whether or not she would take a new job. She noticed a pattern in her life where she struggled so much in making decisions, she was *super risk-adverse*. But it wasn't just big decisions, it was also small decisions. And she was frustrated, that oftentimes, she would be paralyzed by overthinking and just wanted to make a decision. She would seek advice, counsel and research, and not trust herself that whatever decision she made would be a step in the right direction. In a reiki session with her (maybe it was our third session), I received a vision of her on a swing, it was so vivid. She was about eight to ten years old, it was summer and she was wearing a blue and yellow bathing suit, and she was on a swing. She was going higher and higher. I could see her smiling and laughing. She decided to jump. It felt like this was something she had done before; there was a confidence in the decision. I could even feel the lightness in her heart, that she wanted to soar like a bird. But the jump off the swing was quite high and she landed on her arm. She started to cry and that... was that. I relayed the story to her, and she told me she had forgotten that moment. She told me about the cast and how she was in it for months after school had started. She told me how it was wrapped in pink, with her friends' signatures and drawings doodled all over it. That memory was a point of healing for her. We identified this as a core memory, where she took a risk to let go of the swing and she fell, resulting in a major injury. We talked through that moment and, in reality, even though she healed and was seemingly fine, energetically, that fear and risk was held in her body for years. So whenever she took a risk, her mind went to the many ways to keep her safe. This had kept her in a pattern, a cycle, of doubting her decisions in fear of getting hurt. So, energetically, we worked to clear those blocks from many years, so she could free herself and fly again.

But as I tell this story, I am reminded that I, too, took a risk to reveal what I thought was just a figment of my imagination; *was I making this story up in my head?* But when I decided to speak up and share with her, I was not only supporting her healing, I was also healing my inner child who couldn't speak up. This is just one story of many, which soon solidified that I was tapping into my inner wisdom, to see beyond the unseen, and developing a relationship with my confidence in energy healing. When we trust ourselves and our path, we will experience that life itself is a magical thing.

Meditation has been my anchor for healing. In contemplation and connection to self, I have learned that love is the ultimate system of growth, healing and truth. Through stillness, I've come to understand that healing isn't about fixing what is broken or even trying to figure it out... but remembering the wholeness that has always existed within me, *within you.*

In the quiet moments of meditation, I've felt held by something greater than myself, a force that reminds me I am never alone. In the Buddhist teachings of vipassana, there is *the breath*. There is an inhale and an exhale. Each breath is a renewal, each moment an opportunity to align with the vibration of love. And as we exhale, we surrender. It's a surrender to self-compassion and that self-compassion then extends outward to others – our loved ones, our community, and even extended to those we may have difficulties with.

*A story:*

"Do NOT take that tone with me!" I warned.

My daughter was about fourteen. I can't remember entirely what the argument was about, but I remember the heat of it. She yelled at me, her face full of frustration, brows knotted, eyes wide, her whole body leaning forward, propelled by the force of her emotions.

"If I EVER yelled at my mom the way you are yelling at me right now, she would have slapped me across the face. Go to your room." My body was shaking. It was such a visceral experience, a tenseness in my shoulders, the stress permeating my body. "Go, RIGHT NOW!"

I had to slow down – it was too much. I sat down and took some deep breaths. Once my body could calm, I decided I needed to meditate. The noise of the argument took a while to quiet. My thoughts flew from, *My God, if I did that with my mom, she would have literally killed me*, to, *How did I let my daughter disrespect me like this?* Then, the question: *Why am I having such a visceral experience over this? What is being triggered in me?* And that was the aha moment of an awakened consciousness.

Even now, I can see her, caught in a storm of teenage defiance and raw feeling, her voice ringing between us like an unspoken plea to be understood. My daughter was trying to connect with me and I let my wounds speak louder than hers. This was not about me. *My daughter felt safe to yell at me.* She felt safe enough to express her feelings. *She felt safe.*

In that moment, I sobbed. I cried for *little Dinah* who did not feel safe. And I breathed to surrender, to acknowledge her pain and her plea to be heard and loved unconditionally. I understood that she is here too. And I'm here to love her too.

"Can I come in?" I asked softly as I knocked on my daughter's door. Tears in her eyes too, I approached her bed. I sat next to her and apologized for not listening. Fully present, I held space for my daughter, I held space for my healing, and love held space for us all.

Before I began this journey, my days felt like a constant push against the weight of stress, expectations and the invisible burdens I had carried for so long.

A lot of that stress was due to an expectation *that I perceived* others demanded of me, and what I believed others wanted from me – a perception of what we believe, as a society, defines success. And I accepted this outward perception, this expectation, to be my path towards fulfillment.

*Meaning:* Chasing achievement, constantly producing, meeting external standards and molding myself into what I thought would earn validation. I was molding myself into the daughter I thought would gain the love, affection and approval of my mother. And when that didn't work, I molded myself into a successful businesswoman – measured by accomplishments, efficiency, wealth and *how well I could juggle everything without breaking.* I was a wife and mother that fit the idealized image of what I believed a *good* wife and mother should be – selfless, always composed, able to hold everything together with grace. I became a master of adaptation, shifting roles seamlessly, convincing myself that if I could just do more, be more, prove more, then I would finally feel whole, finally feel *enough*.

But beneath the smile and the image, I was exhausted. The weight of those expectations, both real and imagined, pressed into me, shaping my every move, every thought. I wasn't living for myself, I was living for the *approval* I had been chasing my entire life. And yet, no matter how much I gave, how perfectly I performed, that sense of validation remained just out of reach.

As I stepped into a new way of being, something shifted. Meditation became my refuge; a space where the noise softened and I could finally hear myself. The tightness in my body began to release, like knots untying one by one. My breath slowed and deepened – no longer shallow and rushed. Colors seemed richer, the sky more vast, the smallest moments became sacred; sunlight filtering through the leaves, laughter echoing from another room.

Love, the universe and consciousness no longer felt like distant concepts, but living forces woven into every moment. It was the time I made to connect with this vibration. Before, I saw love as something to be given and earned, measured and sometimes withheld. Now, I understand it as the very foundation of existence, an energy that flows endlessly... when we allow it. The universe, once just a backdrop to my life, now feels intimate, guiding me in ways I never noticed before, through synchronicities, intuitive nudges and the gentle unfolding of events that remind me I am always supported.

And consciousness? It has become the space in which everything happens, the stillness beneath the waves of my thoughts. I no longer feel I am at war with myself. Instead, I witness, I soften, I allow. Healing, I've realized, is not about striving to be better, it's about remembering who I have always been.

There was a time when I believed stress was simply woven into the fabric of my life, an inseparable companion to my ambition and my drive to overachieve. It was as natural as breath, as if the Aries fire in me thrived on the pressure, convincing myself that the tension in my shoulders, the racing thoughts, the endless to-do lists were just part of what it meant to succeed.

If I could speak to someone who feels lost right now, I would tell them this: *You are not broken. You are not behind.* You are simply in the space between what was and what will be. And in that space, transformation begins. Every challenge is an invitation to return to love. Every obstacle is an opportunity to heal, to soften, to surrender and to trust.

Healing isn't about fixing ourselves. It's about remembering who we are. Beneath the stress, beneath the fear, beneath the stories, there is a version of you that is whole, radiant and aligned. Your path to peace is not out there – it's within you. And the moment you begin to listen, to surrender, to trust, you will find that you were never truly lost at all.

# Dinah Simpson

Dinah Simpson is the founder of HIGH KI LIVING, where she helps high performers break free from stress and burnout to reclaim their energy, clarity and inner harmony. Dinah integrates energy healing, meditation, sound therapy and breathwork to create a deeply transformative experience for her clients.

After years navigating high-stress corporate environments, she found her way back to peace through ancient healing practices. Today, she empowers others to reconnect to their own wisdom, vitality and truth. Dinah believes that healing is a homecoming to the heart. Beyond her work, Dinah finds joy in quiet moments of meditation, spending time with her children and hiking to reset her energy with nature. She is most fulfilled when witnessing the profound breakthroughs of those she serves.

*May clarity illuminate your path forward, bringing you peace with every step.*

*May your heart remain open, filled with love for yourself and all that surrounds you.*

*May you trust in your journey, knowing that you are exactly where you need to be.*

*May you feel supported, nourished and empowered to embrace the limitless potential within you.*

🌐 www.dinahsimpson.com
📷 @highkiliving
Scan QR code to learn more about Dinah Simpson.

chapter

# 05

## The Sacred Alchemy of Purpose: Awakening to My Soul Mission

*by Lauren Dickinson*

My story doesn't have a dramatic starting point, nor apex of awakening after a tumultuous dark night of the soul. My awakening and pathway on the spiritual journey has been a gentle and steady awareness, a soul realization of the truth of reality and nature of our world. It's not that I haven't had moments of crystal clarity when I knew I was awake, nor that I was spared any dark nights of the soul (there have been a few), it's more that as I sit here now to write these words, I feel the sun shining in through the window and birds chirping in the spring air and sincerely wonder how long it took me to appreciate such simple things in life with mindful awareness. The story I share here is exactly that: a dive into chapters of my own life when I didn't have what I have now, where I didn't know what I know now, and didn't have the vision that the creator has now blessed my soul with. It's been a long and winding road to get here. Even as tears gently fill my eyes with gratitude, I share humbly in these pages the lessons of trust and faith in unnamable things outside of ourselves, which, if we aptly peel back the layers of our projections, we can see that following the path of the heart is ultimately the path of returning home to oneself that it has always been you who has held your own answers within.

As a young girl, I didn't know how *different* I was. I loved school, I loved my friends, yet there was an effect I had on others that I could never place; kids either *loved* me or hated me. And I was looked at as *strange* for being vegetarian. It was never something I was ashamed of, but something I became increasingly aware of, that seemed to rub kids the wrong way. I talked a lot about God and the universe, so I imagine that could have been part of it too! I remember feeling lonely a lot as a child, always preferring to wander in nature by myself, play with my brothers, color or read. I was quiet but never felt self-conscious about it. I see it now as the building blocks of my independent spirit.

At around nine years old, my father started taking us to a metaphysical practitioner, who practiced a healing arts modality called *Alphabiotics*. I knew very little about the purpose of it or why we were going, but I do remember how I felt after each session. I distinctly remember going in feeling one way, perhaps a little scattered and disconnected, and immediately feeling grounded and calm. On one visit,

I remember laying on the alignment table after the process was completed, relaxing and integrating as advised, staring at the large salt lamp on the table in the corner of the room. I clearly remember as if it were yesterday, seeing the light and luminous glow from within. As I stared, it grew brighter in my eyes, filling my senses, until light was all I could see. I would shift my eyes and the room would return to normal. This was my first taste of perceiving energy, and later learned it was perceived from an energetic balancing of the brain, which is the Alphabiotics process.

Later that year, in orchestra class, I had another pivotal experience of awareness. While practicing with the class, the conductor would wave her arms around, her movements so lively and she was so patient with our budding talents as a class. One day, I had memorized the sheet music enough to be able to watch her, as something peculiar was starting to happen around her. We were in the depths of one of my favorite Tchaikovsky songs, a deeply melodious, intense piece; the kind I loved the most. As I let my eyes relax, I started to see plasma-like smoke coming off her body in hues of green and yellow. I snapped back and returned to my sheet music. Looking up, there it was again. I let my eyes relax even more and watched as what looked like the aurora borealis danced around her body. This was the first experience, to my conscious knowledge and memory, of seeing vivid colors around the body and what, in my adulthood, I learned was an aura.

When I finally shared with my mom some of these experiences, she asked why I'd never mentioned it before. My answer? That I didn't know others *couldn't* see them. Over time they became as natural as breathing and it led me as a young adult to decide I wanted to be an energy healer and study with Barbara Brennan in Florida.

High school continued from there, and I went through my fair share of the troubled teenage years. I lost my idea of working with energy, and in retrospect was putting tremendous pressure on myself to figure out what I wanted to do. At the young age of fourteen, I had my first panic attack because I didn't know what I wanted to do with my life.

This was all self-inflicted, as my parents weren't putting pressure on me. I was a good student and had entered into my sophomore year as a 4.0 student. I thought I wanted to go to Harvard or some place highly academic to continue my love for learning and knowledge. I lost this desire too, as I let my grades slip and found myself in the middle of an existential boredom and apathy. By the time senior year hit, I had no idea what my purpose was and spent my home life in my room creating art, as an escapist attempt to placate my soul's illusory sense of freedom. It's no wonder I took to the idea of art school like a flame finding its dance.

Life has a way of carving wisdom into our souls when we least expect it. When into my second year of art college, my artist dreams collapsed under the weight of institutional cruelty – something within me shattered. After the school wasn't delivering on its academic promises, for which many students thereafter transferred, the administration refused to release my transcripts so that I could transfer to another school and sabotaged my good standing financial aid with the lenders. This one moment didn't just close a door to my education for years, it wounded my belief in fairness, in the idea that passion and talent were enough. I carried this wound silently, like a stone in my pocket, feeling its weight with every step. What I couldn't see then, was how this stone was being polished, how its edges were smoothing into something I could one day offer to others.

The universe wasn't finished with its lessons. A couple of years later, I was being broken open in preparation for something far greater than I could comprehend with a series of inexplicable panic attacks that both sent me on a health journey for years, and also back to stay with my parents for a time. I was plucked from my life in one massive sweep of divine intervention; my soul knew what my mind didn't understand until much later, that I needed to be with my family when my father's heart would stop beating. That my hands needed to be there to perform CPR alongside my mother's. That my presence was required, not for my sake, but for my family, and my sixteen-year-old brother who, otherwise, would have been alone that night with my mom.

This is how the wounded healer is born, through experiences that force us beyond what we believe we can endure. My father's death ripped through me like a lightning bolt, illuminating the profound fragility of life, while simultaneously revealing the immense capacity of the human heart to continue beating despite devastating loss. In that bedroom, watching the paramedics take over after our desperate attempts at resuscitation, I was initiated into a visceral understanding of both mortality and the ferocious nature of love.

These wounds became my greatest teachers. The loss of art school taught me that creativity cannot be confined to institutions – it lives in the marrow of our bones, waiting patiently to be expressed. My anxiety attacks showed me the profound connection between mind and body, how our physical selves carry the wisdom our conscious minds often resist. My father's death revealed how present moment awareness is not a spiritual luxury but the only truth that matters when faced with life's impermanence.

When I later found myself drawn to energy medicine, I recognized that I was seeking to heal in others what I had needed most: integration of physical symptoms with emotional wounds, creative expression as a pathway through grief and the recognition that our bodies hold stories our minds cannot yet articulate. My wounds had become my wisdom; not in some abstract, philosophical sense, but in the tangible healing techniques my hands now knew instinctively how to offer.

The concept of the wounded healer isn't romantic – it's devastatingly real. It's the understanding that our deepest pain, when metabolized through presence and compassion, becomes our most profound offering. My grieving heart allowed me to create safe spaces where others could bring their unprocessed sorrows, teaching others, even as life taught me, to trust that even when the path forward seems impossible, something within us knows how to float across the chasm of uncertainty on wings we didn't know we possessed.

We don't heal only in order to help others, although that is the path of most healers, we heal because it is our birthright to become whole.

And in that wholeness, we naturally overflow into service. The wounded healer doesn't use their scars as credentials but as bridges, quiet reminders that they too have walked through darkness and can therefore hold space for others without fear or judgment. In those early years after my father's death, moving through life on autopilot, I couldn't have articulated any of this. But my soul knew. My path from personal healing to facilitating transformation for others unfolded with a quiet inevitability that I now recognize as divine orchestration. After navigating the heartbreak of family tragedy, I found myself standing at a crossroads, uncertain of direction, yet deeply aware that my purpose remained intact, if temporarily obscured.

The universe has its own timing. When I stepped into my first position as a chiropractic assistant, I couldn't have known this was the beginning of a decades-long immersion in the healing arts. There was an immediate resonance. Watching practitioners work with their hands to release pain and restore alignment awakened something dormant within me. Here was work that honored both scientific precision and intuitive awareness, work that acknowledged the body's innate intelligence while offering pathways to enhance its functioning.

As I moved from reception desk to management roles in various wellness centers, I became a sponge for knowledge. Each practice exposed me to different modalities – from structural approaches like chiropractic adjustments to more subtle forms of bodywork and energy medicine. During lunch breaks and after hours, I would often receive treatments, experiencing firsthand how different techniques affected my own system. These experiences became my real education; a direct, embodied understanding that no textbook could provide.

My hunger for healing knowledge led me to countless workshops, self-study mixed with certification programs and intensive retreats. I studied reiki, spinal energetics, polarity therapy, bioenergetics, somatic release work and various forms of meditation; some in self-study, others in certification programs. With each new modality, my understanding deepened, not just through intellectual comprehension, but through integration in my own body. The anxiety attacks that once debilitated me became laboratories for exploring the mind-body connection, while the grief of family loss offered ongoing opportunities to experience how energy moves through emotion when given space to process.

This wasn't the linear career path I'd once envisioned for myself, yet I began to recognize the perfection in how my journey was unfolding. The very experiences that had felt like detours were providing me with a comprehensive understanding of both the healing arts and the practical aspects of running a wellness business.

After years of absorbing knowledge while helping to grow other practitioners" businesses, I began seeing clients privately. My approach naturally integrated the diverse modalities I'd studied, customized to address each person's unique needs. What surprised me was how often clients commented on the quality of presence I brought to our sessions. "There's something about the space you create," they would say, "that makes it feel safe to really let go."

This feedback illuminated something essential; beyond any specific method or technique, healing happens within a container of safety, presence and permission. The most effective sessions occurred when I stepped beyond protocols to meet clients in a space of genuine connection, when I trusted the wisdom of their bodies as much as my own training. This realization became the cornerstone of my evolving practice.

As my client base grew, I noticed patterns in what people sought – not just relief from physical symptoms but reconnection with their authentic selves, recovery of purpose, renewal of creative expression. My sacred practice gradually expanded beyond physical healing to address these deeper yearnings for wholeness.

The vision for group retreats began taking shape during this period. I recognized that while one-on-one sessions created powerful shifts, there was something uniquely transformative about healing in community. The full expression of this vision would have to wait, however, as life once again redirected my path while in Dallas. There, while immersed in the practice of and after certification in the very modality my father introduced us to as a child and where I'd first started becoming aware of my awareness of energy, Alphabiotics, I unexpectedly reconnected with my artistic roots. What I thought had been lost – my creativity – rushed back like a wellspring deep from my soul. This catharsis spurred years of art shows, art fairs and establishing a global collector base. This creative renaissance wasn't a departure from my healing work but a profound complement to it. Through art, I experienced firsthand the transformative power of creative expression – how it bypasses the analytical mind to access deeper truths, how it makes visible the invisible movements of the soul. What I found during this time was the profound connection between the healer and the healing, the creator and the created, through the conduit of the creative. My soul healed on deeper levels than any single modality I'd found to that point, and it has become a catalyst for deepening my healing service to the soul of humanity.

When the pandemic brought me to Mount Shasta, I initially saw it as a temporary shelter in the storm. Instead, it became the fertile ground where all the seeds of my previous experiences could finally take root together. The mountain itself – long recognized as a powerful energy vortex – seemed to amplify my clarity and purpose. Living amongst healing practitioners expanded my understanding of healing beyond the individual body to encompass land, community and collective consciousness.

The catalyst for founding my retreat company came through contrast, witnessing approaches to spiritual facilitation that felt exploitative rather than empowering. After an encounter with spiritual narcissism at a local center, I recognized with absolute clarity what sacred space should never be, and consequently, what I was called to create. My retreat company was born from this vision: creating containers for transformation that honor each participant's innate wisdom while providing genuine, heart-centered facilitation.

Each retreat I now create weaves together energy practices, somatic release work, creative expression and communion with nature in a carefully crafted experience. The structure provides safety while allowing space for spontaneity and emergence. Every group brings together individuals whose stories and struggles mysteriously complement each other, creating opportunities for mirroring and growth that no facilitator could consciously orchestrate. This has deepened my trust in the co-creative nature of healing and divine guidance – how we participate with forces larger than ourselves when we align with purpose and remain open to emergence.

Today, facilitating transformation through retreats brings together all dimensions of my essence: The healer whose hands have learned the language of energy, the artist who understands the sacred geometry of creation, the businesswoman who builds structures to hold sacred space, and the wounded one who has alchemized suffering into wisdom. Each apparent obstacle I'd faced was, in fact, an invitation to deeper embodiment of my gifts. In my most profound moments of revelation often during retreats, I witness the divine mystery of transformation unfolding. These sacred moments affirm what my soul has always known – we are each sovereign co-creators of our lives, our wounds contain the seeds of our most luminous offerings, and our purpose flows through us when we remain faithful to our deepest truth, even through darkness and uncertainty. We are created to create, designed with the innate capacity to heal ourselves and facilitate healing for others, with others, and by inherent design. Even when external circumstances appear to direct our path, *we* remain the still point at the center of our own becoming, the anchor from which our authentic purpose spirals outward, eventually returning to our hearts with greater clarity, power and grace than we could have imagined at the beginning of our journey.

As Ram Dass so eloquently reflected, *We're all just walking each other home.*

# Lauren Dickinson

Lauren Dickinson is the visionary founder and CEO of Orion Retreats, specializing in conscious travel and transformational retreat experiences. With over twenty years in the healing arts, Lauren combines her roles as a consciousness thought leader, coach, artist and retreat facilitator to create transformative programs that empower guests and clients across the globe to awaken to their divinity.

With a well-rounded and practical knowledge base in a wide variety of applications, Lauren skillfully and co-actively facilitates a greater expression of life energy, healing and personal awareness and growth with her clients. Her unique approach is informed by her deep connection to sacred energy centers around the world, including Sedona, Arizona and learning from Aboriginal tribes in Uluru, Australia. Now based in Mount Shasta, California – considered the root chakra of the world – she brings this profound spiritual awareness to her work.

As an international bestselling author and international multimedia artist, Lauren teaches artists and non-artists alike how to tap into their innate creativity and birth their creative genius into the world. Her unique shamanic art therapy and quantum soul coaching processes provide clients with deep and profound self-guided journeys into their inner landscapes, helping them access their creative genius and facilitate deep personal transformation.

⊕ www.orionretreats.com
◎ @orionretreats
Scan QR code to learn more about Lauren Dickinson.

chapter

# 06

# Reclaiming This Body and Becoming HER

*by Michele Marie Neyers*

As a young girl growing up in a small midwestern town, I recall thinking that my body was my playground. With my body I could twirl, skip and dance. I could chase after my pet bunny rabbit, Hopper, and run away from my annoying younger brother. I'd climb trees and pick juicy ripe strawberries from the garden, ride my bike around the block, play hopscotch with my friends, and make clothesline blanket forts in the backyard, where I'd eat warm chocolate chip cookies with a cold glass of milk.

But in my early twenties, everything changed. I began seeing my body as something that needed to be fixed, like a run-down house in need of constant renovation. I spent decades waging war against my perceived flaws and thousands of hours in front of a mirror, silently hating what I saw. I resented my body and punished it repeatedly for betraying me.

Yet there was always an underlying longing to feel at home in my body once again. A place I could belong and feel carefree, the way I did as a child. That longing and remembrance became a compass that would eventually lead to my liberation. I finally stopped waging war and started listening. I softened where I once punished. I began to love the curves and honor the stories and contributions made possible by this body I once despised. And in those acts of kindness and tenderness, I discovered something radical – love; the kind that releases and heals us from the false beliefs once held as truths. This love also brought me to the true purpose for my life.

**The Numbers That Broke Me**

It was yet another bone-chilling, wintry morning in eastern South Dakota as I hurried across the snow-covered campus and ascended the icy stairs into the military annex building. Making my way down the stone staircase to the dark corner room in the basement, I felt the familiar feeling of dread drop into my stomach. Today was my least favorite day of the week. *Weigh-in day.*

As an Air Force ROTC cadet and scholarship recipient, I was required to "report in" weekly to ensure I stayed below the maximum weight requirement: 125lb. That's what a young woman of my age (eighteen) and height (5'2") was expected to weigh. Anything more was unacceptable and would result in disciplinary action, even possible removal from the program. As someone who skated close to the edge of those limits frequently, the pressure of stepping on that scale was very real.

I began to despise that stupid number. 1-2-5. I would hope and pray all week long that the scale would read a number less than that. I didn't care if it was 124.8, it meant the tension was gone for another week. Pulling off shoes, socks, jewelry and anything that would add unnecessary ounces, I would grit my teeth, step on the scale and hold my breath as the scale calibrated and finally settled.

It was during those otherwise carefree freshman and sophomore years of college that I became hyperaware and sensitive to the number displayed on a body scale. Never had that number mattered before. *Weight* was once simply a measurement that held no significance or emotional meaning to me. It had absolutely nothing to do with me or who I was. I was perfectly happy with my body. I loved my hips and other curves, my muscular athletic legs, and had no problem filling out my bra, *thank you very much!*

For the first time, the number on the scale began to mean something. To the military, it meant I wasn't *fit* to be included in their ranks. To me, it meant I was an outsider, a problem, not good enough. The story I told myself was that I was too *heavy* to be valuable. In those weekly trips to the basement, I unconsciously began equating my weight with my self-worth and shaping my self-image to match.

When the time came to take my commission as an Air Force officer at the end of my second year, I declined. Though I had somehow managed to meet the weight requirements (barely) and finish out my last year in the program with honors, intuitively I knew life had other plans for me. Reflecting on this time now, my experience in the military changed the way I looked at my weight, my body and my self-worth. I had unconsciously knitted these experiences into false beliefs about who I was. Those deeply held belief systems had settled within my cells and would infect other areas of my life for the foreseeable future.

## When The Mirror Turned Against Me

After graduating from college, I stopped paying attention to the number on the scale and my weight began to climb steadily. Yo-yo dieting became a way of life. If there was a weight loss program out there, I'd tried it.

When I did have dieting success, oftentimes dropping 30lb or more, I felt on top of the world. I felt unstoppable, not just in my body, but in every area of my life. Not only did I feel like the physical burden had been lifted, but the mental and emotional ones had as well.

When I wasn't dieting, my freezer was usually full of Lean Cuisine and Weight Watchers meals, though there were times when it was filled with frozen pizza, ice cream and highly processed convenience foods. Weekly work travel was a constant reality, so periods of poor eating and a lack of consistent exercise on the road had translated into me being close to 200lb. My thirty-nine-year-old self would have given anything to be my twenty-year-old self, weighing in at 125lb or less.

## The Night Everything Changed

You've no doubt heard stories about people who receive a "wake-up call" coming in the form of a tragic or traumatic event. If we're fortunate, we're only slightly jolted out of the dream state, still alive, but irrevocably changed. For me, a night spent in the ER in my late thirties was enough for me to seriously question my life path.

My heart was racing, which I knew couldn't be a good sign, so I intuitively took some deep breaths. As I lay quietly on the cold, hard surface of the examining table looking into the harsh fluorescent lights,

I could hear the hustle and bustle of nurses and other medical professionals on the opposite side of the curtain. *Why wasn't anyone coming to check on me? Surely, someone experiencing chest pains was a top priority!*

Less than an hour before, I'd been at home, comfortably enjoying a glass of rich, flavorful Merlot. As I took another long sip, I knew something was wrong when my chest felt as if I had an elephant sitting on top of me. All the stress of the week's events became a distant memory, and my mind started spinning with all the possibilities of what was happening. I knew two things for sure; I'd never felt this way before, and I was alone.

Before I knew what was happening, I'd put on my winter coat, flung my purse over my shoulder and picked up my car keys, before flying out the door, jumping into my car, and driving like a crazy person to the twenty-four-hour emergency care center about a mile from my home.

"Chest pains!" I almost screamed at the young woman, as I stood visibly shaking at reception. "I'm having chest pains!" "Okay," the receptionist said calmly. "Go sit down. A nurse will be with you shortly."

I sat on the edge of an uncomfortable waiting room chair and began taking more deep breaths, hoping to stop the uncontrollable shaking I was experiencing, like when the frigid cold gets deep in your bones. As I anxiously waited for the nurse to come and for *someone* to tell me everything would be alright, I closed my eyes and whispered a message to God, the universe or anyone who would listen – *Please, PLEASE let me be okay.*

"Everything sounds fine," the doctor said as he examined me, "but we're going to send you to the emergency room at the hospital – just in case."

Minutes later, I was in the back of a waiting ambulance and wheeled into the ER a short time later. Laying on the stretcher waiting to be officially checked in, I again closed my eyes against the harsh lights and whispered repeatedly – *please, PLEASE let me be okay.*

After the shock of spending the night in the ER had worn off, my life returned to its normal routine, but I felt nothing remotely close to "normal." Thankfully, I'd just had a very bad panic attack and was okay, but I was also irrevocably changed. I had so many questions: *What is "normal"? Do I even want to return to my previous state?* Uncertainty, as I'd never experienced it, washed over me and inhabited my being, as if it was a long-distance guest settling in to stay awhile.

That one night had engrained the reality of my mortality into my conscious awareness. This was a frightening yet loving message, sent to wake me up and remind me, in no uncertain terms, that my life was the greatest gift of all. I knew then I needed to experience life fully through this incredible body I'd been given. The way I related to my body slowly began to shift after that experience, but it would take another fifteen years before the false beliefs I was carrying with me would completely fall away.

## Listening to Learn, Learning to Love

My forties had me exploring health and wellbeing from various perspectives, allowing me to see and relate to my body in a myriad of ways. As I took more of an interest in these topics, and my attention and energy were directed there, my life path lined me up with the right people and opportunities to explore it further. The more I explored, the more I came to realize how little I knew about health and the human body.

I fully leaned into methods for relieving stress, then various types of meditation, regenerative nutrition and alternative modalities, like acupuncture. I started taking better care of my body and learned about food as medicine. I practiced yoga and Pilates. The *perfect* body and weight still alluded me, but I felt the learning path I was on, bumpy though it may have been, was exactly where I needed to be.

What I couldn't know was that the biggest breakthroughs would happen in my early fifties – in surprising ways and from very unexpected sources.

## Divine Interventions and Angelic Truths

It was several years after that night in the ER that I met a clairvoyant spiritual healer from Australia, known as Master John Douglas. I was initially introduced to him at an event hosted in a friend's basement, while he'd been touring the US. I would describe myself at the time as *intrigued, but not ready to truly "see" what was possible.*

Ten years later, I would be *called back* to him, through divinely perfect timing, to complete his advanced elite development course. *Heavenly Mountain*, a private and sacred community just outside of Boone, North Carolina, is a special place. It was here that Master John, through the master healing angels, gifted me (and my fellow spiritual aspirants) with specific activations in my consciousness, energy fields and physical body, allowing me to divine truth in the world around me and to more accurately *dial in* to specific frequencies of matter and energy.

Through the miracle of this body of work, known as *angelic reformation*, many of the false beliefs and self-perceptions I'd held for most of my adult life – especially around my body and self-worth – began to disappear. Many of the recurring thoughts and patterns I had don't exist any longer. Tens of thousands have experienced medical miracles and healings with Master John; this was my personal miracle – to know I had been transformed spiritually and physically in ways I could not explain or fully understand.

## Messages From the Inside Out

Over the past seventeen years, I've become a devoted student (and self-proclaimed nerd) when it comes to study, personal growth and spiritual enlightenment. On a particular day in 2024, I was cuddled up on my velvet blue couch with my sweet cat Sophie, my trusty journal and pen and my latest textbooks on human design and the gene keys; two related yet different perspectives on this ancient and profound wisdom. I was fascinated by them both, thanks in no small part to being inspired by one of my business coaches and mentors. I believed this new element would be a game changer for my clients, but first things first, I started to study myself using this extremely powerful *soul activation system.*

On the human design body graph, the left side lists thirteen qualities or traits that represent the unconscious/body/physiology. Given that I had struggled for decades to truly love the body I had, I decided to begin contemplating my thirteen body traits, individually and holistically, to see what wisdom I would find there.

I began by reviewing a list of all the trait names my coach had given me. These names represent the highest potential or frequency of that trait. Expressions such as "euphoria explorer", "expansion catalyst" and "possibility pioneer" began to come into my awareness. And then "bliss chaser", "committed seeker" and "courageous leader." I let these names wash over me like water. As I sat with them, I was all at once awestruck by their beauty and the tremendous potential my body contained. *Wait, MY body? No way! What did this even mean?*

The apartment was eerily silent. Sophie had fallen into a deep sleep. I listened intently to the silence, waiting for something to happen, though I was uncertain what that could be... until I heard a strong, reverberating voice speak the following question to me:

What if the body you have is the "perfect" one, designed specifically for you to fulfill your unique purpose during this incarnation on planet Earth?

I shook my head in disbelief. *Had that just happened?* As if in direct response to my unspoken question, I heard the voice once again, this time in the form of a direct statement:

Your body is and always has been perfectly designed to fulfill your life's purpose.

As I let those words sink into my being, my sacral responded with a resounding *YES!!* to confirm this internal knowing that I had just heard Truth – with a capital T.

Over the course of the next several months, like a researcher excavating the most precious treasures of the world, I continued to study my design. I was uncovering the truth about ME. My divine blueprint, as God sees me.

During a recent study session, I went in deep on a trait that shows up four times in my body graph and discovered its primary themes are the body, love of self and universal love. I was moved to tears as I read more; tears of recognition and relief, as I began seeing myself and my purpose in the world as clear as day.

**Parting Thoughts**

Healing my relationship with my body and transforming the image I held of myself, didn't happen all at once and continues to this day. It has been a slow, sacred unraveling. A tender return to the truth of who I am. A falling back in love with the parts of myself I previously disowned. And a conscious crafting of an empowered vision of HER – the woman I consciously choose to be and who I AM becoming every day.

As I write this final section, I'm packing for a road trip and bringing my body scale with me. My inner nerd and I are committed to measuring various data points (including body weight) to empower the vision of HER health and vitality as we move towards our sixties decade and beyond. The scale and I have a very different relationship today. I no longer measure my worth by the number on that scale, a reflection in the mirror or anyone else's standards but my own. Instead, I attune to a frequency of my choosing; one that empowers and calls my best self to step forward. This body, exactly as she is, is not just enough, she is divinely and perfectly designed.

This sacred attunement with HER has also become the heart of my coaching work. I guide women who are ready to shed false stories and limiting beliefs, recalibrate and reimagine their self-image, and finally become the HER that is living the life of their dreams.

This body is no longer my burden.
She is my sacred partner.
With HER and through HER, I embody my divine purpose.

# Michele Marie Neyers

Michele Marie Neyers is a mindset mentor and reinvention guide who believes that it's never too late to rewrite the beautiful story of YOU. Her mission is to help heart-centered, spiritually-oriented women re-imagine and change the inner story they believe about themselves so they can embody and experience lives from their divine self-expression. With coaching certifications in mindset, manifestation, and Human Design, as well as her background in education technology, engineering, and physics, Michele empowers her clients with the HER frequency™ method to powerfully align with and fully become the woman they were always designed to be. As the CEO and founder of Juicy Conscious Living LLC, she has influenced the lives of hundreds of women with her teaching, coaching, poetry, and writing. Her other passions include photography, hiking in nature, kayaking, making delicious homemade recipes in her kitchen, and exploring her waterfront community in Annapolis, Maryland.

⊕ www.michelemarieneyers.com
◉ @michele_marie_neyers

Scan QR code to learn more about Michele Marie Neyers.

chapter

# 07

# The Six Heart Illuminations: How Divine Love Transformed My Life's Path

*By Jennifer R Dickens*

On that enchanting night, as I pronam'd (kneeled) in front of a picture of my beloved guru during his birthday commemoration at my spiritual temple, I gently laid my flower offering in front of his candlelit picture. As I reverently gazed into his eyes with love and devotion for his divine support of my deepening spiritual awakening, I suddenly felt a strong energetic vibrational force enter my heart with such intensity that I was almost pushed back screaming. The force came directly from the heart of the picture and when he realized I was about to scream, the force weakened to a mere subtle vibration of love in my heart. I had to maintain my composure because I was in a temple packed with over three hundred devotees patiently waiting their turn to honor their beloved guru.

In a sense of awe and wonderment, I walked back to my seat and sat in the sacred peace and stillness of the ceremony. My heart was buzzing with the cosmic heart activation of the ecstatic love I'd just experienced. I allowed myself to fully receive the radiant joy now emanating, nourishing and awakening my heart. As I silently left the temple that night, I knew I had to discover what this ecstatic energetic force was. This was one of the most defining moments in my spiritual evolution.

My spiritual awakening in my early thirties had preceded this heart awakening experience in my forties. My inner calling to know who "I AM" continued to grow stronger and louder as I followed my heart's guidance and intuition to continuously advance in my personal and spiritual development.

Prior to my spiritual awakening, I had an extensive career in sales and marketing in the financial, professional service and commercial real estate development industries. I worked hard and long hours to achieve positions of higher and higher responsibility; director, vice president, executive team member, you get the picture. Many of my careers and colleagues I thoroughly enjoyed, but after twenty years in the corporate construct, and the ups and downs of the financial market, I was drawn by my heart to pursue a higher calling, fulfilling purposeful work to make the world a better place. But how? Doing what?

Having been laid off because of the market collapse of 2008, I took some time off, traveled and immersed myself in personal retreats to introspect about my life, who I was, what made me happy, and how I could have a positive impact in the world. I evaluated the possibility of becoming a holistic practitioner and healer, but felt a considerable amount of inner resistance. Exploring and contemplating what would be next in my life's unfoldment, what resonated most with my heart at that time was to capitalize on my twenty-plus years of sales and marketing experience to start my own niche marketing agency supporting the growth of natural product brands, holistic universities and integrative medicine doctors. I spent the following ten years content and fulfilled, supporting the health and wellness industry... but, as I spiritually evolved, that contentment didn't last.

Being a yogi for twenty-plus years, and through a series of synchronicities, I found myself drawn more and more to meditation. Then one day while meditating on my bed, a thought popped up in the stillness of my mind; *I wonder if I should have a structured meditation practice?* The pursuit of this path led me to a large meditation temple and spiritual community in Pacific Palisades: *Self Realization Fellowship, Lake Shrine*. I attended a meditation and spiritual lecture and was instantly hooked by the high energetic vibe which resonated within my heart. When I looked into the big brown eyes of Yogananda, there was a deep soul connection, as if I knew him from somewhere, from a time long ago, as if I was a member of his family. His temple and garden grounds felt like home.

I became involved with the community, started serving and couldn't get my Kriya meditation initiation fast enough. The Kriya initiation was the most beautiful ceremony I had ever experienced, as if I was attending my own wedding; a spiritual marriage, with rose petals everywhere, chanting and divine love emanating from my heart like never before. Tears of joy were rolling down my cheeks, my heart was singing and I felt an exuberance from deep within. I knew, at the core of my being, that this path would help me truly know who "I AM." Kriya meditation was a game changer. My spiritual progress, connection to heart wisdom, and knowing who "I AM" was gradually progressing, having many metaphysical, intuitive experiences weekly. It was as if a veil was being lifted, and I was remembering the truth of who "I AM."

I was being guided by a formidable force greater than myself, going deeper and deeper in my meditations, spiritual teachings, divine wisdom. I also explored astrology, numerology, sacred geometry, Kabbalah, ancient Vedic and Egyptian wisdom, Christ consciousness, oracle reading and pendulum divination. I was having a ball experimenting with all these ancient divination and wisdom tools. Rekindling my wizard, light-bearer and goddess gifts from past incarnations, it all felt so familiar, so real and so intuitively guided.

Although I had resisted becoming a practitioner, more and more my heart was guiding me to awaken my divine gifts, to remember who "I AM" and expand my heart capacity to embody more love, light and truth. So I tiptoed into becoming a heart coherence practitioner by becoming a HeartMath® certified coach. As a side business to my marketing agency, I started retaining one-on-one and group coaching clients. I found working with people so fulfilling, rewarding and inspiring – very different to what I was accustomed to, working with business clients as a marketing agency owner.

Then one fateful morning in 2021, during my morning Sadhana (meditation), I started receiving the deepest intuitive insights directing me to explore Yoga Sutra 23 – 32 in Swami Sri Yukteswar's book, *The Holy Science*. I read the sutras, meditated on them and received intuitive insights, and scribed this ancient divinely guided process. Over a period of weeks, it flowed with more and more clarity. I documented it as a six-step process to awaken, purify and illuminate the heart, which takes people from a dark (or heavy) heart to a pure (clean) heart. I was guided to call this process *The Six Heart Illuminations*.

I was inspired, excited and in a state of wonderment. My heart singing and mind wondering... *What am I supposed to do with this program?* An inner dialogue ensued, my heart silently rang out, *Use it with your coaching clients.* I responded: *What?* Heart said, *Yes, follow my lead!* I responded, *Okay.* So, I asked one of my long-time HeartMath® coherence coaching clients, Faith, if she'd be interested in taking this six coaching session program – *The Six Heart Illuminations?* To my astonishment, Faith agreed. Over a three-month period, I led her through *The Six Heart Illuminations* coaching sessions with deeply guided visualization meditations. She absolutely loved it and was strongly heart-illuminated by the end of our sessions. Faith's intuition was strengthened. Feeling more attuned to her inner guidance, she became courageous and started speaking up for herself. She quit her energy-draining job for a more harmonious one. Faith, feeling renewed and replenished, now focused her energy on growing her most intimate relationship with her husband, children, grandchildren and purpose-driven side business. Faith was thrilled, and I was ecstatic with her progress, excited that my intuitively guided *Six Heart Illuminations* program actually works.

**Fulfilling My Higher Purpose**

The realization that there was something subtly but profoundly powerful in *The Six Heart Illumination* process elevated my consciousness and my purpose. I've intuited that *Awakening Divine Love in All Hearts* is now my higher purpose mission. Fulfilling this mission would bring world peace through inner peace. A mission that makes my heart sing with love and joy at the possibility of being a vehicle and catalyst for expanding world peace and love, one person, one community, one nation at a time.

I've been deepening my understanding of the impact of *The Six Heart Illuminations* program, refining and evolving it as I've been guiding people one-on-one and in small groups since 2021. I've established a full-time career *Awakening Divine Love in All Hearts*, helping people release, surrender and let go of what weighs heavy on their hearts – grief, sorrow, resentment, regrets and shame – so they can live life in a light-hearted way, guiding them to live tuned into their heart wisdom, higher self and true divine nature.

Every session supporting my clients brings me inner ease, peace and harmony, and a sense of fulfillment. I'm so grateful I can contribute to the peaceful, heart radiant evolution of humanity, one person at a time. With every client there is a heart-warming story of awakening and realization.

When my client Ananda first joined my classes, he informed me that he didn't trust his heart or the guidance that comes from it, he only trusted his cognitive reasoning. I listened without judgment and enrolled him in the *Building Personal Resilience* and then the *Six Heart Illuminations* programs. After six months of coaching, his perspective completely transformed. He started making (and trusting) intuitive choices for his life. His physical heart health challenges were initially what brought him to seek my resilience guidance, but what he received was so much more. He realized there was more to life than work, that his health and family were more important. There were things he still wanted to experience in life before he became too old to enjoy them. He made the heartfelt intuitive decision to leave a forty-year career at a Fortune 100 company and was unwavering about his decision. He wanted to live the rest of his life dictating how he spent his time, doing what brings joy to his heart and makes him feel more fulfilled.

I've had to go through the heart purification and illuminations journey myself. And I go through it on a regular basis, as I have life experiences which hurt or start shutting down my heart. My heart is continuously awakening, expanding and liberating, in love, my true authentic nature, as divine love expressing itself as Jennifer Dickens. I feel freer and lighter every day. I surrender and allow myself to be guided daily by my soul being, to the best of my ability, starting my days with HeartMath® breath work, Reiki self-healing, Kriya meditation, visualization and intention setting, to be in the flow of divine will, allowing, accepting and receiving. Through surrendering my will to divine will, an omnipresent formidable force, I've discovered the answer to the question of who "I AM" and you can too.

The journey can be rocky and tumultuous, as well as magical, enchanting and joyous. It's a journey and path well worth taking to courageously experience the full expression of life from love, peace, harmony, care, compassion, kindness and joy.

Returning to where this chapter began, with my deep heart activation experience at the birthday commemoration of my guru and feeling a strong energetic vibrational force enter my heart with such intensity that I was almost pushed back screaming – well, after much research, I discovered, the energetic force that came directly from the heart of the picture was something called *Shaktipat*.

In Hinduism, Shaktipat refers to the transmission of spiritual energy upon one person by another or directly from a deity. Shaktipat can be transmitted with a sacred word or mantra, or by a look, thought or touch – the last, usually to the ajna chakra (or third eye) of the recipient. Shaktipat is considered an act of grace on the part of the guru or the divine. It cannot be imposed by force, nor can a receiver make it happen. The very consciousness of the god or guru is held to enter into the self of the disciple, constituting an initiation into the school or the spiritual family of the guru. Shaktipat is described by the yogic texts as *an initiation that activates an inner unfolding of awareness* leading to progressively higher states of consciousness. Over time, through grace and our efforts in spiritual practice, the sense of separation from divinity drops away.

Shaktipat on the heart chakra can help in opening and healing the heart chakra and removing blockages. It can heal past traumas and help us to grow spiritually. When Shaktipat is transmitted to the heart chakra, people feel the opening to vast dimensions, happiness, freedom, openness and unconditional love for all and everything.

This heart chakra Shaktipat as described in Hindu teachings is exactly what I experienced, "an energetic vibrational force entering my heart with intensity," clearing blockages of past hurts, disappointments, resentments and so much more. This was one of the most defining awakening and spiritual moments of my life.

If you'd have told me ten years ago that my career and life would look and feel like it does today, I'd have thought you're insane – *no way, that's not me.* When I was at the height of my career, the stress was so intense, I recall the only thing I wanted was peace of heart and mind. As I deepened my Sadhana (meditation) and awakened my heart, I found that peace of heart and mind I so desperately sought... and so much more.

Today, as I continue to follow my heart, inner guidance and wisdom, I am able to connect and express my true authentic nature and tap into my divinely guided gifts. I never could have imagined how joyous it would be to attune to and fulfill my higher calling, which continues to expand and unfold daily in magnanimous ways.

If any or all of this resonates with your heart, I encourage you to keep following your inner guidance to heart awakening, healing and expanding your capacity to love. If soul liberation and freedom is what you seek, or if becoming a divine embodiment of love heightens your curiosity, I encourage you to follow your heart. Following your heart, inner guidance and soul calling is always the choice toward your divine happiness and joy.

**Simple Heart Connection Practice**

I invite you to take a moment now. To relax and close your eyes, bringing your attention to your breath, breathing a little slower and deeper than you normally would, breathing as if your mouth is in the middle of your heart, taking in each gentle inhale and exhale. Finding a slow steady rhythmic breathing pace. Breathe this way for about three minutes and then ask your heart: *What can I do to deepen my attunement with you?* Then, sit silently and listen for the subtle insights, wisdom and guidance from your heart. You will know if it's heart guidance because it will make your heart sing. Journal and take action on your heart's intuitive insights.

I hope my story has inspired you, stirring within you what's possible when you awaken your heart's wisdom, tap into divine love and live life from the heart.

# Jennifer Dickens

As a HeartMath® Certified Coach, Usui Reiki Master, Six Heart Illumination facilitator and Kriyaban Yogi, Jennifer Dickens has developed a powerfully transformative way of heart expansion and healing, by awakening, purifying and illuminating the emotional, energetic and spiritual heart. Her mission is to awaken divine love in all hearts.

Since 2018, Jennifer has been supporting individuals in stabilizing their mental, emotional and spiritual wellbeing, as well as awakening their hearts to the love and wisdom which resides within. She leads heart-full group and individual programs for everyone ready to transcend their suffering and to live life from love and joy. Jennifer provides gentle, heartfelt guidance and insight into the simplicity of tapping into our true authentic self as divine love.

Jennifer is the founder of Awakening Heart Wisdom, Be Love, Inc. and Whole Life Marketing. She teaches:

- Usui Reiki Level I, II & III training and certification – profound relaxation and energy healing.
- Six Heart Illuminations – a path to heart illumination, shining your inner light and living life from the heart.
- Building Personal Resilience – autonomic nervous system (ANS) and emotional self-regulation.

When not guiding, teaching and marketing, what makes Jennifer's heart sing is traveling to sacred places, dancing, snow skiing, beach volleyball and most of all, deeply spiritual conversations.

⊕ www.jenndickens.com
⊕ www.linktr.ee/beloveinc

Scan QR code to learn more about Jennifer Dickens.

chapter

# 08

# One Spark, Collective Flame – From Inner Power to Uplifting Humanity

*by Tiffani Churchill*

It was seconds between life and death. All survival mechanisms activated, and all senses escalated to the highest alert levels. It was run or be eaten. But by a twist of fate, I walked outside, interrupting the circle of life, the dance between predator and prey. The mountain lion, surprised by my unexpected appearance, abruptly turned and raced away. Ultimately, the deer survived another day. I watched in sheer amazement as the elegant animal slowed, realizing the threat was gone and then shook its whole body. With a final twitch of the tail, it reset its entire system and calmly walked off, in search of the next garden to devour.

Although humans are structured differently, I also had the tools required to quickly shift out of fight or flight, just like the deer. I had been teaching yoga, meditation, and breathwork for over a decade. I had healed my body and transformed my life, so I knew of my innate power. But, like so many people, the tools and practices most beneficial in times of crises are the ones we give up first. After all, as the old Zen proverb states –*You should sit in meditation for twenty minutes, unless you're too busy then you should sit for an hour.* Survival for me was not a moment in time. It had become a way of being. Until, like a person treading water, I lost my strength and began to sink. It started as a normal Tuesday; I dropped my two children off at school and drove down the long country road in Central Florida toward my office. I don't know exactly what the catalyst was for my breakdown, but it was the final piece that brought my whole existence crashing down. Maybe it wasn't one thing at all, but the weight of years – years of enduring, of suppressing, of carrying too much, until there was simply no more space left inside me to contain it.

I loved studying the brain in college. Its intricate inner workings fascinate me to this day. But nothing I learned prepared me for what happens when the mind stops *holding it together*. They say you can lose your sense of time, even your connection to the world around you. That was true for me. When I gained full awareness, I was sitting in the middle of a field surrounded by curious onlookers who seemed as confused by my presence as I was. My face was stained with tears, my feet, somehow missing the black heels I had started the day with, were covered in dirt and my arms were rippled with goosebumps from a damp cold that I was too numb to feel.

I looked up, now fully aware, and said out loud, "I know two things for certain; I have to leave my relationship, and I have to leave my job." I don't know if I was saying this to myself, the crowd of bewildered cows watching me, or to whoever in the heavens might be listening. But those words on that particular day put into motion a stream of events that to many seemed absolutely mind-blowing!

If I had been in full consciousness, my mind would have started to object; that sabotaging self- talk attempting to keep me limited with doubt and unworthiness.

*You can't do that! He controls all of the money. How are you going to leave? It took you six months to find this job. How will you support your children?* But there was no thought about the how, only the pure knowingness that there was no choice. Deep down in all of my being, I KNEW I would not survive on my current life path. Because of this, I let go of all resistance, completely surrendered and opened my heart to what was to come.

Just two years earlier, I had restarted my life – or at least had tried to. Against every instinct, I chose to believe in second chances. My ex-husband knew how to pull every string. Yes, EX! A few well-timed tears, promises of change and expressions of love in just the right moments made me forget the past. I silenced the memories of the messy divorce, the scars of the old wounds and the abuses I swore I would never relive. I clung to the dream of a family, of a marriage reborn and of a new beginning in Florida.

It didn't take long to realize that our zip code was the only thing that changed. The same cycles repeated, only now, I had sacrificed even more of myself to keep everything from falling apart. We moved to a small town with few opportunities, long before remote work was common practice. I had given up my career for this new beginning and it took me months to get an offer to start a new division of a large medical practice. But I was giving everything, including all my savings, to support someone else's ambitions. I felt like I was dying inside.

After prying my heels from the mud, wiping the streaked mascara from my face and trudging over a mile back to my car... something shifted. It was as if I broke open inside, forcing me to see what I'd spent years denying. This wasn't a bad phase, a rough patch or a temporary struggle. This was *the end*. And whether I had planned it or not, I was about to step into something far bigger.

That evening, I took inspired action to initiate the change needed. My nephew in California had recently been diagnosed with leukemia, and more than anything, I wanted to be close to my family as they moved through each heart-breaking day. I reached out to every contact I had there, searching for a way to transfer my life across the country. But there was nothing. No leads. No offers. No escape route.

The very next day I answered my phone to an exhilarated voice saying, "You're never going to believe this...!"A completely unexpected position in a medical practice had opened up, literally, overnight! I had an interview and the position was mine. A month later, I flew my kids to California, and I loaded up a tiny U-Haul with their belongings, my clothes, our dog and two cats, setting out to drive from the east to west coast. In the evenings, I stopped at roadside hotels. The animals were restless from the long days trapped in the car, so none of us were able to sleep. I opened my journal and began to write. I imagined a whole new life; what it looked like, what it felt like, and I wrote every detail as if it were a current experience, a reality already manifested.

I chose Laguna Beach, California, for its top school districts, but with literally $10 in my bank account it seemed like an impossible dream. In a string of awe-inspiring events, I had a home, and it included EVERYTHING I had written out while sitting in those small hotel rooms imagining our new life.

Together my children and I were no longer waiting for a miracle. We were *creating* one.

We stayed in the house for two years until our family grew out of it. My heart had been locked up from my last relationship and I no longer believed in love, but my wise and brilliant daughter longed for my happiness, and continually requested I start dating. I turned to my journal once again. I wrote out what I called the *Impossible List* – a list of extraordinary characteristics – and promised myself, if I ever met a man like that, I would reconsider my vow of spending my life single. Two years later, on a beautiful summer day, I said "I do" to my husband who does not just check all the boxes on my list but exceeds them. Once again, what I created in my mind took shape in my outer world.

Laguna Beach was a thriving community with few rental properties available. I again journaled, meditated on, and imagined our new home. This time I included an ocean view from the kitchen. Then I thought, *Why only from the kitchen* and brought into my experience a home with full ocean views from every room. As I expanded, so did my belief in my own creative power and ability to bring about my desired reality. I set my heart, my mind and my focus on owning a home. As I write this, I sit in my extraordinary space overlooking the red rocks in Sedona in a home once again encompassing everything I imagined. My heart is filled with gratitude.

Over the years, it wasn't just homes I purposely brought into my reality. I experimented daily with the boundaries of human potential, exploring what was possible. I would start with writing out an experience then would choose an image that represented it, as if it were already fulfilled. That image became a symbol; one I would breathe life into during my meditation, feeling it vividly in my mind and heart. I expanded the $10 I had arrived in California with to extraordinary and sacred abundance, imagined and then experienced trips around the world, and celebrated as businesses my husband and I built began to thrive.

Internally I shifted false beliefs, expanded my heart into deeper levels of compassion and brought improved health and vitality into form.

For my entire life I have carried an overpowering fear of public speaking. The kind that people joke about when they say they'd rather die than stand on stage. For me it was real. The idea of being fully seen, exposed and heard was terrifying. My voice would shake. My breath would vanish. My mind would go blank. In my meditations, I imagined being in front of an audience filled with love of the experience and the joy of being in service to something greater than myself. One day this became my reality.

I discovered that when I lived in gratitude, awe and an unwavering knowingness, life unfolded with effortless synchronicity. It was as if I was tapped into a vast and limitless power, *source*, with belief acting as the current that kept everything flowing. But the moment fear crept in, when doubt, stress, or lower emotions took hold, the connection would dissolve. The flow would stop. Possibilities would evade me. The difference was extreme – the expression of Source versus the boundaries of human form. Yet, maintaining that higher frequency required far more discipline than slipping back into the patterns of old limitations.

On a trip to Bali to study with healers, I was sitting in a luxurious hotel room surrounded by lush rice fields. I said out loud, this time in far contrast to my breakdown in the field filled with cows.

*Wow, can my life get any better?* Then I thought, *If I could create all of this, what could we do together?*

This time the curious onlookers were a group of monkeys in a nearby tree. Once again, a momentum began that shifted my whole life.

In my late twenties I had a spiritual teacher who would meditate with me, guiding me into deeper states of consciousness. He explained that he could raise my awareness to levels that, on my own, would take me a lifetime of meditation to achieve. Once my body attuned to this new frequency, I could more easily attain it. It was an initiation into a higher state of being. Inspired by this, I began hosting meditation groups centered on the same philosophy, that a group of us could amplify the energy, elevating ourselves and together uplifting the whole.

I was driven to researching, to exploring ancient wisdom and experimenting to confirm what I intuitively knew; that consciousness when unified could shift reality.

My trip to Bali reignited this passion.

I had scheduled a session with a revered and gifted healer; this time instead of studying I was going to receive. When I arrived at the healing center, she was joined by another woman who appeared frail and evidently unwell. The healer asked for permission for me to join in the session and the woman gave a slight nod of approval.

Instantly my purpose shifted, instead of focusing on myself, I became part of something more profound.

The next day I returned. I soaked my feet in the flower-filled bowl of water anticipating the focus of the healer on me, but I have learned that often when our plans get interrupted, it can be because there is something greater at play. This was evident on this day. Once again, I joined the healer in a ceremony of healing for a woman from her village. This time, our focus was not on a physical body in front of us but on a photograph. Still, it felt powerful, like what we were doing mattered, that this energy was real, and that something unquestionable was at work. I felt more transformed by giving selflessly than if I had received the attention of the healer.

Once home, I joined countless meditation, intention and prayer groups to further explore our connection. Small groups of us would get together in person or remotely, it didn't seem to matter. Now principles of quantum physics such as entanglement and nonlocality are proving this. I witnessed people healing, businesses flourishing unexpectedly and relationships deepening.

One beautiful woman in our group asked if we could hold a meditation for her son who had been living in extensive pain. He was born with a crooked foot and standing on it daily inflamed the experience and suffering. That night, after bartending, he called his mom in joy and disbelief to share that for the first time ever, his evening shift had been pain-free. Three months later, she sent an update that the pain had never returned.

Another instance – a small group of us joined together remotely to focus our collective intention on a region of South Africa that had been enduring a devastating drought. We wanted to explore the impact of our united consciousness, to see what was possible when we aligned our energy for the good of something beyond ourselves. Afterall, rain dancers have done this for centuries! Group members captured screenshots of weather radars, which showed no sign of rain. When our meditation was complete, my phone lit up with more screenshots. This time there were images of droplets falling from the sky. Maybe it was coincidence or maybe it was in response to our coherence. Either way it was a beautiful moment.

I have countless stories of the miracles that transpired from uniting our hearts and minds around a common vision. Even more incredible was my life. I asked if my life could get any better when I sat in Bali, and it DID! Giving to another or to enhancing the world was a gateway to the full unraveling of my heart.

*There was a reciprocal effect – the more I gave, the more I received.*

I no longer had to fight to stay in a connected state or maintain my alignment. The key had been there all along – *Altruism.*

Now like the deer shaking off the effects of the threat, I discovered that shifting my state was effortless when I took the attention off myself and poured my energy and heart outward through meditation and intention. It was an alchemical formula, a sacred exchange and the catalyst for the most transformation I had yet to experience.

This shift led me to one final question, this time I speak it out loud to you the reader: *If a small, connected group could have such profound effects in the life of another, what could we collectively achieve together? Could we change the world?*

I believe we can!

# Tiffani Churchill

Tiffani Churchill is the founder of ALLTRUEistic, a groundbreaking collective meditation and intention app created to unite people in the co-creation of a more evolved future for humanity. Tiffani combines her successful career in the medical and wellness industries with decades of experience teaching yoga, meditation and breathwork. She has a degree in holistic health, a master's certification in energy medicine, and has trained with healers all over the world. She blends science, spirituality and service in all she does.

Upon discovering that she had the ability to bend her reality, Tiffani began to wonder what people could accomplish together. She joined countless meditation, intention, and prayer groups exploring the power of mass consciousness, witnessing astounding outcomes when people unite their hearts and minds around a shared vision. These experiences cemented her belief that connected communities have the power to profoundly change the world.

When Tiffani is not expanding ALLTRUEistic or exploring group consciousness, she is assisting visionaries and dreamers turn their ideas into thriving businesses. She lives an intentionally created life filled with love, purpose, and miracles alongside her extraordinary husband and three children.

⊕ www.alltrueistic.com
◎ @alltrueisticapp
Scan QR code to learn more about Tiffani Churchill.

## Section II:
# From Shadows to Healing

- Which experiences in your past are still longing to be seen, softened, and embraced?

- Are there wounds you've carried so long they've become part of your identity?

- How would your life begin to shift if you opened up to the possibility of healing?

chapter

# 09

# The Courage to Feel

*by Natasha Davidson*

"I don't think you should come."

"What do you mean?"

"I don't think you and the kids should come to Vermont."

I had just quit my job, sold the house, and put all of our stuff on a moving van. My husband and I, and our two young children, were leaving California to start a new chapter of life in Vermont.

"I don't think you and the kids should come to Vermont."

When he said these words, the moving van was almost all the way across the country. He had started working there months prior and I was minutes away from picking the kids up from their last day at school. Classroom teachers had already done their going-away parties for my kids, and each student in class had written a goodbye message.

"I don't think you and the kids should come to Vermont," he repeated.

I spent the next days trying to understand where this message was coming from. *Who would push their family away like that?* When I asked him, he said he was sick in his head and that I would never understand. *It was final.*

The hurt, the abandonment, the betrayal was almost impossible to bear. I had been a devoted wife. Always prioritizing my husband and our kids. How could my husband just abandon me? Where was his sense of responsibility? Did he not honor all of the sacrifices I made for him?

While I was trying to understand, I was also trying to survive. Putting the pieces together after the rug had been pulled out from underneath me. Humbly asking for my job back. Finding a place for the kids and I to live. Putting the kids back in the school they had said goodbye to, hoping they wouldn't be embarrassed or too confused about what was going on. He didn't help. Not one bit. It was all on me.

I began to put my life back together. I spent the next four years as a single mom working hard to do it all; working the traveling corporate sales job, raising two small kids on my own, and trying to find time for myself so I wouldn't fall apart.

Was I happy? No. Was I fulfilled? No. I was just trying to survive.

I hired a part-time nanny to help. I especially needed her when I traveled late at night. And when I went on overnight trips for work, I asked my mom to drive ninety miles to come stay with the kids.

I started to notice my son becoming defiant. I thought that sending him to therapy would help. It was then I realized that I needed to go to therapy. I was exhausted and overwhelmed. I was good at hiding my overwhelm from everyone, but I was especially good at hiding it from myself. I didn't know there was another way to live. The funny thing is that I thought *it was just how life was*.

Things shifted when the therapist asked me if I had any money saved. I said, "Yes, I have an emergency fund." She responded, "What if you view it as an opportunity fund?"

Days later, I left my corporate job. It felt like I was freefalling. It was the first time I didn't have a plan. I had spent my entire life following what I was told to do; be the good Catholic school girl, get the good grades, go to the good university, get the good job, make the big money. Now, I was stepping off a cliff into the unknown.

Deep down I knew – *if I can bounce back after my husband suddenly left me like that, then surely, I can figure out life outside of working in the corporate world.*

I spent those next few months reconnecting with my kids. They hadn't known their mother anymore because I was always gone. Always traveling. Always stressed. Never fully present. Just trying to survive. We went on a long road trip to Oregon and stayed on a farm. It filled my heart. It filled all of our hearts.

When the kids went back to school that fall, I told myself, *If I am going to work, it has to be something I am passionate about.* I had always been passionate about health and nutrition so I signed up to learn how to be a health coach. I thought the training program was going to teach me all about the perfect diet, and I would, in turn, teach others how to eat so that they could be super healthy. At the end of the health coaching program, I was disappointed that they had shared so many different diets but not directed us to recommend a specific one. Up until that point, I felt comfortable being told what to do, so how was I going to move forward without someone giving me clear direction?

At that same time, my mom was experiencing autoimmune symptoms and I wanted to help her. The truth is, I wanted to fix her. She meant the world to me, so I became curious about healing. I was constantly asking the question, "Why do some people heal and other people don't?"

My curiosity led me to a book called *Radical Remission* by Dr. Kelly A Turner. The author had studied hundreds of cases where cancer patients had spontaneously healed. She wanted to understand what these cases had in common, and she arrived at nine key factors:

- Radically change your diet.
- Use herbs and supplements.
- Take control of your health.
- Follow your intuition.
- Release suppressed emotions.
- Increase positive emotions.
- Embrace social support.
- Deepen your spiritual connection.
- Have strong reasons for living.

*Hmmm,* I thought, *I didn't know that unresolved emotions had anything to do with disease in the body.*

This was my first introduction to the idea that emotions are tied to health. I didn't know it at the time, but I was ripe to dive deep into emotional healing.

## The Awakening Experience

*Everything is energy – including you.*

Months later, I was at a BioEnergetics conference learning how to recognize when energy becomes blocked and how to get it flowing freely again. The inspirational speaker on stage, Dr. Sue Morter confirmed:

"The body's energy has to remain in motion if we ever want to be clear and healed and functional at the level that we are destined to be functioning in this life. If we don't resolve some experience that we have, it gets locked in the body which stops the energy flow."

Light bulbs went off. Holy shit. It felt like all the puzzle pieces were coming together.

Healing isn't about eating the right food or finding the right doctor. Healing is about letting go of judgements, misperceptions and resistance. Healing is about taking care of unresolved emotions, about returning back to your true authentic self.

I was so fascinated, I signed up for more classes. I was a sponge soaking it all in. I couldn't get enough. *What other brilliant wisdom could I learn?*

I learned that we create separation by judging people or situations as *bad or wrong*. We create separation by resisting what is. When we create separation in our minds, we create separation in our bodies, which ultimately leads to disease. Disharmony in the mind creates dis-ease in the body.

At that time, I had plenty I could judge as "wrong." Once again, the suppressed anger toward my kids' father bubbled to the surface. Thoughts like, *How could he have done this to me?* flooded my mind.

Now I had the time and space to feel, I finally let myself feel the anger. Years of suppressed anger flooded out of me. I'd been holding it all in, just trying to survive. Putting a pretty smile on my face even though I felt so much pain inside. The truth is, I had been afraid to feel the anger. *I had been so afraid.*

I finally let go of all resistance to feel. I let myself have my anger. I let it flow through me. And because I let myself have it and feel it, it dissolved.

What came out of it was a passion. A powerful passion was rising and emerging from me. Today, I use this passion to serve humanity through emotional healing.

I see people afraid to feel. I see how much they are holding onto, just trying to survive. The overwhelm is too big. They think they just can't process any more, so they get distracted or numb out. I see people living lives that aren't their own. They are living for other people following what they "should" do or what they are told to do. I see how much they are in their heads, trying to figure it all out.

I was that person.

Now I understand that the first step is *feeling*. Because feeling is healing. And when I say feeling, I mean really welcoming in that emotion and sitting with it. Wrapping your arms around it and becoming so close to it that you begin to feel you are merging with it. There is no more separation. There is no more resistance because you have become one with it. You have fully taken it in and accepted it. And acceptance brings peace. No matter what the situation.

Imagine a volcano with hot, liquid magma. The magma oozes out of the volcano and consumes everything in its path. Now imagine that your heart is the volcano and the magma is love. Let the love of your heart consume the feeling. Let it devour it. Let it flow.

It's the resistance to the feeling that creates stress. Our minds love to distract us with other things, in order to NOT feel the feeling we are afraid to feel. Our minds will avoid it at all costs. I know it's painful, it's scary and it takes great courage... but what comes out of it is absolutely incredible.

Out of the chaos and inner turmoil comes balance. You are no longer restless and you are no longer frozen. You are in flow. No longer resistant to life. Accepting life as it comes. In appreciation of what is. Appreciating every single experience. The return to inner peace and harmony is like none other. Once you get a taste of it, you'll want more. It's a form of love that is rich with life.

You come alive. You bite into a summer peach and savor it, feeling the juices running down your face. You laugh like you were a kid. Life is fun and exciting again. Life unfolds naturally with grace and synchronicity. Your mind releases control and you experience a state of deep inner peace that remains unaffected by external circumstances. Things don't trigger you as they once did. Opportunities flow into your life and you boldly take risks. You embrace discomfort and do hard things. You feel truly resilient.

This is what it means to live in the present moment. This is what it means to live in flow. You trust life's timing, and you shift from a reactive, stress-driven life to one of inner peace and wisdom. It's a state of complete acceptance of what is. You see life as one grand adventure. You see life as the gift that it is.

It is an absolute privilege to be in a body on earth at this time. Why not savor it? Why not fully enjoy it?

It is our mind that takes us out of this state of being. The thinking, worried mind has a habit of disconnecting us from the flow when it wants to take over, to try and figure everything out. The mind lacks patience and is uncomfortable in the unknown. I get it, our mind just wants to protect us. But when we are in our heads trying to control our environment, we are creating our own suffering. But there is another way of living. One where you allow more possibility. More opportunities to flow into your life. You go from a life of surviving to a life of thriving.

Trust that you have a higher self that is orchestrating your life on your behalf. You don't have to figure everything out. Be okay with not knowing. Your job is to enjoy it. Life is full of treasure. Your job is to feel.

The beautiful thing is that the body lets you know what to feel. Feeling anxious? It's just your body telling you that you are projecting too far into the future and it's inviting you to come back to the present moment. Because in this moment you are truly okay, right?

Nature is always showing you how to connect to the flow. Our bodies are part of nature and when energy is flowing through your body, energy is flowing through your life.

Sometimes life takes an unexpected turn, and guess what? This redirection is ALWAYS a blessing in disguise. In the moment, it might feel like the worst thing ever. Your mind might freak out. Okay, it WILL freak out. And when you calm down and look back on it later, you'll realize: *Wow, I see why that happened. It led me to awaken more courage, love or passion. It ignited something within me.*

As I reflect on my own life, the words that come to me are: *The redirection was all part of the divine plan.*

Sometimes the mind likes to ask, *Why did I experience that, just for it to end?* I mean, *Why would I get married, if I was just going to get divorced? Why would I do anything, if it's going to end?* Well, it's for the experience of it all. The invitation is not to focus so much on the outcome or the completion of something, the invitation is to savor each experience. The invitation is to be in flow.

Today, I thank my ex-husband for being the catalyst to my awakening. I thank him for being the actor in my movie that played the part of betrayal and abandonment. I thank him for creating chaos so that I could *feel*, and transmute generations of anger that ran through my bloodline. I thank him because this anger awakened passion within me; passion and excitement for life. Passion for this life experience in a body where I get to savor it all. The juicy peach. My feet in the sand. The waves at my feet. The sunlight on my face. The laughter and joy of my children. All of it.

It turns out that the secret to thriving in life is letting go of resistance and allowing yourself to feel – feeling really is healing. True resilience is surrendering knowing that it's all part of the divine plan. I now have a strong sense of self. I'm grounded, solid, courageous. Yet I live in flow, okay not knowing what's next. I live life with an open heart. Ready to love.

I have never had so much energy. So much excitement. So much enthusiasm for life. What a grand adventure this is. Oh, what fun. What a privilege. What a gift.

After recently mentioning to my son that he had been defiant during that period of time, he admitted, "Yeah, Mom, it's cause I didn't want a nanny, I wanted my mom." My children needed me and I am so grateful to have listened. I listened to the quiet whisper that was telling me to surrender. They now have a mom. A mom that is so full of life. A mom that has the capacity to fully love, to be fully present. As I look back, I don't regret any of it.

# Natasha Davidson

Natasha holds a vision for a different way of living: one that breaks free from limitation and opens into peaceful, clear expansion and expression. Her belief is that we are not meant to be stuck in outdated survival patterns, we are meant to awaken to the truth of who we are: loving, powerful, creative beings in harmony with the natural flow of life.

She has devoted her life to helping others by creating Heart Rooted Health, a business dedicated to helping people embody peace and live at the highest levels of life.

Natasha works with the intelligence of the body to reveal what's in priority to shift. Through the BioEnergetic Synchronization Technique (B.E.S.T.), she gently uncovers and releases subconscious interference, allowing the nervous system to stabilize and the energy system to re-align. This creates an opening: more light is able to flow through the system. Clients open to greater levels of energy and higher states of consciousness. Intuitive clarity is strengthened. Physical symptoms commonly resolve on their own. New possibilities emerge and life begins to feel lighter, more aligned, and more inspired.

Natasha works with clients both individually and in group settings. She teaches workshops and shares her wisdom through podcasts and speaking engagements on embodiment and empowerment.

If you feel ready to embody intuitive clarity and create an empowered life, connect with Natasha directly by visiting her website.

🌐 www.heartrootedhealth.com

Scan QR code to learn more about Natasha Davidson.

# chapter 10

## The Choice That Changed Everything

*by Michelle Hays*

I used to believe love was something you fell into. I believed love was something magical that just worked if two people were meant to be. I believed it would come naturally, effortlessly, like breathing. But after years of marriage, I found myself questioning everything. I slowly became disillusioned with love because our spark had faded, our connection felt strained, and I started to wonder if my husband ever really loved me at all.

One day, while my kids were napping, I crawled into bed and let it all out. I cried and cried. No. I wasn't crying, I was sobbing. My whole body involuntarily shook as my tears soaked into the depths of my pillow. I felt overwhelmed by all the feelings and emotions gripping my heart and mind. I felt taken for granted, unappreciated, hopeless, and heartbroken, all at once. I believed I was doing everything I should to be a loving wife and mom. I couldn't understand how or why I could be feeling so unseen, unheard, and unloved. This was not what love was supposed to be like. The only thing that made sense then, was that I must have married the wrong man.

I thought deeply about myself and why I had become a resentful, unhappy wife. I didn't even like myself anymore, thinking what a stranger I had become to myself. I had lost myself in making my husband and children happy. I remember squeezing my eyes shut and trying to catch my breath. Suddenly, I heard a soft, familiar voice; "Mommy, why are you crying?" my little three-year-old asked. I quickly sat up, wiped my tears, forced a smile, and said, "Sometimes mommies get sad too, sweetheart," and then came the question that pierced my heart. "Did I make you sad, Mommy?" "Oh, no, honey! You didn't make me sad," I told her as I gathered her in my arms, held her close, and kissed her precious face, as I managed to pull myself together. "I know what will cheer mommy up... a little ice cream! Would you like to have some ice cream with me?" I asked. "Yes, mommy!" she said.

The next thing I knew, I was sitting across from the man I loved with all my heart, signing our divorce papers. I left the attorney's office feeling drained, afraid, and completely heartbroken. I felt heavy-hearted. I was full of hope and so much love when I got married. I adored my husband and couldn't imagine my life without him. Never in my wildest dreams did I think that we would ever get divorced. Our divorce changed our lives and the lives of our children and families forever. We were now part of the approximately 50% of first marriages that end way before "death do us part." I wholeheartedly believed I married the wrong man. I remember thinking I would fall in love again someday and make a better choice next time. I will find someone who cherishes me, and I will be *happier*.

Like many people who get divorced, I wanted to meet someone new, hoping to fall in love again, *but this time*, I told myself *it would be different*. I created several online dating profiles. I took time to choose the right photos and sincerely described myself, my wants, and deal breakers in detail, as well as the qualities I was hoping for in the man I was looking to meet. I had been talking to my friend Sheryl one evening, and she mentioned that she knew the "perfect" guy for me! She said, "Oh, you two are perfect for each other! His name is Brian, and you'll like him," she said. As she told me, we both enjoyed the same things, are both down to earth, etc., I was feeling wary. I wasn't convinced my friend, Sheryl, could possibly know if I would "like someone." Although I loved my friend, we were very different and valued different things, but of course, I was very curious and oh-so hopeful.

After I got off the phone with Sheryl, I sat silently for a moment. I began slowly tapping the keys on my keyboard, carefully entering his name into the search space on Facebook, and his profile came up immediately. I remember seeing his gentle eyes and slight smile and thought, *oh, at least he is easy on the eyes!* It was March 11, 2010, and Brian chose a lovely restaurant called Truluck's. It was in Mizner Park in Boca Raton (Florida, for those of you who may not know), and we agreed to meet at 7:00 p.m.

That day, I woke up in the morning with a hopeful heart, feeling excited! I went to work, came home, walked my dog, Jackson, and got in the shower. I did my hair, put on my make-up, and chose a classic little black dress for our date. I looked in the mirror and felt good.

I arrived at Truluck's a few minutes past seven – no Brian. I waited. I checked my phone. No messages or calls. *Hmmm*. I started to feel a little annoyed. I thought to myself, *is this guy going to stand me up?* Then, for whatever reason, I decided to call my mom. I told her what was happening, and she said, "Why don't you call him?" I didn't want to call him, but as my mom reminded me, he was Sheryl's friend, and something must have happened. I promised my mom I would call her after our date and tell her how it went... and reluctantly called Brian.

I heard the phone ring once, and Brian quickly picked up and said, "I'll be there in five minutes," and hung up! He didn't even give me a chance to say a word. I stared at my cell phone for a second, allowing what just happened to sink in. I couldn't help but smile because I knew exactly why he didn't give me a chance to say anything. He thought that I might say *let's make it for another night*. He was correct. I was going to say exactly that!

Anyway, true to his words, he came speeding up to the valet in about five minutes, and I watched him rushing out of the car, forgetting to give the valet his keys and the Valet shouting for him. Brian tossed him the keys and then took a moment to regroup at the restaurant's front door (He didn't see me because there were two-way windows.) Brian walked into the restaurant, cool and collected, walked up to me, our eyes met, he gently grabbed my hand, kissed it, and said, "I am so sorry. Will you forgive me?" I don't remember my exact words, but I remember feeling a bit playful and wanting to make him feel at ease, so I said something like, "Don't let it happen again," and we laughed. As the hostess began showing us to our table, "Would you please bring the lady a black napkin?" I heard Brian say to the hostess. "Of course," she said as she smiled and winked at me. Apparently, she was impressed. For a moment, I thought, *what do I need a black napkin for?* But then I quickly realized. Brian requested a black napkin, so I didn't get any white lint on my black dress... brilliant. I was totally impressed. As I was looking at the menu, I was torn between two entrees that both sounded amazing. When Brian asked me what I was getting, I shared my dilemma and, without skipping a beat, he said, "Let's order both of them and share." I was utterly smitten with

Brian at that point. First, he kissed my hand, then the black napkin, and now this... sharing food happens to be one of my favorite things to do. Anyway, to make a long story short, our meals were delicious. We danced in the cocktail lounge after dinner until the music ended. I love to dance. He picked a pink hibiscus and placed it in my hair behind my ear, as we walked over to an after-hours bar called *The Wishing Well*. We didn't want our date to end, but at 1:30 a.m., it was time to go.

I called my mom afterward (she is a night owl) and squealed with delight, telling her everything that had happened on our magical first date. Brian and I have been inseparable since that night. Oh, I forgot to mention one important part of this story – you should know about our conversation at dinner. Brian asked me the strangest question I have ever been asked on a first date. He came right out and asked me, "Do you ever want to get married again?" After pausing momentarily, I said, "I want to be happy." Two years later, I held onto my dad's arm as we walked down the aisle of The Little Pink Church. Brian stood at the altar, his eyes glistening with unshed tears, wearing a look that said everything — *I love you. I choose you.*

The years flew by quickly, as they always do. We laughed, cried, traveled, had fun, bought a boat, enjoyed entertaining, made lots of good friends, spent time with our families, and then, little by little, before we even realized, something started to shift. I began to feel a bit disconnected now and then, and resentment started to build up from all the things I didn't say. Then one afternoon, while we were sitting on the couch watching TV, we started talking, and the next thing I knew, everything escalated. We started arguing. I became furious. I felt my face flush, and honestly, I felt like throwing something! Yikes. So, I decided that rather than saying or doing anything I would regret (I learned that you cannot back take things that you say in anger from my first marriage), I chose to go for a walk... which is precisely what I did. I walked out the front door and slammed it shut. Hard. As I started walking and ruminating, I realized this feeling was familiar. It was happening. I was becoming a resentful, unhappy wife again. I had to take a long, hard look at myself at that point. I was the common denominator. So, I began questioning myself. *Was there something wrong with me? Was I unlovable? Were my expectations of love and marriage unrealistic?* I deeply love my husband, Brian, and I knew without a doubt that I didn't want to get divorced again.

Then came the moment that changed everything. It wasn't anything grand or earth-shattering. It was a choice I made in the middle of an ordinary day, after an argument with my husband, and it changed my entire life. It was a decision to stay committed rather than give up on Brian and our marriage. It was the choice to love my husband, even when I didn't feel like it. While I was on that walk, I intentionally made the choice to focus on all the things I loved and enjoyed about my husband. Those choices led me to a doorway that led me to a truth I had overlooked for many years: love isn't just a feeling or an emotion, *love is a decision*. It's a decision we must make, over and over again in our marriages. Understanding that love is a decision awakened me to a deeper, more authentic kind of love than I could have ever imagined.

No one teaches us how to live together day to day, year after year, or what to expect from love and marriage. We are raised on Hollywood romance, chick flicks, and romantic novels with idyllic romance and never-ending perfection. The couples always seem to figure everything out and allude to living happily ever after. No wonder we become frustrated and disillusioned in our real-life marriages. Research suggests that love hormones, like oxytocin and dopamine, make us giddy when we fall in love, but those hormones eventually wane. I have learned that love will never be enough to sustain a happy marriage. Love is not a sustainable feeling or emotion, because feelings and emotions are fleeting.

Creating a deeply meaningful marriage takes time, attention, and mindfulness. We all want immediate gratification. Developing the deep connections and fulfilling marriages we want requires a conviction to stay together through thick and thin. Love is a feeling, but love without a decision is incomplete. All marriages have challenges; mine, yours, and everyone else's. Remarriage divorce statistics prove it and are even more startling than first-time marriage statistics. Like I once did, many people believe that marrying someone else is the answer. However, statistics show that 67% of all second marriages fail, and an astounding 73% of all third marriages also end in divorce. Clearly, we don't get better at relationships just because we have a new one.

The decisions we make create the marriages we currently have. *Is your marriage everything you hoped for when you said I do?* Was that a, "no"? I get that. Like I've shared. I've been there. I know what feeling unfulfilled and unloved in a marriage is like.

May I share some thoughts with you? Just because you feel unloved doesn't mean you *are* unloved. It's never too late to start over, friend. It's never too late to decide you want more for yourself and your marriage. It is never too late to make small daily changes that will transform your marriage. Learning to develop a stronger, more fulfilling marriage and closing the gap between the marriage you have and the marriage you want, is far less agonizing and stressful than getting divorced will ever be. Love is a skill that can be learned and practiced. You can start over anytime. The marriage you currently have is a direct result of the choices you and your spouse have made. If you want something different, you must do something different. Because when we know better, we can do better. You get to decide and choose your actions, words, and behaviors... every single day. *What will your choices be?*

My heart and mind have been awakened by the realization that love is a decision, which helped me develop a growth mindset that has been a game-changer in my marriage. Embracing the idea that love is a decision can also improve your marriage. I invite you to put your hand over your heart for a moment. Close your eyes after reading this to the end. While your eyes are closed, take a long, deep breath and then recall a time when you felt loved by your spouse. See their face in your mind. Remember how that felt? YOU are loved. Your husband wants to make you happy. He has simply forgotten how. Refrain from complaining and start expressing your desires. (Underneath every complaint lies a hidden desire.)

Tonight, when you get into bed, look at your spouse. First, decide you want *more* for yourself and your marriage. Secondly, open a dialogue and make a pact with your spouse that you would never intentionally hurt one another. Thirdly, focus on one good thing your partner did for you today and express your gratitude. Love is a decision. Choose wisely. Choose each other. Choose love.

By embracing the idea that love is a series of intentional decisions, we can create long-lasting, strong marriages full of trust and intimacy. When we teach this to our children, we can impact how the world thinks about and navigates love and marriage, one intentional, loving decision at a time.

Love is a decision. Love is not something you find or lose, love is something you choose.

# Michelle Hays

Michelle Hays is the founder and host of the Monarch for Love Podcast, a heart-centered Marriage Coach, and a featured columnist for *Lighthouse Point* Magazine and the *Happy Herald*. With decades of personal and professional experience in love, marriage, and personal growth, Michelle offers a compassionate and transformative approach to helping couples reconnect.

She specializes in guiding loving, committed wives, who feel unseen or disconnected, to rediscover their voice, rebuild trust, and reignite the intimacy in their marriages – often in 90 days or less. Her coaching combines deep insight with practical tools, helping women create emotional safety, strengthen communication, and cultivate the kind of love that lasts.

Michelle's work is rooted in the belief that *love is a choice* – and when we choose it with intention, everything can change. Through her podcast, private coaching, and writings, she reminds women that they are not broken, their marriage isn't doomed, and real change is possible.

If you're longing for a deeper, more connected marriage and want a coach who truly sees your heart, Michelle invites you to connect with her.

🌐 www.monarchforlove.com
📷 @monarchforlove

Scan QR code to learn more about Michelle Hays.

## chapter 11

# The Unseen Hand: Whispered Prayers and the Power of Belief

*by Ida Ra Nalbandian*

The phone is ringing in my office. An unknown caller introduces herself as *Maria*. She is my co-worker Arthur's wife.

With a shaken voice she is sharing that Arthur, her husband, is currently in the emergency room and in a very dangerous condition. "Doctors are not sure if he will make it," she says, "he has a serious medical condition."

Gasping, Maria begins by describing the details of the incident. Arthur, while visiting his friend Tony, collapses. Tony performs CPR, a lifesaving technique, during the wait for the paramedics to arrive. Maria's voice is trembling, I can hear her sobbing, her voice full of fear, marked by worry and terror from all the pain she is experiencing. I ask my higher self for guidance on what to say to her, in an attempt to give her some words of comfort.

I am in shock myself, and disbelief from the unexpected. A flash of Arthur's picture appears in my mind, his gentle smile and kind personality forming into an image. Arthur is in his fifties, an active man with a warm, kindness-radiating smile. For the number of years I have known him, he always seemed to be in good health. Our life is like sand on the beach, it changes when the waves arrive to wash things away.

While I look through my mind for calming words, I suddenly feel a voice from the back of my head, urging me to say, "Don't allow any sad forecasts to stay with you right now. If you can, please focus on prayer by visualizing Arthur returning home well and healthy. See it like a slideshow. And, if you can, do this on a frequent basis. The moment you think of him, without delay, allow the slideshow of the desired outcome into your mind, to take over anything else."

I obey the voice and convey the message by assuring her: "When you get calls from family and friends to offer support, ask them to pray with immovable belief for Arthur's wellness, that all is well, and that he is happily, home already, sitting next to you.

"I do understand this is not a common thing," I continue, "yet there were many giants, like Louise Hay, Neville Goddard and Martin Brofman who practiced this technique and succeeded in their efforts to shift the energy imbalance." There have been numerous studies with documented proof done by the HeartMath institute to examine the science behind this phenomenon, also known as united intent-visualization. Dr. Joe Dispenza is another explorer of these kinds of miracles. The list of individuals who have used this to great effect is truly long.

When a technique is not a common habit, it is hard to alter our mind and begin using imagination versus reality, reimagining a scene that is different from what is actually taking place in the moment. However, we can try. By the way, it is free. At my workplace, we had a similar situation when we were activating a mini prayer group during Covid-19 lockdowns, and indeed, we did experience and receive a miracle, and a noteworthy one at that. That's a whole different conversation.

"Do you want to try?" I ask Maria. She replies, "Yes," with tears and a hope in her voice.

"If you agree, I can ask my co-workers who were in a "prayer group" with me during Covid lockdown to join us. Would you like that?"

I explain to Maria that we will chime in with our prayers by visualizing Arthur returning home healthy and happy. Belief is the fuel for the vehicle of our prayer, without faith, the vehicle is out of gas, it can't move. She agrees once more, curious to try this option.

"We'll start our prayer as soon as I contact them and seek assistance from the healing forces of the universe to amplify our prayer-request and witness Arthur recover soon."

I continue on, "Maria, one more thing you could do is to call every temple, church and prayer center near you. They usually accept prayer requests, so ask them to pray for Arthur's quick recovery."

Maria agrees with everything I share. Tiny notes of strength come back to her voice, some energy of an invisible power giving her a shoulder to lean on.

I conclude with firm assurance, "Please remember. Miracles exist when we believe in them, and trust that they are done. The energetic universe is our partner in all that we ask for, and it delivers *only* after we display faith. Doubts are not allowed; they are viruses that are designed to make our wish sick and forget its way to the destination. Our job is to remember to remain in the vehicle of faith that these viruses of disbelief won't destroy our potential results."

Maria's voice is getting calmer by the minute. We say goodbye and promise to stay strong and seek assistance in prayer from different sources.

I commit to prayer and will ask others to do so as well. She says, "I will keep you posted." Her voice is firm and determined, the trembling is gone. Now, she has hope.

I put down the phone, contemplating what just took place. *Where did this firm, leading voice from the back of my head come from?* This is the second time this voice had made itself clear. It takes over with such eagerness. I thank the voice for its assistance in comforting and reassuring others who need it.

Even though this was the very first time I connected with Maria, there is no doubt in my mind that she understood what I meant. I knew she could help her husband by using her own unseen powers, by activating a portal for prayer.

A memory flash flows into my mind. Back in March 2020, during the Covid-19 lockdowns, as department manager, I was given a task to deliver difficult news to everyone in our workplace, before going home and waiting for further guidance, without knowing if anyone could keep their job. That day, when I delivered the message, some emotional numbness took over me. Looking for some inside help, I held on to my keys in the pocket of my jacket, hoping to receive support from a solid object. At that moment, the world appeared extra unstable, like a big ocean rogue wave smashing things, and I could only watch, frozen.

A few years back during my travels, I purchased a keychain with very attractive miniature keys, each one engraved with a decorative word. They are the following: *Wisdom, Faith, Love, Prosperity.* I keep the keychain on my set of keys as a needed reminder for the four energies I enjoy having in abundance. And now, at that strenuous moment, I held my hand around them, touching and feeling each one.

Shortly after I delivered the news to my co-workers, I saw their facial expressions become frozen and terrified. I saw how this news devastated them and brought intense fear, regardless of how gently I chose to deliver the frightful message. My words stole hope from their hearts. They stood up in front of me in complete silence, some of them staring at the floor, unable to even look up.

While observing all this, with my hand still grasping the keys, I felt something break off the keychain. Curious, I took the key out to see what had taken place. One of the little keys had broken off. I read the engraved word: inscribed was *Faith.*

*What was, and is, the universe trying to tell me through that one word? I* kept staring at the key and the word *Faith*... I seek answers within myself. *What does this word actually mean? How do I stay with it? Why did this key break off and not the others?*

It seems that I needed to take a step forward without seeing the road. When the rug is pulled from underneath everyone's feet, what do I hold on to keep my balance?

Suddenly this strong voice came from the back of my head and urged me to say the following:

I understand it is very difficult news for all of us. At this moment, it may appear that there is no hope for us to hold on to, right here, right now. However, there is one thing which with certainty worked for humans of old and continues working for those who choose to use it. It is an internally focused intent, *a prayer*. To put it simply, our mind is an electric plug that needs to connect to the outlet of the universe to source its electricity. When we plug it in the right way, the universe provides the requested assistance. And when many join their efforts to unite them in their intent, the miracles happen faster.

Today, I ask those of you who can join me to choose prayer over despair, and to go home with the belief that is expressed in the following mantra: *Even though I don't know what will happen, I am safe, and I am protected. The universe is finding many ways to grant me what I need. All is well in my world.* I encourage those people to repeat it over and over regardless of what current events mask themselves as a reality.

Some of the employees stared down in gloom while others gathered their belongings to go home. A few came and found me to seek more details. I explained to them that everyone has a power within them, and it requires willful activation and use, because no one can do it for us. "After the dark night, the sun comes out, so please remember this simple truth. A few of us agree to pray together and visualize that we are fulfilling our responsibilities, we are working, we are happy, and that all is well in our world."

That day we went home with a commitment to explore daily prayer. Shortly afterward, our employer began contacting our team and others in the organization, giving us numerous tasks for remote work, as well as additional assignments for outdoor programs. No employee was left without an assignment, and everyone would be paid after completing the required services, unless they wished to do otherwise.

When the time came for us to return back to work after the lockdown, our "prayer team" commented on how the manifestation of miracles is a true possibility. We don't claim any ownership of happenings, as rather we see ourselves as energetic partners with the positive forces of the universe that can activate miracles for the greater good and benefit of all. The most important detail in this process is not to claim credit for the results and brag about them, but rather to just observe and thank the universe for its assistance. We witnessed in our lives what Dr. Joe Dispenza and many other giants in the field try to teach us is a possible tool to use for a good cause.

Now, in the present, I face another situation that can also be remedied with an activation of prayer. I contact our "prayer team" and ask if they can join me in prayers for Arthur's wellness and recovery.

We all agree to unite our efforts. We agree to have one vibrant image in our minds; one of Arthur walking through our office door in his favorite green shirt, greeting us and smiling. That is the prayer we would imagine in a strong and vivid scene.

I keep playing this image in my mind over and over, many times a day, holding on to the feeling of joy from the welcoming scene, watching Arthur returning to work. Together, we pray and pray as the days go by, our faith remaining strong and unwavering.

While we remain committed, Maria texts me saying the following: *There is some miraculous progress taking place, something is shifting, our prayers are certainly working, let's continue...* Later, I call her back to find out more. Her voice is more confident, and the energy of hope is sprouting. She says that Arthur is feeling a little better, and that he asked for food, while the doctors are in shock from this unforeseen improvement, and express newfound hope for his recovery.

I share the news of the good progress with our "prayer team." Ultra happy, we continue our energetic efforts to visualize Arthur's return to work.

We continually get more good news from Maria, and then more, and more... until eventually, she calls me to share that Arthur is checking out of the hospital and heading for the physical therapy center. We persist in our effort of prayer.

Then, I get a call from Arthur himself asking to meet and discuss his return to work with me.

My heart pounds from joy and gratitude that the universe helped him to recover in such a short time. Though this news I do not share with our team, hoping to let them experience the surprise of his return on their own.

It's Monday, and Arthur shows up to work, to absolutely everyone's surprise. He is wearing his favorite outwear, the green shirt and gray pants. The same green shirt we imagined he would wear walking in through the front office door.

Miracle? Intentional manifestation? What am I witnessing? Life certainly is a marathon of choices.

While Arthur and I are chatting about how the medical team and doctors took care of him, and how everyone involved themselves with their prayers speeding up his physical recovery, one of the members of our "prayer team" passes by my office. I wave, asking him to stop by. He pops his head in with curiosity and sees the surprise, shouting, "No way! You're back! So happy to see you, man. OMG and you are wearing the green shirt... wow!" And then he turns his head my way with a mischievous smile asking, "How can this be?" I smile and remain silent in delight.

This miraculous and quick recovery news passes quickly throughout our "prayer team." We humbly thank the universal energies for their partnership and support.

Surpassing the known, we can find other solutions. This gives us the wings to insist on choosing a path that makes our heart and soul sing, rather than a path of despair that does otherwise. To develop a capacity to choose wisely, one's circumstances need to be altered, if they are within our choice. Then our power can be claimed and used. Amen!

I send this story out to the world to help all who may benefit from it.

# Ida Ra Nalbandian

Ida Ra Nalbandian is a former university lecturer in philology, comparative literature and linguistics.

An accomplished author and contributing writer, Ida Ra Nalbandian is dedicated to exploring the power of language and literature to inspire change. With a mission to promote self-awareness, attentive choices, kindness and the expansion of the greater good, her work seeks to cultivate deeper understanding and a more compassionate world.

Ida Ra Nalbandian has published multiple books, including *Does God Have a Bicycle,* and *Jacob's Magic Vegetables: How Loving Kindness Grows.* Her work has earned recognition with *Jacob's Magic Vegetables: How Loving Kindness Grows* making it to the Amazon Bestseller List and being named Dreamvisions 7 Radio and TV Network Children's Book of the Month.

In addition, she is a contributing writer to numerous publications:
• *Portals: Energetic Doorways to Mystical Experiences Between Worlds* by Freddy Silva.
• *Wellness GPS: Get Prepared for Success with All Things Wellness: More True Stories of the Heart, Spirit, Mind and Body.*
• *A Daily Gift of Hope: A Collection of Stories from Hopeful Hearts Around the Globe.*
• *A Daily Gift of Kindness: A Collection of Stories from Kind Hearts Around the Globe.*

⊕ www.vahagnfoundation.org
Scan QR code to learn more about Ida Ra Nalbandian.

chapter

# 12

# Whispers of the Heart: A Ten-Year-Old's Path to Healing

*by Deborah Kane*

***"The truth doesn't shout; it rises in the quiet."***

In February 1970, I was ten years old and just beginning to feel a sense of safety. I was just beginning to let my guard down and looking forward to waking up in the morning. However, this day, the air felt heavy and my stomach was tight with tension, as if the world itself was holding its breath.

We were gathered in the living room, my siblings and me, cross-legged on the worn rug. My mother was about to speak, and there was something in the way she held herself, something I couldn't quite name, but it made me feel that this moment, whatever was about to unfold, mattered.

And then, he walked in. The room seemed to lose its breath all at once. He entered through the front door, the beam of sunlight from the window casting only his shadow across the floor. I couldn't see his face clearly, but I didn't need to.

My father. This man who had taken so much from us – who terrorized, humiliated, controlled and disgraced us – was back. The one who shattered any sense of separation I had worked so hard to rebuild in his absence, was here to stay.

My body went rigid. My hands gripped the rug beneath me, nails digging into the fibers. I began rocking back and forth, a slow rhythmic motion I couldn't control. My thoughts raced, wild and frantic, a tornado of questions spinning inside my head: *Why is he here? How is he here?* The judge, the police, the social worker, they all said he wasn't allowed here. Everyone said it. Everyone... except my mother.

I felt my body shrink, retreating inward, as if I could disappear into the floor – crawl so deep inside myself that I might cease to exist.

The room felt unmoored, floating somewhere just beyond reach. Voices surrounded me – his, hers, my siblings – but they were muffled, distant, as if I were submerged underwater. Separated. The more I withdrew, the less I felt like a participant. I became an observer, frozen in thought.

I trusted my mother. I watched her closely, studying her face, sensing the weight of something I couldn't yet comprehend. I couldn't speak. Trauma lingered; an invisible barrier that kept my questions locked away. My chest tightened, air trapped somewhere between my ribs and my heart, stuck – unable to move in or out.

My world shifted that day. I sat in a place where everything felt wrong, uncertain. Familiar, yet somehow more dangerous. I felt exposed, vulnerable, unsure of how to make even the smallest move out of the living room.

I was ten years old when I understood what it meant to be powerless. Ten – when I learned that standing tall didn't always mean fighting back. Ten – when I learned there was touch that healed and touch that hurt. Ten – when I realized that silence could carry as much weight as words. I learned that trauma lingered in tension, shaping every tomorrow. I learned that some commitments, some sacrifices, are made without ever being spoken.

There were triggers that echoed in the past, teachers who challenged and guided, treatment that offered hope and training that built resilience. I learned that safety is not a guarantee but a fragile hope, slipping through my fingers, no matter how tightly I tried to hold on.

Yet, even then, I knew – deeply knew – there was more to life than this.

And in this knowing, I noticed something unshakable within me. A presence, subtle yet peaceful, like a glimmer in the darkest moments. Something I felt, but didn't know how to access. It came in dreams, where fear couldn't reach as easily, in moments of despair, when everything else dissolved into raw feeling. There wasn't time to explore its meaning. Survival required focus.

While others sought comfort in familiarity, I learned to compartmentalize; one life at home, another beyond it. Though safety felt out of reach, I glimpsed a way forward. Curiosity became both my refuge and my guide. I watched. I studied the rhythms of people, the way words could wound or heal, the way silence could be a fortress or a prison. I searched for answers: *Why did people behave as they did? Why did some wield power while others crumbled? Why was kindness so rare, yet so transformative when it appeared?*

All of it – a journey, trying to get to the truth.

As my instincts sharpened, I learned to see beneath the surface of words and actions. Patterns emerged. Truths revealed themselves in the spaces between what people said and what they left unspoken. But knowing wasn't the same as trusting. Trust required something I wasn't sure I had. When the weight of the world became too much, I turned to my secret weapon: sleep. Sleep was my superpower. It wasn't just an escape, it was clarity, reflection and the key to my next steps.

In dreams, fear lost its grip. Possibilities stretched beyond the limits of my waking world. Maybe that was my first glimpse of something steady, something safe, though I didn't yet recognize it. Sleep wasn't merely a reset, it was restoration – a sacred space where my mind wove meaning from the tangled threads of reality and despair. When everything else dissolved into raw emotion, sleep became the refuge where peace lived, where the glimmers emerged, where survival finally loosened its hold.

Perhaps sleep was where I first began to access the truth. At the time, I didn't know if I could trust it. Maybe it felt like a trick of the mind, an illusion, a false hope. Or maybe it was simply too quiet, too subtle, drowned out by the relentless noise of fear, responsibility and hypervigilance.

And yet, even as sleep offered its truth, something else began to stir.

Over time, I noticed a quiet peace settling in as I walked. Being outside softened the noise in my mind, allowing me to slip into a rhythm beyond thought. With each step, tension eased from my body, and a lightness took its place. It was more than a presence, it was connection. It felt forgiving, hopeful, like a whisper of something I had once glimpsed in a dream, now within reach.

Step by step, breath by breath, survival loosened its grip.

Eventually, I began seeking relief. At first, my efforts were clumsy. I reached for peace but found only the numbing comfort of escape. Years passed – years of blackouts, shame and regret – before I was pulled back into action. Through reading, classes and therapy, I began to uncover new ways to understand, to trust and to question beliefs I had once thought were unchangeable.

Little by little, exhausted from my relentless pursuit of answers, I surrendered.

I realized relief wasn't something to stumble into. Healing and self-discovery weren't about endlessly preparing for the next step or planning my way forward. The only action that would truly make a difference was learning how to cultivate calmness itself.

Therapy answered many of my external questions and expanded my capacity to cope, but restlessness remained. Then, my sister introduced me to a reiki healer. By that point, I was depleted, exhausted from the endless pursuit of answers and ready to try something new.

My first session left me stunned. Instead of seeking explanations, I was guided inward; to feel, to breathe, to recognize discomfort, to sit with emotions rather than escape them. Even in my unease, I felt relief. Safe. I didn't have the words to describe it, but I knew I was accessing something familiar.

For the first time, I wasn't searching for meaning, nor was I required to speak. I was simply guided to follow my breath, to feel the places within that hurt, to listen. And in that quiet allowance, the glimmer I had been seeking began to reveal itself.

Reiki wasn't just a practice, it was an awakening. It showed me how to create space for calm and how to connect with my body and spirit in a way that felt expansive, not corrective. It wasn't about fixing anything, it was about stillness, trust and discovery. I wasn't searching for healing, I was stepping into it. It was then I realized that healing wasn't something to chase, it was something to nurture.

Healing and self-discovery are often framed as actions; something *to do, to achieve*. But the truth doesn't shout, it rises in the quiet. The more you choose stillness, the more clearly you hear *your* truth. Not the one you've been given, not the one shaped by social expectations, comparison or unattainable loyalty but the one that has always been yours. And when you start to hear it, you'll know – it's time to let it lead you.

When you're feeling overwhelmed, uncertain or lost in the noise, remember stillness is a choice. It's not something you passively wait for, it's something you actively create. And with practice, it becomes your way of being.

Here are a few steps to help you begin:

**Breathe with intention** – Transitioning from one task to another can feel overwhelming, especially for those who have experienced trauma. These shifts can trigger stress and anxiety. Breathwork is a powerful practice that helps calm the mind, ease the heart and brings you back to the present moment. Start by taking a few minutes between transitions – before work, during lunch or after work. Explore simple breathing techniques such as deep breathing or box breathing. Over time, you'll begin to notice how these moments of intentional breathing help reduce the overwhelm and bring clarity to your thoughts.
*Reflection:* Notice how you feel after practicing intentional breathing. Does it help you feel more centered?

**Create quiet space** – Creating space for quiet is crucial for building inner trust, especially for those who have experienced trauma. Disconnecting from the noise around you, whether that's technology, people or external distractions, can be incredibly restorative. Try sitting quietly for just five minutes each day or take a walk in nature to reset your nervous system. These moments are not about doing, they're about being. By making *quiet* a regular practice, you allow yourself to reconnect with your inner voice and strengthen your sense of safety.

*Reflection*: How does it feel to spend time in stillness? What emotions or thoughts come up during those moments of quiet?

**Embrace gentle practices** – While practices like reiki and therapy can be powerful healing tools, healing looks different for everyone. Find what resonates with you – whether it's meditation, journaling, tapping, acupressure or sound healing. These practices help you reconnect with the truth of who you are and restore your spirit. There's no "right" way – what matters is finding practices that nourish you. Start by exploring one practice and see how it makes you feel.

*Reflection*: What practice feels most natural to you? How does it help you feel more connected to yourself?

**Trust the process** – Healing from trauma takes time, and the internal fears of not feeling safe often need plenty of reassurance. Be patient with yourself and trust that the quiet moments you create are full of joy, creativity, wisdom and answers. At first, sitting in stillness may feel unfamiliar or uncomfortable, but over time, you'll start to sense something deeper within you. This essence has always been there, waiting for you to reconnect with it. Healing isn't about perfection, it's about creating space for what has always been within you to emerge.

*Reflection:* As you sit with stillness, do you begin to recognize something new or familiar within yourself? What is it?

I was ten years old when I first learned about pain and powerlessness. But I am no longer that child, trapped in silence and uncertainty. I have learned to trust – not just in others, but in myself. I have learned to reflect, to understand that while my past has shaped me, it does not define me. I am safe.

I have reshaped the stories I once believed were unchangeable. I have challenged the limits placed upon me. But the true transformation didn't happen in a single moment. It unfolded gradually, through a willingness to deeply examine the experiences that shaped my childhood, my relationships, my education, my work. Each experience left an imprint, shaping me in ways I never questioned... until I did.

Until I was willing to examine what I had been taught, what I had internalized and what I truly wanted to hold on to, versus what I needed to release, I remained trapped, a hostage in the role of observer. Reflection alone was not enough. For so long, survival had been deafening; the constant chatter of past wounds, the echoes of fear, the relentless push to prove, to protect, to anticipate what came next. Yet, even in my deepest despair, glimmers of peace never left me. Understanding my past helped me make sense of my story, stillness gave me the opportunity to step beyond it. In that quiet space, I awakened something that had always been there – my spirit, my intuition, my inner guide.

Perhaps you've spent years searching, questioning or carrying stories that no longer serve you. Perhaps survival has been loud for you, too. But beneath all the noise, something deeper is waiting to be heard.

So I ask you: When was the last time you were still? When was the last time you truly listened – not to the world around you – but to the quiet wisdom within?

Stillness may begin as a personal practice, but its impact ripples outward. When we listen, not just to ourselves, but to one another, we create space for healing, understanding and connection. Our shared stories remind us to remember that we are not alone on this journey.

Let's walk along this path together. Let's listen, explore and rediscover the wisdom within. In the quiet, we don't just find ourselves, we reclaim our stories, our voices and the power to move forward with clarity and purpose.

*"In the quiet, I found my words. In the stillness, I uncovered my truth."*
– Mary Oliver

 # Deborah Kane

Debbie is a writer, speaker and storyteller with a passion for empowering others to recognize the transformative power of their narratives. She holds a master's degree in educational counseling and a bachelor's degree in social science and women's studies. With twenty-five years of experience working directly with individuals diagnosed with mental health disorders, Debbie has dedicated her career to fostering understanding, connection and growth.

In 2020, Debbie embarked on a four-year journey of self-discovery, cultivating deeper compassion, trust and openness. This inward exploration led to remarkable personal and professional growth. She has completed training with Bessel Van Der Kolk, the acclaimed author of *The Body Keeps the Score*, and recently honed her speaking and writing skills under the guidance of world-renowned speaker Lisa Nichols.

Debbie's search for meaning and her unwavering commitment to personal and collective growth have inspired her to guide human service agencies, employees and college students. Her mission is to help these groups explore their inner narratives, develop emotional resilience and unlock their full potential to make a meaningful impact on the lives they serve.

✉ dkanestc@yahoo.com
◎ @dkanestc4rg
Scan QR code to learn more about Deborah Kane.

chapter

# 13

# Off the Roller-Coaster of Pain and Into the Light

*by Ragan Thomson*

My name is Ragan Thomson, once known as Ragan O'Reilly. I came from a family lineage rich in achievement, where ambition and success were foundational traits, normalized as a way to a happy life. My family's expectations loomed over me like shadows, pushing me to excel in every facet of my life, especially in sports. I aimed to be the embodiment of my family's pride, stepping into the role of a star athlete, with tennis being my chosen major discipline.

As I immersed myself in the world of tennis, the pressure intensified. Every match became a battleground, not just for victory, but for the love and approval I desperately craved, particularly from my father. My mother, who I loved very much, was distant and cold in her parenting, which caused me to focus on the conditional affection of my father even more. Therefore, winning meant validation, while losing felt like relinquishing affection. The stakes were impossibly high, and soon, the relentless drive to perform became overwhelming. I was trapped in a cycle where success was tied to self-worth, leading me to equate every point won with a semblance of love.

As the pursuit consumed me, the toll was devastating. I reached a breaking point where the sport I once loved now felt like a life-or-death situation. I realized I was at my sickest – both physically and emotionally – when grappling with bulimia and anorexia. In a moment of clarity, I made the shocking decision to stop playing at the peak of my career, at age eighteen. It was an act of rebellion against the pressures that dictated my life... and a massive cry for help. I remember the look of total disappointment on my father's face; a painful mix of misunderstanding and sorrow. He could not fathom my choice, yet deep down, I understood that if I continued in this destructive cycle, I wouldn't survive. I needed to reclaim my life and, in that moment, confront my deepest fears about love and worthiness, away from the sport that had defined me.

The decision to stop playing tennis, once perceived as a potential liberating moment, soon plunged me into a dark downward spiral, filled with struggle and pain. Instead of the relief I sought, I was met with crushing disappointment from my father. In an attempt at understanding, he joined me in a couple of sports psychology sessions, but I could feel the chasm of our relationship widening. With his arms crossed and gaze averted, he embodied my greatest fear; that my love, and in turn, his, was conditional, tethered solely to my performance on the court.

This realization consumed me, deepening the sense of isolation I had grown accustomed to. Spiraling into despair, the lack of affection from my mother and father pushed me further into an identity crisis. Battling overwhelming depression and anxiety, I grappled with perfectionism and body dysmorphia, losing sight of who I truly was. The darkness loomed heavy, leading me to a place where existence felt unbearable.

After the choice to not play tennis, an identity crisis ensued. I found myself spiraling downward feeling lost and depressed, experiencing a disconnect with myself and my family, which began to create the feeling of being on an emotional roller-coaster, enveloped in a profound well of pain and sadness, colored by extreme internal highs and lows.

Yet, amidst this turmoil, something deep within me, the essence of my soul, whispered, *Hang on, there's more to life yet to come.* In the face of suffocating pain, my focus began to shift. I started to feel within the love I felt for others and the connections they shared with me. It became clear that this love was the lifeline I needed to continue. I learned to hold onto the light of those relationships in my heart, ultimately allowing them to guide me through the darkness and choose to remain in a physical body.

Growing up in an Irish Catholic culture, rich with tradition, I had always felt a curiosity to explore other religions and cultures, beyond what was presented to me as the only option. My spiritual explorations began, and took immense courage, often with me feeling I was abandoning my family. My father has also shared his concerns about this choice, many times, leading me to feel as if I had, once again, disappointed him. I learned that the search for more, that was underway, was at the risk of me losing all that was dear in some way, according to the identity structure I had created of myself.

Still, a deep calling was leading me to seek a deeper relationship with God, and I studied religious studies in college for a bit, creating a feeling and a connection to all religions, all peoples and spirituality beyond the church walls. It was this connection I found that gave me courage to keep going... although I was still experiencing feeling lonely, abandoned and depressed, as deep down, I had no idea who I was without being within the identity of a star athlete and meeting the expectations of the outside world. During these most tumultuous times, the years passed, and I hit a wall, as they say. I was ready to get off the roller coaster; the feeling of being low and yet so high at moments.

The search for a spiritual mentor began; a guide to help navigate the deepest pain within and to help awaken me into who I truly was, free of all the pain. And as the saying goes, "Your teacher appears when the student is ready." When I met her, the connection was immediate. I remember looking into her eyes and feeling the peace she had accessed within me... and that was what I wanted more than anything.

Session by session, the healing began. The light of her presence illuminated the dust upon my soul, gradually removing the layers that obscured my inner light. The metaphor of peeling an artichoke comes to mind (each layer representing wounds, pain and karma) and with time, peeling back layer after layer, eventually coming to the deepest inner work within the heart. Spirit, gentle and loving, never gave me more than I could handle, guiding me through each step with grace.

With each layer removed, I experienced deep healing, sometimes instantaneously. The intuitive guidance I received during these sessions was transformative. My mentor's insights, delivered with compassion, resonated with truths I already knew but had not yet embraced. Her role was a beacon, lighting the path to self-discovery and spiritual awakening.

This awakening journey expanded quickly, and it was as if a cork had been let off my energy system. Suddenly, the once stifled human was becoming a brilliant butterfly. In fact, I still remember the moment she shared I was to be a *teacher of teachers*, *a healer of healers,* and rather than blocking what we heard, we could feel the truth in it.

Slowly and with great commitment to the path, I moved from feeling overwhelmed by life's emotions to experiencing a calm, peaceful connection to the divine. It was through this transformative journey that I truly rediscovered my healing gifts and began to use them, not only for my benefit, but to help others find their paths to healing and peace. The roller coaster had stopped, and I was finally ready to step off, into a life vibrantly reconnected to my spiritual essence.

As I continued on this path of healing, I became acutely aware that this journey was not merely about overcoming pain, it was about transforming my relationship with it. I began to see that my struggles were not obstacles but rather essential teachers. With each session, I learned to embrace the parts of myself I had long ignored; the sadness, the fear and the doubt. It was as if the layers of my emotional armor were finally being stripped away, revealing the raw, unfiltered essence of who I truly was.

This process of peeling back those layers was not always easy. There were moments when the pain felt overwhelming, as if I were being asked to face the darkest corners of my soul. I vividly recall the many sessions where I was guided to confront the deep-seated fears, limiting beliefs and extreme judgment of myself, that had haunted me for years. I still remember the immense courage required. It was as if all the training in sports had cultivated higher qualities within me that I could now utilize, such as much needed courage, determination, perseverance and inner discipline to keep showing up and healing.

But through the gentle guidance of my mentor, I learned to approach the fragmented parts of myself with compassion, empathy and love. I took a deep breath each time and, instead of running away, I imagined extending my hand towards myself and wrapping myself in a loving hug. Slowly... old parts of Ragan began to dissolve into the light, after each one received what was needed to do so. I realized that fear was a pain I had once tried to escape through food addiction, and then later, drugs and alcohol. Fear loses its power when faced with love and acceptance. I felt a profound sense of liberation wash over me, and I understood that healing was not about banishing pain but about integrating it into the tapestry of my being.

The process of awakening involved more than just one-on-one sessions; it was a holistic journey encompassing various practices that enriched my spiritual life. Meditation became a cornerstone of my daily routine, providing a sanctuary of stillness where I could reconnect with my inner self. I embraced different forms of meditation, from mindfulness to guided imagery, each offering unique insights. It felt like an adventure into my own psyche, where I discovered hidden treasures of wisdom.

Nature also played a pivotal role in my awakening. On weekends, I sought refuge in the forests and mountains surrounding my home. The serenity of the natural world spoke to me in ways words could not. I would sit by riversides, oceans or streams, feeling the cool water flow over my hands, or meditate beneath the wide expanse of the sky, allowing the clouds to drift lazily overhead. In those moments, I felt a deep connection to love, to beauty and to God, serving as a reminder that I was a part of something much larger than myself in the expansiveness of the natural world.

As my understanding deepened, I found community with others on similar journeys. I attended workshops and spiritual retreats, where I met like-minded souls seeking healing and freedom from within. Sharing stories and experiences with others created a sense of belonging that was both comforting and invigorating. It was inspiring to witness how each person navigated their own path, yet we all resonated with the same yearning for connection, purpose and peace.

Through these experiences and deeper soul connections with others on the path, I began to uncover the healing gifts that had always resided within me. It was as if a veil had been lifted, allowing me to see the intuition I had long suppressed. I started practicing energy healing and intuitive readings, understanding that my own healing journey had equipped me with the tools to guide others. It was a thrilling realization that my pain had purpose; it had prepared me to help others navigate their own emotional landscapes.

I remember my first session as a healer for another individual. With eager anticipation, I set the space, lighting candles, prepared my singing bowls and began playing soft music that they would experience when walking into my office. As I tuned into their energy, I felt a tingling sensation of joy, bliss and euphoric lightning shoot through my body, which proved this was a divine blessing occurring and we had now become a conduit of the light of spirit to move through to help the soul I was serving.

As I immersed myself in these experiences, I found that my journey was not just about personal healing, it became a path of facilitation and guidance for others. I was called to be a conduit for healing, channeling the wisdom and love of the universe to support those around me. It was a humbling realization; my awakening process had not only transformed my life, but it was also equipping me to help others embark on their own journeys of self-discovery.

Yet, I soon understood that this role as a facilitator came with its own set of challenges. Each time I opened myself to others, I also opened the door to my own vulnerabilities. The more I taught and shared, the deeper I delved into my own unresolved traumas. I was reminded of the profound question that often echoed in my mind: *Do you choose the light, or do you choose the dark?*

This question became a mantra for me. In moments of uncertainty and fear, it served as a compass, guiding me back to my center. I learned that choosing the light meant embracing courage, compassion and unconditional love, not just for others but for myself. It was in these moments of deepest fear when I grappled with feelings of inadequacy, loneliness and past rejections that the power of my choice became most significant.

Reflecting on my childhood, I realized how pivotal experiences had shaped my understanding of worthiness and goodness. I saw myself, in the past, as lost, unworthy and not good enough. These judgments and beliefs lingered well into adulthood, influencing my relationships and self-esteem. It fueled a cycle of self-doubt that whispered insidiously in my ear, *You are not enough. You are unworthy of love.* But through my spiritual awakening, I learned to question and confront these shadows. I recognized that I was not defined by my past experiences or my father's perceptions; I was a being of light, infinitely capable of love and compassion.

I began to ask myself, *What if I chose to see my wounds not as limitations, but as pathways to greater understanding? What if the moments of abandonment and rejection were invitations to discover the depths of my resilience?* Slowly, I began to reshape my narrative, finding beauty in the scars that had once felt like chains.

In the face of my deepest fears, I learned to respond with compassion rather than judgment. I found solace in meditative practices, where I would sit with my fear, allowing it to exist without trying to push it away. In those moments of stillness, I realized my fears weren't enemies, they were teachers. Each one offered a lesson, urging me to look deeper and uncover hidden strengths.

As I continued to facilitate healing sessions for others, I began to recognize the shared struggles that many people face. The themes of worthiness, fear of death, abandonment and pain echoed across different lives, uniting us in our humanity. It was both heartbreaking and beautiful. In these sessions, I witnessed the incredible resilience of the human heart, as clients found their voices and started to reclaim their stories and heal their lives, as I had through awareness, deep inner self-reflection, forgiveness and experiencing pure unconditional love as the antidote to healing all with courage.

Together, we explored the themes of light and dark, encouraging individuals to sit with their shadows and embrace them with pure love, acceptance and forgiveness rather than run from them. We discussed how the light dissolves the dark. By acknowledging both the light and the dark parts of ourselves, we embraced our wholeness. The light magnifies our strengths, while the dark deepens our understanding of empathy and compassion.

Through this process, I learned the significance of unconditional love, not just for others but for myself, especially in moments of struggle. This love became a powerful force that dismantled the walls of self-doubt and the lack of self-worth I had so carefully constructed. I began to understand that love is not contingent on perfection, it thrives in vulnerability and authenticity.

The lessons continued to unfold, and with each passing day, I felt myself being woken further by spirit. I sat in meditation, seeking guidance and clarity. The messages that flowed through me were clear: *it is not enough to simply exist, we must choose to live with conscious and loving intention.* We are given choices in every moment, and I wanted to make mine count, not just for myself but for the collective.

*What do you choose?* became a pivotal question in myself. It was a call to action, inviting individuals to explore their choices in times of fear and uncertainty. Do they choose to succumb to feelings of inadequacy, or do they step into their power and embrace their true selves? The answers vary from person to person, but every choice made in alignment with love and compassion moves us closer to our authentic selves.

# Ragan Thomson

Ragan Thomson is a spiritual teacher, intuitive transformational healer and world service activist devoted to guiding souls toward deep healing, self-discovery and divine remembrance of who we really are at a soul level. Through her meditations, retreats and sacred teachings, she creates space for profound transformation, helping individuals release inner wounds, awaken their true essence and step into greater alignment with their soul's purpose. Ragan serves as a facilitator at Unity Spiritual Center in Santa Barbara and shares her guided meditations on Insight Timer, extending her healing work to a global audience. Rooted in the belief that inner peace leads to collective awakening, Ragan's mission is to help humanity move into greater love, unity and oneness – one soul at a time.

🌐 www.raganthomson.com
📷 @ragan_thomson
Scan QR code to learn more about Ragan Thomson.

chapter

# 14

# The Journey to My Heart

*by Laura Muirhead*

There I was, lying on the cold tile floor of my bathroom. I couldn't stop the tears from flowing down my already swollen face or my body from shaking with emotion. That was when I knew something had to change.

Have you experienced a profound moment of realization in your life? You know, an aha moment or what might feel like a lightning strike that wakes you up? Or, similar to this story, have you found yourself at a breaking point that made you realize something had to change?

Many people do. But that's not my story – the story above, I mean. My experience hasn't been like that. Awakening my heart has been a lifelong journey.

Growing up in a world where conformity was valued over individuality, where in fact it was the rule of the day, it was a challenge to hold on to my authenticity. My life didn't start that way, but after my parents' divorce when I was nine years old, my dad married again. I lived with him and his new wife. Imagine if everything in your life changed... especially the rules of the house, including how you dress, how your hair is cut (to mirror your new stepsisters), and even what you eat is closely monitored. I realize, of course, that parents are meant to guide your behavior, but there is a difference between guidance and control.

Even with my self-expression being repressed, I did my best to hold on to some of my true self. When I was old enough to babysit and earn my own money, I would buy some of my own clothes. I graduated from high school early and took the first opportunity I could to move out of the house. To this day, I often discover that I'm still breaking free of some of those old ideas and coming back to myself.

Attending church was an additional change in my life during that time. When I found that particular church a bit uncomfortable, I chose another religion that felt more welcoming. I suppose as a young adult there was a hope of fitting in somewhere. Ultimately, I found those beliefs were not aligned for me, and I stepped away, though I do value having an understanding of teachings from both of those experiences.

My twenties were a time of exploring and reconnecting with myself. I went to college, first taking art classes which ended up not feeling *quite right* for me. I knew my heart wanted a different direction, to pursue a degree in graphics, so I changed colleges. Before transferring from the first one, though, I was able to explore a photography class and had an unexpected astronomy class I also enjoyed.

Those years included me fulfilling a personal passion of learning to fly. At twenty-five, I achieved a long-standing goal of getting a private pilot's license. I bought my first house, got married and divorced – still on the journey of finding my way to myself.

There were a variety of jobs, from office work to postal employee, and I even spent a short time as a kitchen designer. The ones that felt like the best fit were in lending and real estate. I even held a real estate license and worked for mortgage companies during that time.

As you may have noticed, I'm multi-passionate and like wearing different hats. I have a huge respect for people who find their one true calling in life, but that isn't me. I love variety. This has also played out when I wear my entrepreneur's hat.

My first venture was a bread store that didn't end well. My passion for horses, riding and showing led me to building a horse stable from a cornfield up. I dabbled with embroidery at one point. When I found I had a passion for ceramics and working with clay, I opened a pottery and art studio. That allowed me to wear my artist's hat and bridge many of my artistic endeavors. My studio had a retail space offering my photography and handmade pottery, as well as my artwork on greeting cards, mugs, pillows and tote bags. My spiritual side also came out to play in that space by offering workshops delving into crystal, tea leaf reading, chakras, card reading and even mediumship.

The common thread through everything has been working with numbers and finance. My husband already owned his company when we married. Soon after, I joined him as CFO and vice president of our multimillion-dollar a year family business. I proudly wear that hat, interchanging it with my others to find a fulfilling balance that I love.

My personal journey has shown me many twists and turns along the way. It's somewhat like following a path in nature; you come across unexpected blocks, maybe a fallen tree that leads you on a detour or a rocky area that is more challenging. Maybe you reach a summit that opens up to an amazing view, and then you come across a meandering river that allows you to float along with its gentle flow.

I've had so many of these unexpected experiences, that for a long time, I knew I wanted to write a book, sharing my stories with the hope of inspiring others who read it. Those stories came together in my published memoir, *A Funny Thing Happened on the Way to My Life*.

These are all part of my unfolding awakening.

I followed my intuition when it led me to buying a winning lottery ticket. Years later, we had a devastating fire that burned our dream house to the ground. The obvious extremes of these situations are not lost on me.

The biggest challenge for me, though, was discovering that my dad, the man who I lived with when my parents divorced, is not really my dad. That was a journey in itself.

It took seven years, from when I first had the hint that he wasn't my biological father, to confirming the truth of it all. Even with that many years to wonder and, you would think, come to terms with the idea, the confirmation of this knowledge hit me with the force of a lightning bolt!

There are so many layers to finding your way back to yourself after something like that. A whole side of my family tree crumbled, limb by limb. Finding out the truth about my "real" father was tough. There was the huge challenge of knowing I share some of his physical traits... it was uncomfortable knowing that I look like HIM.

Talk about identity theft!

My entire life story shifted. Everything I knew... everything I'd been told... for my entire life... was a lie.

There were many years of trying to work through so many feelings, the biggest one was *anger*. What finally helped me in moving through and accepting it... accepting myself... is gratitude.

I was listening to the story of a man who had been a star athlete. In fact, he was on his way to becoming a professional athlete. That was his life's path. Then he had an accident. They weren't sure if he would ever walk again, let alone play sport. A devastating blow for sure. Well, he *was* able to walk again, but he couldn't play sport. As he told it, that was a major shift in his life; he went on to be a very successful motivational speaker and bestselling author.

He ended his talk by saying that what helped him was *gratitude*. He found gratitude in his situation because, had he not had a life-changing accident, he wouldn't be who he is and wouldn't have written his books and touched so many lives. The challenge was offered *to find gratitude in your own situations*.

Thinking of my difficult challenge, at first, I couldn't see how there could be any gratitude in it. *What could it possibly be? Where could I find the gratitude?*

It didn't take too long before it hit me. The gratitude is that I am me. Just to let you know, the estimated odds of any one of us being born, at all, is about one in 400 trillion. So, I realized that had I been born to any two other people, I would not be who I am. It came down to science. That is where I was able to find the gratitude. I am a miracle. We all are.

As I mentioned, for years I had the seed of desire in my heart to share my life stories. There were things that held me back, even though I felt a big part of me showing up authentically was to tell the truth about my life. It was overwhelming to think about the potential outcome. There was the fear of visibility, which, for so many of us, is a challenge. And there was the fear of everyone knowing the true story and how it would affect other people who hadn't been willing to share the truth, or those who didn't know it.

Even as I was writing my memoir, I wasn't sure I was ready for my story to be out in the world. Luckily, I have a supportive, understanding publisher who encouraged me along the way. Plus, I was not meant to be the writer in my family in the first place, though that's a story for another day.

Writing and publishing my memoir has brought unexpected twists of its own.

I never would have imagined being on a billboard in the middle of Times Square in New York City (!)... but that's one of the incredible things that happened by saying *yes* to moving forward with telling my story and writing my book. I was surrounded by my family and friends too. It was a dream, I didn't know I had, come true.

The idea of allowing more than you think is possible into your life is a powerful shift. When you release the fear, step into trust, and say *yes* to what feels aligned, the universe meets you in ways you never could have planned.

Since that day in New York City, so many more incredible opportunities have opened up for me. And so many amazing people have come into my world. I've had opportunities to collaborate with other women worldwide. I am speaking at international events and on the virtual stage. Adventures in international travel, with book signings, are on my calendar. And more books and author projects are in the works. I realize this is the power of telling my story and truly being aligned with your heart and soul.

You don't have to be a writer and tell your story; that is what is working for me. Do what is right for you and what lights you up. It's so important for each of us to be authentically ourselves. It's where and when the magic happens.

I've often wondered why I've had so many *A Funny Thing Happened on the Way to My Life* experiences in one lifetime. One of my mentors helped me to understand. On a human level, some of these things may not be the most desirable or fun. Of course, many of them have been challenging for me as well. For my soul, though, my soul is enjoying all of it and somehow needs it. My soul even agreed to all of it before I was born. Knowing this has put things into perspective for me.

Each of the ups and downs, each experience, has been an opportunity to learn and grow. Looking for and finding gratitude is a game changer. I realize that for my entire life, I have had natural tools, unique to me, that have served me in being able to stay true to myself, as well as help me reframe my experiences to see the positive outcomes.

I have leaned into these tools so many times, and a few years ago, I realized I wanted to share them to help support others. That is why I created my signature program, the *Queen Code*. It helps people establish better boundaries or what I call *personal policies*. Then came the *Queen Code Oracle Card Deck* that can be used as a companion to the *Queen Code*... but works well on its own when used for daily guidance and journaling, helping to connect with your inner guidance; your intuition.

Gratitude served me well in navigating the months after our house fire. It was important to be grateful for what we still had, and it helped us to move forward in rebuilding our lives. We were able to take advantage of opportunities that would have been different, or might not have shown up at all, had we stayed in that house. That included leading to me opening my studio.

It's not only having gratitude for the big things in our lives, but it's also so important to express gratitude for the day-to-day things that might be considered small. Gratitude is one of the highest vibrations, right up there with peace.

So you see, for me, awakening has truly been a journey; a journey that continues to unfold in ways I never could have planned. Along the way, I've learned how important it is to be true to myself. This includes following my intuition and saying *yes* to what feels aligned for me. It also includes finding the balance between wearing my business hat and my creative hat. I am happiest when I can do both. What drives me forward is finding ways to support and inspire others, whether that is through the words that I write, the *Queen Code*, the *Queen Code Oracle Card Deck*, or my photography and artwork. Often, I may not know how I might be helping someone. I was reminded of that just the other day when a friend told me that something I said had inspired her.

This is the ripple effect I love; the one that happens when we show up as our authentic selves and share our unique gifts and voices with the world.

Here is something I want to share with you. Hopefully, It will inspire you: "Imagine when the ripples we create become waves – start today!" – Laura Muirhead

That is the magic of this journey – when you show up as your authentic self, you never know who you might be lighting the way for.

# Laura Muirhead

Laura Muirhead is an internationally acclaimed author, accomplished artist and the CFO of her family's multimillion-dollar company. She is also the creator of the *Queen Code* program and the *Queen Code Oracle Card Deck*, which guide multi-passionate women to find clarity, set boundaries and elevate both life and business, stepping into their full potential. Laura's work bridges creativity and business, demonstrating that success can be achieved on both sides of the spectrum.

Her personal journey is as dynamic as her professional life – she is a licensed pilot, an energy healer and the author of *A Funny Thing Happened on the Way to My Life,* as well as a beloved children's book and three journals. Laura's life story is one of resilience and reinvention. From navigating the unexpected twists of life to rebuilding after a devastating house fire, she draws inspiration from her experiences to empower others.

Laura enjoys photography and exploring the world. She splits her time between homes in New Jersey and Michigan. Laura cherishes time with her husband, grown children, close friends, two Labrador retrievers and a life filled with creativity and adventure. Learn more about Laura by visiting lauramuirhead.com

⊕ www.afunnythinghappenedonthewaytomylife.com
◎ @laura_muirhead_

Scan QR code to learn more about Laura Muirhead.

chapter

# 15

# No Hair. No Mask. Just Me.
A Radical Reclamation of Self-Worth and Truth

*by Sara Hunter*

I stood there holding a chunk of hair in my hand.

It was *mine*.

*This can't be real,* I told myself.

My whole body trembled with disbelief. I wanted to scream, but everything collapsed in on itself, stealing my voice before I could let it out.

That morning began like any other. Everyone woke up early, preparing to explore my husband's hometown while we were visiting his family. As I stepped into the garage to grab a picnic blanket and sunscreen, I reached up to tighten my ponytail. Running my fingers through my hair, I felt something smooth on the back of my head. A prickly sensation lit up my spine, as I rushed to the bathroom to see what was happening. My breath caught in my throat. I blinked. Then again. I squeezed my eyes tight, hoping I'd imagined it. But no matter what I tried, a bald patch the size of a silver dollar was shining back at me.

It was as if my brain short-circuited, unable to process what my eyes could not unsee.

Outside the bathroom door, I heard my family getting ready and I somehow found the courage to step out of the bathroom and get through the rest of the day and the rest of our trip. By the time we returned home to Colorado, one week later, another dime-sized patch had appeared on the top of my head.

With each day that passed, I watched as more and more hair came out; in my brush, the shower, on my clothes. Between sobs of disbelief, I tried creams, prescriptions, oils, steroid injections, supplements – anything to try to stop the hair loss, or at least slow it down. A dermatologist told me, "There's no way you'll lose all of your hair, but even if you did, you'll look great!" I know she meant well, but I wanted to scream. Her words skimmed the surface of something so deep and personal. I wasn't mourning beauty – I was mourning control, identity and a privileged sense of security. Within four months of discovering the first bald spot, 85% of my hair had fallen out.

These months were incredibly distressing. It felt like an exposure of all of my *ugliness*. I was being stripped of my dignity, as if I'd done something wrong and needed to be punished. It felt unfair; yet somehow, I felt equally ashamed for how hard this was hitting me relative to the greater suffering in the world.

I began working closely with a naturopath who helped me address what we learned was a severe form of leaky gut. Because while my hair was falling out, my health was also rapidly declining. But after eight months of seeing her twice a week, I grew back a full head of hair. I couldn't explain the triumph! I felt on top of the world, as though I had climbed the most arduous of mountains. The sense of pride that I had somehow "beat it", was indescribable.

Little did I know, though, my journey was not over. There was more for me to go through; more than just surviving another traumatic event and wearing some kind of badge for it. This time, it was going to be deeper.

The following summer, walking our dog in the woods, I brushed against a spider web. Instinctively, I reached up to wipe it away, and my fingers closed around a handful of hair.

Blood drained from my body.

*No, no, no, no, no, no*

A shot of freezing cold electricity surged through my body. I stood there in silence until a guttural cry ripped from my chest, *WHY IS THIS HAPPENING?*

I couldn't bear to tell my husband and daughters that all the work I had done to heal hadn't actually worked. This time around, everything happened at lightning speed and 100% of my hair fell out within a week

– along with my eyebrows, eyelashes and every feeling of safety and security. If I felt I was being punished the first time around, this was next level. Like the scrubbing of the wounds; the *deep clean* of the inner debris that was keeping me from the healing I needed to experience.

This time, I felt something had to be here *for* me and not just against me. I didn't know what the "something" was, but looking back from where I am now, I can see it was my awakening.

Looking back over my life, this was not the first time I'd had my sense of safety and security shattered. It happened when I was ten years old, just after my brother died. It was tragic and had sent my family into a tailspin. The life I'd known up until that day fractured in ways I was unequipped to handle on my own. But my parents, overwhelmed and crippled by their own grief, simply couldn't be there for me. Understandably so.

Yet, I was left with a gaping, bleeding psychic wound. So instead of being able to see my parents' withdrawal as their way of dealing with incomprehensible grief, I internalized it as rejection – I understood it to mean that *I* was too much for them, a burden, unworthy of being seen or loved. Everything I ever knew was blown to pieces. As they turned away from me, I turned away from them, vowing to never need them again.

But the truth was – I did need my parents. I *did* need to be seen, loved and valued. But if I couldn't get love or validation from the people who were supposed to give it to me, then I would force the world to *see* me.

If I wasn't going to be seen, I would make sure I stood out.
If I wasn't going to be held, I would ensure I was recognized.
If I couldn't be loved, I would at least be noticed.

Rather than seeking approval through perfection, I rebelled and bucked the expectations of what I thought I was supposed to be. Over time, I began wearing my pain, instead of feeling it, through darker, punk rock, edgy styles. I was always playing with my appearance, shaping my image in a way that controlled how others perceived me.

But it wasn't solely about standing out. I wore my pain like a barrier. *See me, but don't come close – if you do, you'll just leave.* So, while I longed to be seen, the thought of anyone wanting to get to know me terrified me to my bones.

For years, though, it worked. I thrived on my ability to turn heads. People didn't notice, though, it was only a plea for love that I wore like a chain and beggar's sign around my neck. Even still, *acknowledgment* became a high I chased more than any drug I could get my hands on. If I could experience, even for one shallow moment, that somebody knew I existed, then I somehow felt secure.

But while it gave me a sense of power, it was built on a fragile foundation. It depended on others noticing me, which required constant maintenance because, if I wasn't standing out, then *who would notice me? How would I know if I was worthy of anything?*

As I got older, my rebellious style softened, but my need to control remained strong. By my thirties, I'd spent decades living in a state of hyper-independence, guarding the truth of who I was from the world and keeping people at arm's length. I was convinced that *needing nothing* meant I could never be let down or hurt by anyone. I knew I was strong enough to survive on my own.

Yet, beneath that independence was tremendous conflict. On the one hand, I had a growing and unsettling urge to break free from the cage I had built around my heart, but on the other hand, I had an even greater fear that bound me to silence. Even as I saw every kind of professional I could, I still had no idea where to begin to set myself free. I was searching for someone – *anyone* – who could help me figure out what was wrong or *why I was the way I was.* I was growing desperate to touch something real, to unlock the part of me that I knew was buried deep beneath the surface. But no matter how much I searched, I could never reach the true version of myself that split off so many years ago.

And then – I lost my hair. The thing I had spent my whole life controlling was ripped away from me. It certainly didn't feel like an *awakening* at the time. All I knew, as I stood there staring in the mirror at my naked face and head, was that I could no longer pretend. My appearance had been my weapon of self-preservation. It was how I had shaped my identity – *on my terms.* And now, it was gone.

Nausea swarmed through my body as my deepest fears rushed to the surface to taunt me. *Everyone I loved would now see how ugly I truly am.*

I was confronted with the terrifying realization that I had never – *not once* – felt safe, loved or whole. And without my hair to hide behind, people would recoil. They were going to see my ugliness. *My husband was never going to look at me again.*

For the first time in my life, I had to face myself. Full on. No mask, no distractions, no barriers. To see beyond my curated image and face the fear that wounded me in the first place. Yet I not only had to face myself, I had another truth to contend with: *This world has always told me that my value is tied to how I look. That women are only desirable, worthy or lovable if they are deemed beautiful.* I had spent years standing apart from those expectations, rebelling against them – but I still existed *within* them. I had defined myself through my differences, but I was still playing the same game. And now, I had been forcibly removed from it.

As days blurred into weeks, I kept finding myself at a crossroads. I could numb myself, retreat into hiding, and shove this unbearable truth back down... or, I could listen. I could surrender to what this moment was asking of me. I could stand up and become the mother my daughters desperately needed. *Was I going to let the fear of being unlovable destroy me? Or was I going to show my girls that love – true, unshakable love – was never meant to be earned?*

I had my answer. I knew that what I modeled for my girls mattered more than I could ever fathom. *But how?* How was I going to stand on my own two feet, face my family, face the world, and find the strength to keep going?

And then, it struck me – if I was going to navigate this with any measure of grace, *I had to love myself through it.* And if I was going to love myself in this way, I had to believe – *truly believe* – that I was worthy of it.

It took months of trying to force my way into healing; through pep talks, toxic positivity and clinging to the belief that *if I just had more faith in the divine, I would finally feel whole.* It took letting wave after wave of grief move through me; the grief for the little girl who lost more than her brother that day. Yet even after all the trying, the striving and the reaching, I found myself with the same painful question: *Am I truly worthy?* Until one day, I couldn't ask the question anymore, I had to do something different.

For most of my life, it didn't matter how much love, support or success I had, I couldn't hold onto it. It was like trying to fill a pitcher with holes in the bottom. So I took the discussion off the table, once and for all. I decided fully, in my mind, body and spirit, that *my worth* would no longer be something I had to earn, prove or defend. As long as it was a topic that could be debated, I was bound to fall into the cracks and lose myself again. No more proving. No more apologizing. No more waiting to be whole.

It was this decision and declaration that secured something in me. But there was still more work to do and holes to fill. This was only the beginning. What was I going to believe to be true about my life? What narrative would I choose to tell myself... and fully invest in... that would support my growth and expansion? Continuing any sort of victim storyline was going to suck the life and energy from those around me. I had a duty to protect the hearts, energy and spirit of my family, so I made the conscious decision to take a good hard look at the story I was spinning. Rather than asking God "Why?" I decided to accept this as something I may never fully understand, *and that was just going to have to be okay.* I chose to believe it would be used to break the generational shame that cursed the women in my family. The more I accepted it, the more I found something I could actually buy into, and that sealed yet another hole.

By this time, I had come remarkably far. I was deep in my transformation, no longer debating or defending my worth, and no longer believing I was being punished for something I didn't realize I'd done. Unexpectedly, almost as if the background noise had cleared, I began to hear my inner voice in a way that was undeniable. I had not been raised to listen to my intuition, rather, I was taught that our hearts deceive us. Yet, I found that by listening to what I needed, when I needed it, more flow came into my life. There were days when I still felt fragile, so if I didn't have the energy to go out in public, then I would give myself permission not to go. Or if I did have the energetic and emotional bandwidth to get out and be seen, then I would head out the door, head held high, with a smile shining brightly on my face! It became essential that I checked in with myself first, because I was experiencing, on a deep level, what it meant to live in authenticity and alignment.

Even as those months were challenging in every way, something was undeniably shifting in me. *I was awakening.* It took the full dismantling of every coping pattern I'd ever created, and the collapse of the wall I thought was protecting me, for me to finally see a way forward.

It's been over a decade since I've been living as a bald woman. From my perspective now, losing my hair broke me open so I could finally wake up to the truth of who I am. While my sense of worth is still as secure as it was when I decided it was no longer debatable, I still have moments where I miss having hair. What is more than how I have adapted to being bald, is how I have rescued my inner child from the shackles of shame and unworthiness. I am now free and unashamed of who I am at my core.

This isn't just a story about losing hair, it's a journey of deep awakening and reclamation. Maybe you still have a gorgeous head of hair. Maybe your armor looks different. Not all wounds look like mine, as most are invisible or deeply buried, but one thing is true for all of us; we find ways to survive. Maybe, like me, you've spent years building an identity around something – your work, your achievements, your independence, your ability to be palatable to the people around you – because deep down you fear your worthiness or value.

Through my work over the past twenty years, I've found that we commonly learn to cope in these ways:

- Proving.
- Pretending.
- Protecting.
- Perfecting.
- Pleasing.
- Placating.
- Problem-solving (fixing or rescuing).
- Performing.
- Procrastinating.
- Projecting.

Do any of these sound familiar, as ways you have learned to cope?

All these strategies keep us safe, at some point. But what if what you've been doing, is the very thing keeping you *asleep*? What if the very thing you've used to protect yourself is now the thing holding you back?

If you feel like you are waking up to something in yourself right now, I boldly invite you to explore it. Here are some journaling prompts that may help you get started:

1. *What would change in my life and how, if I declared with 100% certainty, that "I AM WORTHY'?*
2. *What strategies have I used to protect myself? What am I most afraid would happen if I stopped using them?*
3. *What would awaken in me if I no longer had to prove, perform, please, placate, etc.?*

Friend, this is deep and powerful work that I believe we are all built for. We aren't created to live in muted or defended versions of ourselves. Maybe that is why you have felt unsettled for so long. Know that there is help, and hope, and that you don't have to go through the process of returning back home to yourself alone.

# Sara Hunter

Sara Hunter is a transformational coach, licensed professional counselor, and founder of The Rooted Woman Collective. With over eighteen years of experience in therapeutic and transformational work, Sara guides emotionally intelligent, visionary and spiritually curious women who are ready to break free from old patterns and come home to their true selves.

Her mission is to help women reclaim their inner wisdom, embody their worth and root down into an unshakeable confidence, so they can live, love and create from a place of deep truth and alignment.

Through trauma-informed coaching, embodiment practices and somatic work, Sara creates profoundly safe spaces for women to shed their protective strategies and reconnect with the parts of themselves they've long silenced.

Sara has worked with hundreds of women across the globe and continues to expand her impact through writing, speaking, and engaging in women's circles.

🌐 www.therootedwomancollective.com
📷 @therootedwomancollective
Scan QR code to learn more about Sara Hunter.

## chapter 16

# Anchored in Earth, Ascending in Spirit: The Tightrope Between Two Worlds

*by John Klug*

## *Life Before My Awakening*

I woke suddenly to my father knocking on my bedroom door, "John, I need to talk to you." I was groggy, having gone to bed late after working into the early morning at the restaurant. He said very seriously, "Your mother and I are concerned about the hours you're keeping and how some nights you don't even come home." Turns out I occasionally slept in my car to avoid waking my family. Father continued by asking, "Are you taking drugs, John?" I was shocked. *Do my parents even know who I am?* The truth was, I was working myself to exhaustion almost every night; a product of the German work ethic instilled in me by my father from an early age. To be accused of using drugs was like a slap in the face. My denial made little difference to my father. He continued, "Your mother and I feel you are setting a poor example for your brothers and sisters. You've dropped out of college and do as you please without concern for your family or future. We think it would be best if you move out. Go and waste your life somewhere else."

After sleeping overnight in my car for several days, I moved into my best friend's house. Mike's parents set up a bed for me in their basement, and I did the same as before; work long hours and sleep late into the day. Over a very short period, a relationship blossomed with a server I worked with at the restaurant. We later moved into an apartment together. As my father said, I was like a cork floating in the ocean. I had no purpose or direction other than satisfying my immediate needs.

"John, I'm pregnant." It took me several minutes to understand what my girlfriend was saying. I launched immediately into the five stages of grief. Once I reached acceptance, my only thought was... *I'm going to be a father. I'll do whatever it takes to be the best parent I can be, and I sure as hell won't make the same mistakes my parents did with me.* Now, I had a purpose!

The first step was to earn more money! Looking through the classified ads in the Sunday newspaper, I came across an ad posted by a small company seeking a computer programmer, listing all the skills I had gained in my high school studies. I applied and, to my surprise, got a call for an interview. Shortly after, the company offered me a job. I began to earn enough money to take care of all the necessities. Life was pretty good!

The second step was to... wait, what second step? Get a better car, save to buy a house, return to college, finish my degree? Nothing inspired me. The only thing I wanted was to explore my immediate interests; programming, electronics, car repair and anything technical in nature. My everyday experience showed me little more than burdens and restrictions on my freedom, and it convinced me *life is not fair!* There had to be more than just sleeping, working and spending a few hours with my family. There had to be.

## *The Awakening Experience*

### The est Training

It was just after 6pm on the second Sunday. At that moment, the trainer said something that instantly changed everything. He said, "You are a machine." It doesn't seem like much on the surface but at that moment, my life changed, after all the hours spent inside that simple hotel ballroom outside Chicago. Something happened that had never happened to me in my twenty years of life; my mind went still. The little voice constantly chattering away in the back of my mind stopped. It was completely silent! I had "gotten" it! Everything I had heard in the days and hours leading up to this moment made sense. My epiphany filled me with great hope and joy for the future. I had a vague sense of what my life could be. I was on the highest high I had ever experienced. Now I had something to go on.

I rejoined my good friend Mike, who had taken the training with me. As we walked down the hallway to leave, *she* stood there blocking my path, looking deeply into my eyes – the one I had locked eyes with several times throughout the training. As I walked closer to her, she stopped me and said, "John, I know you like me, and I like you," expressed without pretext, just as we had learned. I was lost in the moment, melting into her embrace. I could feel the sexual tension rising inside me. "Why don't you come up to my room?" Mike's voice brought me back to reality, "John, we gotta go." She protested, saying, "You get it now, don't you?" encouraging me to let go of my past limitations and embrace my heart's desire, just as we had learned in "the training."

Thoughts raced through my mind... *I can't do this; I'm married, I have a child and my friend is my ride back home,* but my heart was saying, *Stay.* At that moment, I realized life was more complicated than it seemed just a moment before. "Trust me... I want nothing more than to stay with you, but I have to go." The look of disappointment on her face devastated me. My overwhelming sadness sent me into a tailspin I was not to recover from anytime soon. Little did I realize, this decision would lead to a series of events that would change the course of my life.

This was my first experience with the tightrope between two worlds; the outer world demanding my conformity to social norms and the inner world urging me to explore my heart's desire. Later, I discovered that this theme had played out over and over. I didn't know how to balance my inner and outer worlds. Perhaps she would have played a significant role in my awakening, though of course, I will never know. Ultimately, it contrasted the nature of my circumstances with my potential future, helping me to see how following my heart might have brought great joy and accelerated growth.

**The Conversations for Action Workshop**

The Conversations for Action workshop is based on the work of Terry Winograd and Fernando Flores. The one thing I learned in that workshop that stuck out was their analysis of effective communication. They taught how communication comes down to five elements:

- Proposals
- Requests
- Promises
- Offers
- Invitations

Everything else was what they termed "weather reporting" – communication that doesn't result in action. Seeing how this concept played out in the workshop caused another profound shift in my thinking. I realized I now possessed a strategy for operating in everyday reality and, more specifically, a key for communicating effectively.

Left unaddressed by this workshop were the quiet yet insistent urgings of my heart's desire. The dilemma remained: *How can I bring my heart's desire to life?* I was more successful in the physical world with what I had learned. That success brought in more income, allowing me to indulge my new-found passion for reading spiritually oriented books. The extra income became the means to bridge my outer and inner worlds for several years. The more successful I became, the more opportunity there was to learn about spirituality. I had found a path forward!

### The Seth Material: *The Nature of Personal Reality*

The book, *The Nature of Personal Reality*, written by Jane Roberts and Robert F Butts, pulled me in like no other; I must have read it in just a few days. I was fascinated, inspired and eager to learn everything that Seth had to teach. What an incredible thing! I had access to Seth's teachings with no more effort than reading a book. One of the most impactful ideas Seth brought forth was... "You create your reality." This concept, coupled with what I had taken from the est training, resulted in the realization I created my perception of reality. In practice, it is much more complicated and nuanced than that. If I create my reality, that must mean there's some mechanism for creating the outer reality I perceive. Through Seth's teachings, I learned that my thoughts and beliefs, regardless of whether I'm aware of them, are used to create my reality. What shows up in life follows our thoughts and beliefs. Now, I had a means to bring my dreams to life!

***Opening to Channel* by Sanaya Roman and Duane Packer**

In the years after reading the Seth material, I was obsessed with channeled messages. I had read dozens of books, each book bringing me another piece of the puzzle of how to fulfill my heart's desire. One day, browsing the shelves of my favorite bookstore, I discovered *Opening to Channel*. As I eagerly read that book, I entertained the idea that I could channel. Just think of it; communicating with wise spirits and grander beings than myself. If I could do that, it would kick my life into overdrive. As I continued to read, I began to think, *Why not? Why not me?*

I jumped into the exercises outlined in the book, diligently practicing the automatic writing exercises discussed. I would sit on my couch after my two children had gone to bed and begin writing. I was a single father at the time, and life was hectic. Each day was pretty much wake up, have breakfast, get the kids ready for school, get the kids to school, get myself to work, work my eight-hour day and then come home, make dinner, go through my kid's homework and their papers, and play followed by bath time, and getting ready for bed. After bedtime stories, "me time" arrived at nine o'clock. Even though I was exhausted, I was passionate about spending time with my notebook and the automatic writing exercises. After some time, I became frustrated with the exercises. Even though I could see helpful messages not in my own words, it was too laborious, too chaotic.

And, of course, the book *Opening to Channel* was all about verbal channeling; automatic writing was simply a means to that end. I wanted to learn how to do that, but I didn't have a way to do it for myself. It was just me and my kids. *Could they be the audience for any personalities I might randomly channel?* Not at ages five and seven. Because I lived far from friends, I felt I couldn't move forward. Again, I was walking the tightrope between worlds. *How am I going to learn? How am I going to practice verbal channeling? How will I experience what brings me such an incredible sense of purpose?*

Using what I'd learned up to that point, I put my request out to the universe. Believe it or not, in a short time, I stumbled upon a poster advertising a workshop based on the book *Opening to Channel* taught by a woman personally trained by Sanaya Roman. I signed up immediately, working with my ex-wife to coordinate the kid's visitation schedule around the weekend of the workshop.

The workshop was incredible; I learned so much so quickly. I couldn't wait for the advanced class! Thankfully, the advanced class opened the following month, and again, the experience swept me away in the magic of *Opening to Channel.* Our teacher introduced us to an entity named Bartholomew. After some instruction, we paired up and took turns connecting with Bartholomew. The things he purportedly had to say! But hey, we were students. Can you imagine the level of patience Bartholomew had to possess? His energy was loving and compassionate, and I could sense his dedication to helping his students learn their craft.

We prepared for our most demanding practice session on the last day, near the end of the workshop. But while the other students partnered up, my teacher brought in someone from the outside for me to partner with. This session was not just practice, this was the real thing. I remember feeling overwhelming emotions throughout the session. The pure, unconditional love that poured through me brought me and my "practice partner" to tears. It was beyond anything I had ever felt, so intense I could barely get the words out at times. Was it Bartholomew speaking? I had no way of knowing. She was given information about her physical condition in such a raw and tangible fashion, things I had no way of knowing, and left no doubt that a very wise and compassionate energy was working with us. Afterward, the teacher approached me and said, "Well, John, you're ready to channel for your own clients." I was now a channel!

Many years passed as I practiced my craft, working with friends, family and others I met along the way. Again, I began to struggle with breaking free of the status quo and working as a channel full-time. *How could I afford to make such a drastic change? How would I support my children and pay for all the things life demanded of me?*

**Golden Arrow**

Golden Arrow is a group consciousness similar to my and everyone else's higher self. Even though I cannot remember the question I posed to Golden Arrow, nor the exact wording of their answer, what they said had a powerful impact. Thinking back to the years since I learned to channel, the greatest obstacle to fully embracing my role as a channel was the idea I was *responsible for the message.* In the few words Golden Arrow spoke, I realized I had everything backward; I behaved like the channeling was all about me. I felt responsible for the message and worried the words spoken while channeling might cause people difficulties or lead them astray. Suddenly, I realized people were not coming to see me, the channel, they were coming to hear Jonathon. I instantly thought, *I am the instrument through which Jonathon speaks. He's responsible for the message, not me. I'm not the star of the show; Jonathon is. I'm his humble servant. I'm the instrument. I'm the channeler. My job is to let go and let Jonathon come forward. By doing that, I'm allowing Jonathon to deliver his message with extraordinary clarity and impact.* Finally, I was free.

**Life After My Awakening**

The est training taught me I had a choice, the Conversations for Action workshop showed me how to be an effective communicator, the Seth Material helped me unlock the power of conscious manifestation, *Opening to Channel* introduced me to the powerful gift of channeling, and finally, Golden Arrow freed me from the prison I had created, allowing Jonathon to take the spotlight.

I am now actively transitioning from my corporate career to a life centered on service to others. I participated in my first Conscious Life Expo and am actively seeking other expos and spiritual fairs to attend. I'm investing in a professional website, social media, and the tools needed to present my work in the most professional manner possible.

I now understand that I am Jonathon, and Jonathon is me. Gathering the courage to follow my heart has allowed me to open to new worlds, whereas before, my life resembled a fallen leaf, going wherever the wind blew. I now have a strong compass because I'm living from my heart's desire, and I experience the greatest joy in living this way. With that joy comes grace. And so, you too will have the same as you follow your own heart's desire!

# John Klug

My name is John Klug, and I channel a personality named Jonathon. Jonathon represents my soul collective – the combined wisdom and experiences from my past, present and future lives. We originate from Sirius B and carry the energy of ascended masters, which gives our work a profound spiritual purpose. I'm dedicated to guiding and supporting others on their spiritual journeys.

Jonathon helps individuals navigate the complexities of living in the third dimension, offering support as they ascend to higher states of consciousness. This journey can lead to greater clarity and a renewed focus on what truly matters to you. His teachings are grounded in common sense, and he shares wisdom in a practical and relatable way.

My goal is to reach a wider audience with these insights. To achieve that goal, I am transitioning from a corporate career to full-time channeling, providing personalized sessions via Zoom and participating in gatherings nationwide.

My journey into channeling began in 1990 with automatic writing, followed by formal training in Sanaya Roman's *Opening to Channel* program. I have also studied with Carla Rueckert, known for her work on *The Law of One, The Ra Material.* Additionally, I facilitate a weekly Zoom gathering where anyone can engage directly with Jonathon.

⊕ www.jonathon456.org
⊕ www.youtube.com/@jonathon456
Scan QR code to learn more about John Klug.

## Section III:
# Breaking Open, Breaking Free

- When have you chosen freedom, even if fear was trying to hold you back?

- Is there a pattern you're ready to release?

- What would freedom feel like in your body, your mind, and your spirit?

chapter

# 17

# Shattered Innocence: A Child of War

*by Toni Ghazi*

**A Fragile Normal**

I learned to tell the difference between the sound of thunder and the sound of bombs before I learned how to write my name. In my earliest memory, I am five years old, clutching my toy truck as the ground shakes and the walls tremble around me. Mama pulls me into the bathroom – she says it's the safest room because it has no big windows – and we huddle on the cold tile floor. My heart is pounding so loudly I can hear it in my ears. *Boom. Boom. Boom. Is that my heartbeat or another distant explosion?* I squeeze my eyes shut and hold my breath, my entire small body frozen in fear, waiting for the next thunderous blast to pass.

By daylight, life tries to pretend it's normal. I wake up to the smell of flatbread warming on our stove and mama's gentle hand smoothing my hair. She smiles at me like nothing is wrong, like we didn't spend half the night with our hearts in our throats. "Good morning, habibi," she whispers, her voice calm but her eyes tired and red. I nod and try to smile back. Mornings are usually quiet; the guns and rockets seem to sleep at sunrise... at least for a little while. Baba sips tea at the rickety kitchen table, a radio pressed to his ear. The radio crackles with news I don't fully understand; words like *ceasefire, militia, shelling*. I swing my legs under the chair, nibbling at my bread, pretending I'm not listening. But I am. Every child I know has learned to listen to the whispers of war.

I haven't been to school in weeks. Fighting in the city closed all the schools. I miss my friends and even my teacher's chalky drawings on the board. Mama says insha'Allah (God willing) I'll go back soon, but I see the doubt in her eyes. Instead of school, I spend the day in our apartment. I'm not allowed to play outside; it's too dangerous. So, I sit by my window, coloring with my crayons. I draw a big yellow sun over a peaceful house with a garden. In my picture, no bombs fall from the sky. It's a world I barely remember or maybe just dream of.

Mama tries her best to make life feel normal. She helps me line up my toy cars and sings me silly songs, even as distant booms make the dishes rattle. In the afternoon, the sun paints golden stripes on our living room floor. I crawl into them and pretend my toys are racing through golden deserts. Mama claps along softly, and for a few minutes, I feel like a regular little boy. I even forget to be afraid.

**Night of Terror**

That night, I am jarred awake by a thunderous blast that rattles our entire building. It feels like the world is shaking apart. My ears ring and a framed photo falls off the wall with a crash of shattering glass. I hear baba shout in alarm. My brother starts screaming, and my own voice is trapped in my throat, a silent cry. Another explosion booms even closer this time, and the lights flicker out, plunging us into darkness.

"Mama!" I finally shriek, my voice high and broken. Mama rushes to my room, grabs me and my brother, and we run to the bathroom. Baba is right behind us, flashlight in hand. We curl up on the floor, the four of us pressed together. My heart drums against my ribs so fast it hurts. In the flashlight's weak beam, I see dust dancing in the air like ghostly snow. The house shakes again as a third blast echoes, and I clench my teeth so hard I taste blood.

The sounds of war are all around. Distant *tat-tat-tat* of gunfire, the whistle of rockets overhead, the ground-shaking *BOOM* of impact. Each one makes me flinch and bite down a whimper. Mama holds us tight, humming a shaky lullaby to try and drown out the chaos. I feel her trembling too; even parents are terrified, though they try to be brave for us.

Suddenly, a deafening blast erupts just outside. The bathroom door blows shut and something heavy crashes elsewhere in the building. The tile floor bucks under us as if hit by an earthquake. I bury my face in Mama's shoulder, a scream ripping out of me. My whole body is shaking uncontrollably, frozen yet quivering, every muscle locked in terror.

Then, just as quickly, an eerie silence falls. Only the distant rumble of fighting and my brother's faint sobs remain. Baba coughs, waving dust out of the air. "We have to leave," he says, voice grim. He pries the bathroom door open. Outside, our apartment is still standing, but part of the building next door is gone. Through the gaping hole in the wall, I see flames and smoke in the night sky.

We step into the hall, and my knees nearly give way. The corridor is filled with rubble and smoke. Neighbors shout urgent warnings. I see a woman from upstairs limping down, blood streaming from a cut on her forehead. Mama shields my eyes, but between her fingers I glimpse more than I should: destruction, people hurt, everything dark and chaotic.

On the street, it's like stepping into a nightmare. The smell of smoke and burning plastic chokes me. Under the flicker of fires, buildings that once stood proud, are now skeletons with jagged teeth of concrete. We hurry along the street, keeping low. My hand is locked in Mama's, and I'm afraid to blink or breathe. Sirens wail in the distance and someone is crying out for help nearby. In a panic, I wonder about my friend Kareem who lives down this street; *Did he and his family escape in time?* The thought of anything happening to him makes my heart squeeze painfully.

We pass a figure lying on the pavement. In the dim orange glow, I realize it's a man, not moving. I stare at his still face and the dark pool around him. My stomach lurches violently as I understand he's dead. I want to scream or look away, but I can't. Mama pulls me close to her skirt to shield me from the sight, but it's too late – I will never forget that image. I feel something inside me break, certain that nothing will ever be safe again.

At last, we reach a crowded basement that someone has opened as a shelter. Dozens of neighbors are huddled together in the damp gloom. Mama finds a spot for us against a wall. My whole body is trembling and I can't unclench my jaw. A neighbor presses a cup of water into my hands; I didn't even realize I was thirsty until the water touches my lips. I drink in small gulps, spilling a bit because I can't steady my hands.

In the candlelit dark, I catch sight of other kids my age with the same wide, haunted eyes. No words pass between us; our silence speaks for us. My heart is still hammering, and I curl into Mama's side trying to make myself as small as possible. She strokes my dusty hair and whispers that we're safe here. Safe. The word has lost its meaning.

I try to speak to ask about our home, or what happened, but my voice cracks. "M-m-mama..." is all that comes out. She hushes me gently. Wrapped in my mother's arms, I finally let the tears flow. I cry for what feels like hours, until exhaustion overtakes fear and I drift into a shallow, haunted sleep.

**Scars of Fear**

By morning, the bombardment stops. The city is eerily quiet as pale sunlight filters through smoky clouds. We survived the night, but nothing is the same. In the days that follow, we stay with my aunt in a safer part of the city. Our apartment is still standing, but I can't forget the hole in the building next door, the faces in the dark, the man lying still on the ground.

Everyone says I'm lucky to be alive, but I don't feel lucky. The war has left wounds inside me that no one can see. I jump at every loud sound, a door slam or a dropped pan sending a jolt of panic through my veins. Nightmares wake me up with a pounding heart and gasping breath. Worst of all, when I try to talk about what happened, my voice falters. Words stick in my throat. A stutter that wasn't there before has taken hold. "M-m-mama, I s-saw..." is all I manage before breaking down in sobs. It's as if the horror of that night tangled up my tongue.

Mama and Baba try to comfort me. They hold me close and say it's okay, that I'm safe now. Mama promises me the war will end one day, that I'll grow up in peace. I want to believe her. I nod and smile weakly, but inside I'm not sure what safety means anymore. How can I feel safe when I know what bombs can do?

Still, in this darkness, there are tiny sparks of light. My family is one of them; mama's gentle hugs, baba's silly attempts to cheer me up with magic tricks using a deck of old cards. One evening, the power comes back on and my aunt plays a song on the radio. Baba grabs mama's hand and they start to dance slowly in the living room, swaying together amid the flicker of oil lamps. I watch them and manage a small smile. Watching them sway, I feel a tiny glimmer of hope.

**Dawn of a New Day**

Months pass and the war that has filled my entire childhood is finally coming to an end. One day, the guns go silent. The adults whisper the news we hardly dare believe: a ceasefire, maybe even peace. The silence feels alien and fragile. I stand on the balcony of my aunt's house, my toy truck in my arms, listening to a city without explosions. The only sounds are distant cars and birds. Birds! I haven't heard them over the din of war in so long.

In the coming weeks, we return to our old neighborhood to rebuild. School reopens, and I even go back to class. I'm nervous around the other children and still stutter when I'm anxious, but no one laughs; everyone here has their scars. We all flinch at loud noises, but slowly, together, we heal bit by bit.

One afternoon, my friend Kareem (he survived too) and I sit on a wall eating ripe oranges. Juice dribbles down our chins and for the first time in forever, I hear myself laugh at a joke he tells. The sound surprises me; it's a bright, silly giggle, the laugh of a child who still lives inside me somewhere. Kareem laughs with me, and the sun feels warm on our faces. In that moment, with the taste of sweet orange on my tongue and laughter in the air, I feel something loosen in my chest. The fear that had made me stutter and hide is still there, but I learn to live with it.

That night, I fell asleep in my own little bed under a mended roof. My truck is tucked under my arm. The city outside is calm. As I close my eyes, my heart beats steadily. I'm still that child who endured nights of terror, and those memories will always be with me. My stutter remains, a quiet echo of those years, a part of me that never left. But now I'm also a child who has seen a new morning, who dares to imagine a future beyond the war. And as I drift off to sleep, I finally feel a small piece of my lost innocence return, like a shy sunrise after a long, dark night.

That future came with a gift I never expected; clarity. A deep awareness awakened in me. I began to see the truth hidden beneath all the fear – that I was never truly broken. That love, especially the love I discovered within myself, had always been there. I learned that I am not confined by past beliefs, fears, or circumstances. I am more than what I endured. I am free to create, to speak, to grow, even if my voice shakes. I realized that the possibilities before me are limitless. And as I drift off to sleep, I finally feel a small piece of my lost innocence return, like a shy sunrise after a long, dark night – lighting the path to who I was always meant to become.

 Toni Ghazi

Toni Ghazi is a spiritual catalyst, paradigm shifter, and cosmic channel who helps individuals break free from limitation and step into a fearless, empowered way of being. Serving as a direct conduit for the Praying-Mantis Beings of the Antares Stargate, Toni bridges dimensions—offering transmissions of higher intelligence, healing frequencies, and soul-level remembrance from benevolent extraterrestrial guides devoted to humanity's evolution.

Known for his bold, transformative presence, Toni's work is designed for those ready to challenge old paradigms, release fear, and reclaim their true essence. His offerings—ranging from live transmissions and workshops to one-on-one sessions—activate dormant inner codes, helping people dismantle outdated programming and reconnect with their inner power and divine purpose.

Toni combines multidimensional insight with grounded tools to guide individuals toward wholeness, authenticity, and sovereignty. His approach empowers both men and women to reclaim their voice, align with their truth, and live with unapologetic clarity and intention.

With a mission rooted in unity consciousness, Toni invites seekers, visionaries, and truth-tellers to remember who they really are and co-create a world where magic, multidimensionality, and spiritual mastery are not the exception—but the new norm.

🌐 www.tonighazi.com
📷 @theantareanheart

Scan QR code to learn more about Toni Ghazi.

chapter

# 18

# Streetwise and Soul-led: From Surviving to Rewiring

*by Shannon Shade*

It must have been around 2 am when I woke up in a comfortable yet unfamiliar bed, momentarily forgetting why I was there. Then, I remembered... and suddenly, I wished I could forget. One of my closest childhood friends had taken his life, and his family had paid for me to come to the funeral, letting me stay in their home. Their house was on a quiet, peaceful farm, tucked away in the middle of nowhere. And I sure wasn't used to silence these days. *Maybe that's what woke me up, the sheer stillness,* I thought to myself. As I lay there, trying to will myself back to sleep, that's when I saw them.

Three glowing orbs hovered a few feet below the ceiling, directly above the foot of my bed. They were perfectly round, glowing with a soft white light, just like little full moons. They weren't huge, but they weren't small, about the size of grapefruits. They felt alive, friendly and gentle. I sensed that they were curious about me and checking in. As they moved around each other slowly, perfectly, orbiting like a trinity of spirit beings, my conscious mind began forming theories. *Was this orchestrated by my deceased friend? Or was this a spirit team? Angels with a message? Was I hallucinating because of grief?* One thing I knew for sure was that I wasn't dreaming. I was trying to understand when suddenly, my thoughts shifted to my friend and the tragedy. A wave of sadness washed over me, followed by a twinge of fear as I realized that this experience was beyond ordinary.

Yet, the very instant I felt fear, the orbs bolted across the left side of the room, fast like lightning, and disappeared, almost as if through a portal before they hit the wall to go out. I absolutely knew in that moment that they didn't want to scare me. I felt they were there to give me a cosmic high five and to let me know my friend was still existing and that all was well.

That morning, I hesitantly told my friend's family about what I'd experienced, and to my surprise, one of them shared a similar story.

This wasn't grief messing with my mind. This was real! I had always experienced unusual encounters and I had seen mysterious things before. But this was one of the first times I saw something so vivid with my physical eyes. I had felt an undeniable personality within those orbs. For weeks to come, I sensed they were still near, rooting for me, protecting me. And that protection? Holy hell, did I need it.

The same parents who paid for me to attend the funeral paid for my ticket back. But back to what? I was nineteen, almost homeless, surviving off food banks and attending church sermons to get a bowl of stew. I was living off East Hastings in Vancouver, one of the worst places in Canada. I had a roof over my head, but the floors were made of dirt. Bars were on the windows, the streets were full of addicts and street fights were the norm. Ginseng brandy was the drink of choice for those with little money (myself included), and it was literally killing people. Almost everywhere you looked, the people and situations were physical manifestations of trauma. Many people had conditions that no one knew how to name back then. They were lost in the system before anyone knew how to find them.

As I rode the long, sixteen-hour bus ride back to Vancouver, devising a plan to move ASAP, the bus pulled over for a break. I decided to get off the bus, stretch my legs, and grab some snacks at the nearby convenience store. As I did, I suddenly recalled a strange incident that had occurred just weeks ago in the city, before my friend's passing. I'd been traveling on the local city bus. It was just another ordinary day on the same route I had been taking for months. But what happened next was not ordinary. In fact, it defied logic.

I stood up to get off at my stop, when behind me, a voice rang out, sharp, almost robotic and impossible to ignore: "SIT DOWN." I didn't even look behind me. I froze and quickly sat back down. Instantly, the bus screeched to a forceful halt as another vehicle cut it off. Everyone on the bus was launched forward. A woman who was standing near me in the aisle went flying. She was badly hurt. I was shaken but unharmed. I spun around to see who or what it was that told me to sit, half expecting to see something straight out of a sci-fi movie. But there were only a few people, all just as shocked as I was. I didn't bother asking if they heard the voice because something told me they'd just look at me like I was from Mars.

Back in the convenience store, as I recalled this memory, time got away from me. I spent so long thinking about that bizarre bus moment, I kind of forgot I was actually supposed to be reboarding the other bus, the one that was, you know, taking me back to the city.

Staring at the chip aisle like I was in a trance, I snapped out of my thoughts when the lady working at the till asked me, "Hey, kid, isn't that your bus leaving?" I looked out the window, and my stomach dropped. The bus back to Vancouver was pulling away without me.

I ran as fast as I could, and the other passengers noticed, thankfully, so the bus driver stopped and let me back on.

Once I was back on, I realized I had a ton of snacks in my arms, all of which I had completely forgotten to pay for in the rush, nor did I have time to. This struck me as funny, and for the first time in weeks, I had a good laugh before eventually drifting off to sleep for the rest of the trip.

When I arrived in Vancouver, I didn't have much to pack because most of my stuff was gone. My boyfriend at the time, who was a drug dealer, and a lousy one at that, had pawned nearly everything I owned while I was away. Honestly, he was so bad at dealing, he owed his customers money. I was so ready to kick him to the curb. And unlike the loss I was already carrying, losing him wouldn't sting nearly as much. The weight of my friend's passing was heavy, and I already missed him dearly. I couldn't begin to imagine what he had been going through, the pain and turmoil in his mind that led him to that moment, when he took his own life. But at the same time, I had conflicting emotions because the psychological and emotional impact was massive for everyone. It shattered something inside all of us. But sorting through this tsunami of confusing emotions would have to wait. It was time to get my life together.

As I packed, I thought back to simpler times, like when I was five or six, draping a blanket over my back and letting the warm air from the heater vent lift it like a superhero's cape. I'd pretend I was a superhero. I would literally pray to the heavens, begging the gods or whoever was in charge to turn me into one. I wanted it SO badly.

And then there was music. Music was a must-have. I'd lock myself in my room, blast my favorite songs, and sing until my throat hurt. I also wanted to be a singer and would imagine *rocking the world.* I prayed to the universe to let my voice be heard. But times changed as I got a bit older.

I was eight years old when my parents ended their marriage. Even at that young age, I knew it was for the best. They were unhappy together, and some part of me understood this was the right decision for them. But that didn't make things easier. The years ahead would be tough, but somehow, through everything, I always had a sense that someone or something was steering me away from the worst of it.

And then, around age nine, something happened where I knew, truly knew, that something was watching over me. My mom had been dating a farmer, and one sunny afternoon while visiting his home, I went outside and crawled into an opening in a stack of old hay bales. It was warm, cozy, and safe. But suddenly, something felt off.

A feeling hit me, GET OUT! NOW! It wasn't a voice or a conscious thought. It was a full-body knowing that if I didn't move right then, something bad was going to happen.

Without hesitating, I scrambled out, and the moment my feet hit the ground, flames started to shoot up behind me.

The hay had caught fire. My mother's boyfriend had lit it, not knowing I was inside. I stood there, staring at the flames, feeling oddly safe, while he turned as pale as a ghost and proceeded to tell me that this situation almost gave him a heart attack. Even at that young age, I understood that I had been protected. And actually, I was turning into a protector of sorts myself.

By the time I was nine, I was babysitting kids. This was not unusual in the eighties. Things were different back then, and many adults didn't think twice about leaving a young child in charge of others, especially in a super small town like the one I lived in. I didn't know much about taking care of kids, but I figured it out. And when they wouldn't sleep, I would pretend to hypnotize them. And it worked, they'd sleep!

As a kid and later as a teenager, I had a lot of freedom and not much guidance. I started dating too young and lived a rebellious life. Yet, at the same time, I was mature, responsible and careful. Somehow, despite finding myself in precarious situations more times than I could count, I walked away unscathed most of the time. My family had its own struggles, and while there was love, there wasn't always a clear path forward when it came to pursuing my dreams. *Still, I kept chasing them anyway.*

That mix of early responsibility, freedom without direction and a deep longing for more is what made me pack my bags at eighteen and head to a big city with almost nothing. My dreams were clear: I wanted to become a rockstar. The bravery was there and the rebel in me was ready. I was rocking a black leather jacket, big hair and so much eyeliner that even after I washed my face, it still looked like too much. The eyeliner was planned. And that was about all that was. I didn't have a real plan. Not for surviving, and not for chasing dreams. I just knew I had to try. But the city had its own plans for me, and it wasn't pretty.

Which brings us back to Vancouver, back to the major turning point. Nineteen years old, surviving in the toughest part of the city. When my dear friend took his life, it changed everything. As I left that scene behind, I decided that since something was so clearly trying to make sure that I survived all these years, I may as well start putting in the effort to live... and I mean really live.

Leaving the survival grind was just the beginning; it took me four more years before I finally began moving forward in a more positive direction. I went to university. Studied music. Sang. Performed internationally. Worked as an improv performance artist for decades.

Taught music and led rock-style programs for kids, both locally and abroad. The musical, creative and spiritual sides of me continued to grow, and I felt deeply connected to each one.

It was a bold life, but still not the easiest one. And decades later, the weight of the past, the survival mode I had lived in for so long, finally caught up with me. The trauma I had buried from so many places and seasons in my life was clawing its way out. Anxiety crept in, and my ability to handle stress wore thin. Trauma lived in my body and mind, affecting me in ways I could no longer ignore. It was time to heal the old wounds. Spirituality had carried me through, but now the work was more about the body and the mind, where the pain of the past had taken root.

That's when I discovered hypnotherapy, or maybe it discovered me, and I started healing in ways I never thought possible. I rewired the survival patterns, the fight-or-flight reactions, the deep-seated wounds, the limiting beliefs. I changed how I identified with my past. And as I healed, I knew I wanted to help others do the same. I became a clinical hypnotherapist. And just like music, this wasn't just a job, it was a calling. But this time, it wasn't about performance. It was about serving, and helping others heal. It turns out that all those years as a kid pretending to have superpowers and a voice that could reach the stars were not only preparing me for this life, but also creating it. After all, those early years are when the subconscious mind is wide open and unguarded to every belief, every story and every dream. That was then, but here's what matters now.

I've had moments that were deep, dark and heavy. There were moments when I could have been gone, but something kept me here. Something greater. Yet, this isn't a story about floating in the light. It's about walking through the fire, feeling the weight of it all, and still choosing to rise. I've had mystical experiences. I've been guided. But the real awakening wasn't just a spiritual one, it was a human one. It was realizing that even with all the spiritual insight, my healing had to include my human self: the body, the mind and the heart. That, too, is sacred. That, too, is awakening. Embracing all of it. The human and the divine, the mystical and the messy, the pain and the possibilities.

Knowing that you can hold both and still move forward.

So, if you're struggling in life, please remember this: You have already made it through some of your darkest moments. There is light at the end of the tunnel. You might not even see the tunnel right now. But it's there. You may discover that whether you're having a bad day or a dark night of the soul, this is just a chapter of your life story, not the whole book. It might feel like a long and exhausting passage, but one day, you may revisit this chapter and see it with fresh eyes. Sooner or later, you can rewrite how that chapter lives in your heart, mind and body. Add to it whatever feels right to you, a touch of humor, a little wisdom, even a sense of purpose. And as you do, you're not just changing the story, you're changing the way your system processes it: mentally, emotionally and physically. It's not that you are rewriting the truth of your story, rather you are no longer letting the wounds define the narrative. And can you imagine how it will feel when that new perspective resonates with you on all levels?

That's the power YOU have. Your spirit is strong, and your mind is marvelous. Best of all, there is something greater guiding you, a wisdom beyond words and your joy is its deepest desire. Call it spirit, intuition, the higher self. Whatever it is, it's whispering to you:

"Keep going. Even though sometimes it's hard."

And one day, you'll be so damn glad you did.

# Shannon Shade

Shannon Shade, RCH, is a registered and accredited clinical hypnotherapist offering sessions both online and in-person. She combines trauma-informed techniques with a deep understanding of neuroplasticity and nervous system regulation. Alongside her formal training, she brings lived experience, sharpened instincts, and the ability to meet people where they are. Her work is guided by both science and soul, blending evidence-based methods with deep intuition and a creative force that helps clients rewrite their inner stories and reclaim their true selves. Shannon's writing has been featured in *Mediumship: Sacred Communications with Loved Ones Across the Veil* by Suzanne Giesemann. She offers a safe, supportive space for those ready to move beyond survival and step into authenticity and healing. Ready to reclaim your story? There are chapters ahead you have not even imagined yet.

⊕ www.shannonshypnotherapy.com
◎ @shannonshadehypnotherapy
Scan QR code to learn more about Shannon Shade.

chapter

# 19

## Finding Heaven on Earth After Living Through Hell

*by Martin Lewis*

The transformation process from a life of struggles and anger to experiencing literal *Heaven on Earth* is my awakening story. I'd like to share the journey with you.

We live in very polarized times (c. 2024-25). Political parties and the mainstream media are pushing an agenda of us versus them... that's how they get their riches. Navigating a path through the polarity, to find spiritual riches of my own is the focus of my awakening.

Challenges arise when people declare allegiance to a political movement or religion over finding a path of peaceful co-existence. It's a problem when which *flag* a neighbor chooses to fly in their front yard becomes more important than living with them in harmony. My awakening is about a path to loving all with mercy, forgiveness and compassion as guiding principles. My path is finding joy and not drowning in the vast negativity being put out by power structures.

**Background Story**

From an early age, I felt a strong connection to the teachings of Jesus; kindness, compassion, mercy, forgiveness, love. Those approaches to life resonated strongly with me. It didn't take much convincing, at Sunday school, to get me on board with the Christian Church. It also helped that my denomination was very much based on the teachings of Jesus. I was focused on the meaning or lesson being taught more than merely memorizing words (and misapplying the memorized words out of context). Keeping active in the church led to public baptism at age eleven. At this point, I'm fully synched with the positive aspects of the Christian religion and came up out of the water with an active metaphysical connection. I could feel the golden orange energy from "God" (would now call this a connection with the energy of source, the all-that-is) and a mental connection with the divine. It was truly amazing to have a metaphysical connection that could give advice on choices you're getting ready to make. I quickly found it was to my benefit to follow the advice. Doing things I'd received "not a good idea" advice about, always made for, shall I say, a disappointing experience. After my awakening, I now know this to be a connection with my primary spirit guides, the *Order of Melchizedek*. There would be other lucid experiences, primarily prophetic dreams, but the experiences were limited in scope and impact.

While there was never a wounding incident and resultant fleeing from the Christian religion, there was a falling away as I grew older. Getting up early to hear the same message retold over and over seemed not worth the effort while in college. After college, life became very busy. Serving on active duty in the military, getting married, having children, and enduring all the demands military service brings with it; tours in combat zones added extended separations and post-traumatic stress disorder challenges on return. Throughout these types of challenges, faith in the baseline teachings of kindness, compassion, mercy, forgiveness and love for all, still resonated with me. Church dogma, that a person's sexual orientation had to be judged, didn't. Why would an otherwise outstanding, commendable person be excluded from a church (or heaven!) because they didn't follow an arbitrary rule? That didn't resonate with me, felt as though something was off – too much rule following. It didn't match my views on the baseline message. I found myself falling further and further away from organized religion. Taking part in small group discussions felt fine, but attending an organized service was definitely not happening.

One aspect of religious doctrine I didn't catch taking a hold on me was believing myself *to be right*. So, seeing something as "right" or "wrong" put me fully in the grasp of duality. So, if I saw views on racism as "wrong" or if I saw views on abortion as "wrong", I put the side I disagreed with in judgment. Total fail on my part.

**Entering Dark Night of the Soul**

After twenty-five years in the military, the toll began to show in the form of chronic migraines, joint and back pain, post-traumatic stress disorder and depression. A twelve-year *dark night of the soul* period would follow. Divorce, re-marriage, COVID lockdown and a move under duress during the COVID period increased stress. All this led to a slow build of anger with common stressors: loss of career, separation from kids, continuing pain and challenges controlling emotions.

**Transition Away from Dark Night of the Soul**

My dark night of the soul would end in the Summer of 2024. Some of my first steps out of the period included finding books aligned with my current level of awakening. Books telling of extraterrestrial influence in Sumer[1] and in the Biblical stories caught my attention. A book on Christ Consciousness attributed to the Order of Melchizedek also caught my attention. These had my interest in late spring, and with the school year ending in June 2024, it was time to make vacation plans.

With my youngest turning five years old, we decided to take him to Disneyland. It would be a road trip stopping in Phoenix before going on to Disneyland. Follow on trips to Monterey and San Francisco would be the extent of the outward trip, retracing the path back to double the vacation experience, only substituting in Hollywood for Disneyland on the return.

My anger would reach a peak in the days leading up to the trip. First my laptop died and was replaced with a tower unit (less travel convenient but hopefully sturdier). Travel plans came together slowly. Agreed in principle but not in details. The lack of details led to disharmony and frustration. After a pinnacle of frustration, calling off the trip in the afternoon one day and then agreeing to plans for the trip later the same night, led to a decision to go with the flow and make the most of the final trip plan.

The trip itself was mostly calm and straightforward. Until arriving at Disneyland that is. Staying at the hotel in the themepark grounds, was totally fine. The weather was a different story. Despite temperatures

---

[1] Sumer is the earliest known civilization, located in the historical region of southern Mesopotamia.

in the low 80s F, the sunshine was some of the most intense I've experienced. Unexpected sunburn slowed us down and led to an early return to the hotel.

Without my laptop, playing any of my favorite video games was off the entertainment menu. Turning to YouTube videos in limited free time became a way to occupy myself for a few minutes. The ones that YouTube's algorithm kept feeding me included near death experiences (NDEs), people channeling angels or ascended masters, and stories of extraterrestrial influence on the Bible. I found these fascinating. The awakening lid was starting to swing open!

The awakening lid came flying off one day. A NDE video came on of a young person who died unexpectedly and met with his spirit family. The person had led a good life, being for fairness and against racism, discrimination, cruelty, etc... The person liked the other side and asked to stay. They were sent back because there were important lessons still to be learned. While the person had been for "good" causes, they had also been against the "bad." So much so that hate of the "bad" things was in the person's heart. I saw a perfect mirror image of the approaches in my life. I had to learn the same lesson as shown on the NDE video.

During this time, I continued to read the Christ Consciousness book. The subject and teachings were fascinating to me (it was one of my favorite books then and remains so to this day). I found the verbiage used somewhat difficult, to the point of slowing my progress through the book. A video channeling ascended masters came on around this time, covering the subject of Christ Consciousness. One ascended master covered Christ Consciousness so well, I felt I'd gained equal insight in thirty seconds of video as in the three hundred pages of my favorite book. At the time, I'd never heard of Quan Yin[2] before and knew nothing about her. That would soon change!

---

[2] Quan Yin is a revered Bodhisattva in East Asian Buddhism, often translated as "Goddess of Mercy" or "she who hears the cries of the world."

The return trip would be pleasant and a chance to start integrating my new insights. A couple of lucid experiences pushed my awakening further along. Before heading to Hollywood, we made a day trip to Big Sur from Monterey. At this time California Highway 1 was closed just south of the Esalen Institute. The morning of our trip to Big Sur, I read a book review by a staff member of the Esalen Institute. This was my first encounter with the synchronicities a person recognizes after awakening. Turned around on Highway 1 near the entrance to the Esalen Institute, I felt the most immediate frequency rise I've ever encountered, strong enough to require pulling the car over for a short acclimation. We went to Hollywood the next day and made a trip to the Los Angeles County Museum. I had a lucid dream vision of seeing Quan Yin walking across the museum grounds as a message that she was actually close by.

**Spiritual Growth**

On the return drive from Hollywood, I started to internalize the lessons learned in the first full week of my awakening. It became crystal clear to me that having no hate in my heart would require loving the "other" political party in America (both leaders and voters). This became an understanding that more was needed than "loving the sinner and hating the sin." The important combination was loving the person and forgiving the actions... doing both unconditionally. The understanding that flowed forward was: *Don't judge. Don't hate. There is no room for hate in your heart, only room for love. Try to understand others. Even if it means their beliefs and your beliefs are fundamentally different, that's okay. It also means you don't have to try and change anyone's views.*

**Metatron/Quan Yin Connections**

My most explosive spiritual growth was upon returning home. I picked up a book of channeled teachings by Archangel Metatron[3].

---
[3] Robbie Mackenzie and Archangel Metatron, *Metatron, This is the Clarion Call*, (2011)

After starting the book, Metatron appeared to me in a dream and provided the key message: *Everything is source, the all-that-is. There are no other players or actors. We each are individual aspects (often called fractals) of source.*

With that understanding, the key is to love all, accept all people. It's okay to disagree using your discernment. I love unconditionally, regardless of differing social, political or religious views. I will love the person but can still choose not to love what they represent. Even the things I don't resonate with (in my discernment) are sent love – not scorn or derision. Not love with the intent of supporting the actions I don't support but love to soften the impact and the nature of intent I don't support. This approach doesn't mean you have to suddenly become best friends with people doing things you don't support. No need even to have them over for dinner. That part about not judging other people is key when putting forth unconditional love.

Choose to live a heart-centered life. Choose love over fear. When you take this approach, you naturally keep only love in your heart (and keep out fear and hate!).

Shortly after the dream experience with Metatron, Quan Yin also visited in a dream to ask if I'd accept a more direct connection with her. This I did and began to look for information about her views and teachings.

Her message works well with the message Metatron provided. *Show mercy when dealing with others. Show the same mercy when dealing with yourself. Compassion, kindness and forgiveness are key and fundamental concepts to incorporate into your life.*

**Self-Healing**

Use your memories and personal views as cobblestones and building blocks, not as roadblocks. They provide you a vantage point to see yourself and others (who are having a different experience).

As part of forgiving unconditionally, I forgive myself and anyone else involved and the memory of what happened. I don't try to see the event or interaction as either good or bad. It simply is an event I was involved in. I accept that the event took place and thank it for providing a learning experience. I thank it for providing a way to see myself and life with additional insight. Here's an example:

As a young child (let's say four years old), I spent a week with my grandparents who lived a five- or six-hour car ride away. At that time, my grandfather was the most incredible person in the world to me. So one night, I wanted him to read my bedtime story. He got caught up in a business call and couldn't read the book to me – and I declined repeated offers from my grandmother to read the book in his place . When bedtime arrived, and the business call wasn't concluded, I was sent to bed without a story. Four-year-old me didn't understand and was very disappointed. In time and understanding how the world works, the memory takes on new meaning. As an adult having raised five boys, I fully understand much of what my grandmother went through raising six boys. Now I forgive myself for being a demanding child, forgive my grandmother for setting and maintaining boundaries, and forgive the memory for holding any hurt. I now see the memory as neutral; it serves only as a reference point for understanding people and life in general. In the forgiving, note that there is no part where something was right or wrong. It simply was and there is no judgment.

## Conclusion

No need to convert others! Only have unconditional love for others, no judgment.

Love self, love others... love mistakes you've made, as they are chances to learn and be better .

Use your experiences to expand compassion; have a wider and kinder view of the world.

In your healing process, lessons learned are valuable... you don't have to discard them. All don't have to be sweet and gilded.

A message of hope... Earth's *dark night of the soul* is going on right now... greatness comes out the other side. Heaven on Earth? We can have it now!

 # Martin Lewis

Martin serves as a messenger of divine insights and as Herald of the coming Golden Age for humanity and Earth. He works with his divine partners to spread a message of love for all, mercy, compassion and forgiveness.

Emphasizing non-duality and embracing oneness, Martin's message is to live in harmony with others and the environment. Removing all fear from daily life while increasing joy and expansion of the soul is Martin's view on the purpose of life.

The coming Golden Age is the ascended time for humanity and planet Earth (living in 5D). This time will be a literal "heaven on Earth" period for every living being.

⊕ www.larimardragon.com
◎ @martinmelchizedek

Scan QR code to learn more about Martin Lewis.

chapter

# 20

# Don't Fall Asleep Now: The Dream that Changed Everything

*by Marlu Harris*

**The Breakdown**

Have you heard people talk about their amazing insights while showering? Some claim to download enlightened messages from the universe that reveal the secret to life and other brilliant ideas.

My most memorable shower vision was knocking back a handful of Klonopin[1] and swallowing hard. And you know what I thought then?

*They'll be sorry.*

Stumbling out of the shower, I grabbed a towel and slid to the bathroom floor. I held my head in my hands, shocked at the suicidal thinking.

*Okay, okay, you've got this. You're a therapist. You're not going to do anything. Get up. Get dressed. Get help.*

My inner voice was surprisingly kind that day. Thank God someone was looking out for me.

*How did I get here, anyway?*

Prescription anti-depressants and anti-anxiety medication had not eliminated the pain from fifteen years of constant conflict with my ex-husband. But was that a reason to end my life? Looking back, I realized the emotional unraveling had started two years earlier when a new crisis erupted.

"Mom, I feel like I don't want to live anymore," my sixteen-year-old son Nathan cried over the phone. As a licensed psychotherapist, I've worked in many capacities. That day, I was counseling military families at an Air Force base three hours away.

---

[1] Klonopin (clonazepam) is a commonly prescribed anti-anxiety medication. Often used to calm the nervous system, it can be deeply sedating and potentially habit-forming when used over time.

"Oh, honey, what's wrong?"

"Can you come home?" he asked.

I sprung into action and secured an immediate appointment for his psychological evaluation. I was all about doing and taking action. It stung when a colleague questioned why I didn't drive back immediately. I didn't think to go home, wrap my arms around him and tell him I loved him.

My ex was aware of Nathan's suicidal thoughts but never informed me, which made him an easy target for my rage. I channeled my fear and helplessness into blame. But beneath the anger, I was drifting, like a helium balloon rising higher and higher. My son held the string, his grip loosening, the thread slipping through his fingers. I was powerless to close the distance between us. I didn't realize how far away I floated until it was too late.

Fifteen years of fighting had worn me down. Nearly every court date and attempt to protect my son had backfired. When Nathan called me crying, I did what I always did; I took action. I stopped traveling for work, I stopped scheduling evening clients and I kept fighting the never-ending war. I thought I was fighting for justice, but I didn't realize that my fixation on proving I was right was driving everyone away. I damaged friendships and almost lost my son.

In the weeks that followed, Nathan's suicidal thoughts gave way to something else – episodes of uncontrollable vomiting. After a year of countless tests and doctor visits, he was finally diagnosed with a rare condition called Cyclic Vomiting Syndrome (CVS).

With Nathan confined at home most of the time, we decided to get an emotional support dog. His father had initially agreed to share puppy time with me. However, after three visits, he forbade the puppy. When I thought Nathan's father and I had decided on the CVS diagnosis and treatment plan for our son, he sent a letter to Nathan's psychiatrist stating:

*I strongly believe Nathan's mother has Munchausen-by-proxy[2], and she is making my son sick to get attention.*

I felt betrayed again. Yet somehow, this revelation fueled me even more.

"He's punishing me for fighting for our child," I'd say to anyone who would listen.

I fought so hard, yet I was losing my son. His illness isolated him, and my resentment isolated me. One day, after a fiery argument, I snapped. I told Nathan to stay at his father's. I expected him to be gone for a few days, but it was weeks before he agreed to even be in the same room with me – and only then, in the therapist's office.

My bitterness deepened when Nathan left and I was home alone, caring for the puppy I'd gotten for him. I continued to blame everything outside myself for our suffering. I couldn't see how tightly I was clinging to control or how deeply that control was rooted in fear.

Now, I was the villain. Everything was my fault. Two years of fighting for Nathan, battling illness and sabotage, led to that moment alone in the shower when everything broke.

*They'll be sorry when I'm dead.*

Standing in the shower, I pictured my palm full of little yellow pills, my body splayed across the tile floor. The vision was absurd. I knew I would never follow through, but to even *think* the thought was hitting bottom for me.

---

[2] Factitious disorder imposed on another (FDIA) is the clinical term used in the DSM-5 for what was previously called Munchausen syndrome by proxy. It involves a caregiver deliberately fabricating or causing illness in someone under their care, usually a young child, in order to gain attention or sympathy. This diagnosis requires near-complete control over the dependent's medical care, which would not apply to an adolescent living in a shared custody arrangement. In this case, Nathan's psychiatrist, who had been treating him for over a year and had ruled out other possible causes – including bulimia – dismissed the allegation immediately, stating that it did not meet the diagnostic criteria in any way.

I resumed therapy with the addition of a third anti-depressant. Nathan and I engaged in months of painful, heart-wrenching, but ultimately healing, therapy sessions. We listened more carefully and made efforts to understand each other better. After six long months, he returned home.

Then, I had a dream that would change my life forever.

## The Dream

*The dream is expressed in the present tense as if it's happening now.*

My boyfriend Eric and I are snuggling beneath the covers, watching TV. We are eighteen years old. As I nod off, he nudges me and whispers, "Don't fall asleep now."

His warm touch and soothing voice shake me awake, and I open my eyes to his gaze.

"I won't," I say as I rub my forehead along his neck.

He leans over to kiss me, but I stop him.

"You're not going to leave me, are you?"

"I will never leave you," he says. "I will love you forever."

He kisses me softly. An electrical current of warmth and pleasure flows through my body from head to toe, unearthing sensations I've never known. His kiss awakens the sleeping beauty, activating an emergence of unsurpassed ecstasy. An energy of urgency, excitement and passion springs forth. My body, mind and soul are wrapped up in a raving, writhing, otherworldly sensation beyond sexuality. I'm in heaven.

Suddenly, I'm cloaked in magic, protected by the promise of everlasting love.

*Eric is back, and he'll never leave me again. He promised.*

I allow myself to awaken slowly. Wrapped in the sweet glow of love, the vivid emotional transcendence of the dream envelops me like a cuddly blanket. As my consciousness drifts into complete wakeful awareness, it hits me.

Eric wasn't coming back. Eric was dead.

Countless feelings, memories and images flooded my mind.

*Eric broke up with me at nineteen. He died at twenty-nine. I haven't thought about him in years. I don't know the man who killed him. So why is Eric showing up in my life now?*

I became obsessed with discovering the meaning of the dream.

But first, I cried. I cried over Eric's death as if it had happened yesterday. Unstoppable tears broke through at inopportune times. Sometimes, it hit me while making a call or eating a meal. When I was driving, I had to pull over as the tears fell so hard that my vision blurred.

Weeks had passed since my dream encounter, and I was still grieving. Shaken to the core, I felt unequipped to handle the onslaught of sadness.

One day, my therapist said, "I just can't help you with this dream anymore."

I was stunned, and yet her honesty turned out to be a gift. It enabled me to step into the spiritual realm. I reached out to Shelley Stockwell, a psychic who had helped one of my clients after the death of her teenage daughter.

Shelley went into a trance and began channeling Eric. Suddenly, it felt like Eric was right there speaking directly to me.

*I loved you so much. You were the only love of my life.*

*I fucked up my life. If I had not fucked up my life, I would have married you, and we would have had non-fucked up kids.*

*I want you to experience the kind of love we had,* Eric said through Shelley. *You deserve love.*

We hadn't spoken in thirty-five years, not since that last phone call when Eric reminisced about our psychedelic trips, laughing at how we used to drop acid like candy. He promised to come to our high school reunion that year, but he never did.

*I've been trying to reach your son but haven't been able to. He is hurting. You need to hold space for him like you do for everyone else.*

Mentioning my son surprised me even more.

*I want to play at your wedding. Save me a seat.*

Eric was a gifted guitar player. I wasn't even dating anyone.

*I hope that pears become your favorite fruit. I want you to think of me whenever you eat one because we made a swell pair.*

A pear orchard surrounded his house, providing cover for the illegal marijuana crop that eventually got him killed.

He used to say, "You can't see the plants unless you're in a plane."

*I have to go now because she's not very good.*

Shelley's head dropped forward. Eric was gone.

The two-hour session blew me away. I felt compassion for how I had judged myself and the impossible situation we'd been through. My guilt softened. I had contemplated investigating Eric's murder or writing about his killer on death row in San Quentin, but that wasn't the meaning. The dream was about reconnecting with my heart.

*Don't fall asleep now*, he had said.

## The Awakening

Eric's kiss activated something brilliant beyond what my physical mind and body could comprehend. It opened a portal to unimaginable splendor outside time and place. My dream catalyzed my awakening. I began showing up for myself.

After channeling Eric's message, Shelley hypnotized me and asked if I could see or hear any guides. A name came through: Sonia. I didn't know who Sonia was, and I didn't associate the name with angels.

When I searched "Sonia" and "spirit guide", *Ask Your Guides* by Sonia Choquette appeared. Two months later, I took my son to Chicago for Sonia's *Create Your Heart's Desire* workshop. Soon after, I traveled alone to Paris for her intimate summer salon. It was the first time I'd done something so bold. Sitting in her Paris apartment, in a quiet circle with five other women, something within me stirred, but I couldn't explain it.

"I can't talk about this to anyone," I said.

"Yes, you can," Sonia said. "Name it and claim it. Say: I lead a charmed and guided life."

I still couldn't completely trust myself, but her instructions permitted me to stop hiding. I posted the words on Facebook with a photo of Sonia and me. And that changed everything.

Back home, I consulted a psychic at Mystic Journey in Venice, California. I kept asking her to contact Eric, but during our third session, she gently stopped me.

"You have layers of energetic residue stuck in your system, and you must clear it," she said. "You need to meditate."

She instructed me to scrub with Dead Sea salts in the shower while repeating, *I am clearing emotional debris.* It was simple, but powerful. She recommended I start listening to Deepak Chopra's meditations. With compassion and firmness, she was redirecting my focus from my obsession with Eric to the healing I needed within myself.

I began the *21-Day Meditation Experience* with Deepak Chopra and Oprah Winfrey. I listened every night. My sleep deepened. My energy returned. A sense of peace settled in. I didn't realize how much of myself I had lost until pieces of me began to return. After years of chronic PTSD, stuck in survival mode, bonding through blame and complaint, I was feeling free again.

Six months later, I realized something remarkable; I no longer needed the medication.

Under my doctor's care, I slowly titrated off the anti-depressants, anti-anxiety medication and prescription pain meds I had taken daily for at least ten years.[3]

With my energy and curiosity back online, I began exploring new modalities. I considered pursuing a doctoral degree but instead decided to study the courses that piqued my interest. I named my program PhMe and bought the domain. I was shaping a unique education, one course at a time.

I completed an Akashic Records Practitioner Certification[4] and began writing intently, trying to make sense of the emotional disconnection I felt from my family of origin. As a single mother, the loss of both

---

[3] **Meditation is My Medication.** For over a decade, I relied on a daily cocktail of prescriptions. Now I rely on meditation. I often tell my clients, "I'm not a medical doctor, so I can't prescribe medication—but I can prescribe meditation."
**Meditation is My Medication** is more than a motto—it's printed on my business card and is one of the affirmations in my *Manifest Miracles Oracle Deck.*

[4] "The Akashic Field is the constant and enduring memory of the universe. It holds the record of all that ever happened on Earth and in the cosmos and relates it to all that is yet to happen." – Ervin Laszlo, Science and the Akashic Field: An Integral Theory of Everything (Rochester, VT: Inner Traditions, 2004), 3.11

parents before Nathan's birth, combined with the pain of estrangement from my siblings, weighed heavily on me. Through the Akashic Records and numerous writing workshops, I began to understand how inherited pain and unconscious patterns shape our lives. My memoir became my hero's journey.

Not long after beginning the memoir, I was diagnosed with breast cancer. At first, I was shocked and scared. Then I made a conscious decision to channel that fear into love, a choice that became my mantra: *#treatingcancerwithlove.* That shift changed everything.

The type of cancer was slow-growing and intuitively, I knew it had been developing since my divorce through years of unresolved conflict and emotional pain. I chose to view cancer as a messenger rather than an enemy. I began treating my body with loving kindness. I located a Jungian analyst to help decipher my vivid dreams. Today, I remain cancer-free, filled with gratitude for the wisdom and healing that came through love.

I trained in Rapid Transformational Therapy® (RTT) with founder Marisa Peer and began hypnotizing clients. Then, I discovered Dr. Joe Dispenza. His teachings on the quantum field, meditation and energy confirmed what I had sensed intuitively. We are powerful creators capable of healing, transformation and multidimensional expansion.

Something extraordinary happened during a live retreat in Mexico. Surrounded by two thousand people and immersed in meditation, I began speaking in tongues, known as the Language of Light.

When I had the opportunity to meet Dr. Joe in person, I asked about my light language.

"Just surrender to it," he said. "And don't get hung up on the phenomenon."

Light Language opened a portal. Soon after, I began voice-channeling a collective of ascended masters, archangels and intergalactic guides who call themselves the Council of Light. The Council speaks through me with clarity, love and an Irish accent. Their presence is unmistakable. They're with me when I access the Akashic Records, my monthly Mystic Mastermind group, my Manifest Miracles Oracle Deck and my live journeys. I am truly blessed.

**From Darkness to Radiance**

Ten years ago, I dreamed a dream that called to my soul and woke me up. I didn't know where it would lead – I only knew I had to follow. At the time, I was in such deep despair I considered ending my life. I am no longer that woman on the bathroom floor.

One of the biggest traps we fall into, especially as women, is seeking validation outside ourselves. That's how we give our power away. I spent years bonding through blame and complaining, not realizing I was dimming my own light to connect.

Awareness of victim mentality is key. I had to change *Why is this happening to me?* to *What can I learn from this experience?*

Solitude is sacred. Guidance comes through stillness.

In that quiet space, I remember Eric's message:

*Don't fall asleep now.*
A call to stay conscious, present, and awake to my soul's purpose.

*I will never leave you.*
A reminder that I am never alone; love and guidance are always with me.

*I will love you forever.*
The eternal truth of unconditional love that lives within me.

Eric's message was the voice of my soul.

And that changed everything.

## Marlu Harris

**Marlu Harris, LMFT, RTT® Hypnotherapist**

Marlu Harris is a Licensed Marriage and Family Therapist, RTT® Hypnotherapist, Akashic Records Practitioner, and Light Language Channel. A life-changing dream ignited her soul awakening and inspired her to expand her psychotherapy practice into a multidimensional path of healing and transformation.

With over 30 years as a psychotherapist, Marlu blends psychological insight with energy healing and quantum awareness to support profound inner change. When traditional academic programs no longer fully aligned, Marlu created *PhMe™ (Personal Harmonic Me)* – not a degree, but a frequency – a soul-centered modality designed to guide others home to their unique soul rhythm and purpose.

Marlu has attended over ten advanced retreats with Dr. Joe Dispenza, completed initial training through his NeuroChange Solutions program, and is a member of his Inner Health Coalition – a global group of healthcare professionals exploring the integration of expanded consciousness and meditation in clinical care.

Marlu is the creator of the *Manifest Miracles Oracle Deck* and leads a monthly Mystic Mastermind group for Akashic Records exploration and soul alignment.

⊕ www.marluharris.com
◎ @marluharris

Scan QR code to learn more about Marlu Harris.

chapter

# 21

# Journey in Becoming an African Violet

*By Gretta Chamberlain*

*An African violet can appear to be a delicate and fragile flower, which is in constant need of nurturance to survive. However, it represents an inner spiritual strength which gives it the ability to withstand adverse and dire conditions, and to persevere until it reaches a state of balance and tranquility. In addition, as a mystical symbol, it represents courage, introspection and transformation.*

I am inviting you to follow me through my self-imposed journey, in which I examine how I have morphed into my totem, *the African violet*. I am viewing this as an experience in self-transformation and a process that catapults me deeper into my spirit and the knowing of who I am.

Throughout my adult existence on Earth, I have periodically examined my life to determine what I have accomplished and what lessons I have learned, as well as which ones are left in my personal coffer to still experience. As part of this introspective scrutinization, I have taken into account my aging process and what part it plays in the development of my spirituality and me as a human being. Consequently, I have posed several questions to myself concerning this process.

One is, *Am I actualizing my life's purpose and expressing my full-life potential in service to humanity?*

At this point in time, I have chosen to look at my role in existence through this question. Therefore, I am examining myself in relationship to purpose and self-engendered potential and using this writing opportunity to facilitate this introspective examination of my presence in this world as an Elder. Because of my ongoing advancement in age, I have now earned the title of Elder in my community. This is an important accolade for me because it implies I have reached a point in my life that reflects wisdom and grace. Since I have been given this new status in life, I have chosen to begin this self-analysis by examining the patriarchal lineage of my mother and how it influenced my life.

In beginning this excavation of self, I chose to examine the epigenetics I inherited from my mother. By selecting her as my parent, I elected to be born into a family whose members have a proclivity to live long lives. For example, my mother's grandfather, my great-grandfather, lived to be one hundred years old. While his mother, my great-great grandmother, lived to be one hundred and three years old. From this, I recognize that I come from a family whose physicality is strong and I have inherited the genes to follow in their footsteps.

Because of the epigenetics, there are other paths which I am instinctively following, similar to those of my ancestral lineage. One of which is the development of my psychic abilities. As a child, I would predict unknown outcomes, remotely travel to other locations giving full accounts of what I had seen, notify the family of upcoming deaths, hear voices calling my name and see earth-bounds (ghosts). My mother was very protective of me in this area. She would often warn me about telling people not part of the immediate family that I had these abilities. At the time, as a seven-year-old, it was difficult for me to comprehend the true significance of her advice. Later, I learned she was not only shielding me from the scrutiny of others, but herself as well, because she too possessed those capabilities. Once again, epigenetics has proven its presence.

Another incident involves the transition of my great-grandmother. Because of this, my great-grandfather came to live with my mother and me. This was the time when I was first introduced to the healing process known as "the-laying-on-of-hands." At the age of thirteen, my great-grandfather, Willie, told me about his experiences living in Louisiana. He stated that he would travel in a horse-drawn wagon from town to town selling medicinal elixirs and "laying-on-of hands" on people who requested his healing assistance. I was intrigued by this conversation. I asked him what that term meant and how he did that. He explained that he would place a penny between his two hands and rub them together with great speed and intensity to produce tremendous heat. Next, he would place his hands on the ailing part of the person's body. Upon this placement, the individual would be instantly healed! I knew Willie didn't fabricate information, so I accepted his explanation with wonder and amazement. Little did I know, that one day, I would request from *The Realm of Beings*, my ethereal support team, to be able to replicate this restorative process and use it in my energy healing practice. (Later in this chapter, I'll inform you of their immediate response.)

Later, years appeared to be moving slowly for me, as I transitioned from being a teenager into becoming a responsible adult during a time in American history that was challenging for people of my coloration. On a Sunday, when I was ten years old, while walking home with my mother from church, I excitedly told her that I wanted to become a medical doctor, more specifically a surgeon. She looked amazed as she continued to walk, but gave me no response. I realized later that she didn't know how to help me accomplish this desire, nor did she believe I could achieve this dream, because the times of my childhood in which I was existing, were totally against this happening for a child living in one room and sleeping in the same bed with her mother, a single parent.

Later, as a teenager, I contemplated becoming a scientist but was again discouraged by my mother. She suggested I become a teacher. Her reasoning was typical for the time in which I was living. I was disappointed in her suggestion, based on her belief that I would always have a job, which was extremely important in the Negro community. Hence, I became a teacher and worked in school situations that were considered *unsavory*. These were harrowing times for me. However, through these experiences, my personality went through an overhaul and I found myself becoming a more resilient person; someone who could weather the storm and accept adversity, rather than succumbing to the perceived unfairness in my life experiences, and matriarchal decisions formed out of fear and lack of unconditional love, as I had in the past.

Well, I survived teaching school for three years with fifty students in my last self-contained fifth-grade class. After that experience, I decided to look for a teaching assignment in another country. I wanted to travel internationally, explore different cultures and learn to speak additional languages. So, I sent my résumé to various schools and educational systems throughout the world. I also decided to investigate the Peace Corps to see what it offered. Finally, I made my decision to join this organization and was sent to Sierra Leone, West Africa. There I learned how to survive without running water, bathing in a stream, having no electricity, and dealing with army ants. I embraced every moment of my experience, which taught me to be self-reliant and to appreciate myself, internally and externally.

For the first time in my present life, I felt I was home. As a child, I would often tell my mother that I wanted to go home. Her response was always to tell me that *I was home*, but, for some reason, I never believed her. So, those thoughts and their emotions were carried throughout my adulthood, until I reached the continent of Africa. Once there, my life began to move through a rapid spiral of change. My dreams even changed to reflect that I was on the African continent, and no longer in the States.

People came to visit daily to welcome me. My house was like a revolving door; I always had visitors. Because I was still learning the language, I would sit in front of the person. periodically nodding and saying the Temne greeting, which would usually continue for fifteen to twenty minutes. After an hour's visit, they would prepare to leave, and we would spend at least five to ten minutes saying *goodbye*, as I thanked them for coming. These types of experiences taught me to develop more patience and to become more accepting of others. After several visitations from people in the village, a young man appeared at my door. We visited with each other for several hours and determined we had a great deal in common. As time progressed, we spent more and more time together. Eventually, we decided to marry.

This union became a pivotal point in my life and a passage into the world of spirits and spirituality. It was during this time that I was introduced to various types of mysticism, which encompassed the conjuring of spirits, the production of unworldly magic, and exposure to the *Seventh Book of Moses;* a magical text allegedly composed by Moses and stemming from the Kabbalah and the Talmud. It contained magical drawings with instructions in their purpose and usage, with incantations for conjuring ethereal beings. Needless to say, I was intrigued, yet frightened at the same time, to participate in such rituals. My husband, Mohammed, advised me to only attempt it if I was strong enough to face the spirit with strength and fortitude. Well, my curiosity overrode my fear. I drew my chosen figure on the floor, stepped into the center of the pentagram, and said the incantation. I waited with bated breath. I said the conjuring words several times but to no avail. Nothing happened. I was both relieved and disappointed. It was after this experience that I vowed never to attempt such a spiritual venture again. However, little did I know that this was a precursor to my life's vocation.

As time passed, I learned more and more about West African culture from my husband and more about him. One thing I noticed, was that on occasion, he would literally pass out. I informed him about this behavior which he never remembered experiencing. I suggested seeing a physician in the city but he refused, saying there was nothing wrong and to stop worrying about it. Well, his fainting continued but transferred itself to bedtime talk. Mohammed began to hold conversations with me while he was sleeping, and in the morning would not remember anything that was said. Being a curious person, I began to engage freely in these nightly discussions and enjoyed asking questions to clarify the purpose of their existence and why they were communicating with me. This communication continued for weeks. I learned they were a group of seven and had been with me since my childhood. They were the voices who called my name, as I ran up and down the stairs in my great-grandparents' old Victorian home. The one, who had the strongest and more intense voice, was called *Father* by me. Over weeks of communication with them, I knew that they loved and cared for me, and I was never alone. I was their child, and they protected and guided me through all of my African trials and tribulations; the loss of my child, my bout with alcoholism and the death of Mohammed, my husband.

Before my husband's death, I received a visitation from my ethereal group requesting I return home with them. They appeared as though they were coming out of the ceiling in my bedroom. They were moving in a downward direction and getting closer to me as I lay in my bed. This was the first time they appeared to me in corporal bodies which were in the form of seven round gold balls about two inches in diameter. They spoke to me in speech that sounded very slow and slurred. They said, *We have come to bring you back.* Of course, I found this announcement to be very disconcerting, even though, I knew they were looking out for my good. However, I replied that *I was not leaving*; I had to keep my commitments and complete my tasks. So, I did not waiver. After speaking my request three times, they eventually stopped moving toward me, accepted my decision, and disappeared. During this time, several thoughts were rapidly moving through my consciousness, one of which was that I realized I was one of them – an Arcturian, entrusted with certain responsibilities, which I was determined to accomplish before exiting this reality.

After four years of spiritual evolvement in Africa, I returned home, a little wiser and a little braver. The African part of my journey led me to study various areas in metaphysical thought from Ernest Holmes to Alice Bailey, and others. I found myself studying the occult, as it was called in the early 1900s. I was fascinated by Existence and sought answers to my many questions concerning it. As an extension of my learning, in my late thirties I was introduced to Dr. Irene Hickman, who taught me the process of going remote (not remote viewing) and how to deal with entities of low vibration. From her teaching, I became exposed to individuals who are not human but come from various parts of this and other universes. Of course, at this time, my *Realm of Beings* stepped consciously back into my life and began to teach me everything I know. Consequently, my education is on-going and endless. I am in a constant state of mind expansion, with a deepening in transcendence and an increase in cosmic energy.

At present, I am given missions which support not only Earth, but the entire Universe. These are given to me by my *Realm of Beings* or by the three Gods, who created this particular universe. On occasion, I am summoned by the Universal Federation, which is the governing body of this universe, and given various tasks I must fulfill, like protection of various planets, participation in battles in space, periodically giving Earth energy and assisting individuals, human and non-human, in their self-healing processes.

In conclusion, I have found my life to be one of wonder and amazement. I am grateful for all my experiences, including the challenging ones, and those supportive of me in evolving into an African violet. I have remarried several times and have thirteen children. One is a humanoid daughter, and the rest have a reptilian father, known as Datar, whom I married. Together, he and I work for the betterment of all species in this universe. Through our union, we support the mandate of the three Gods, which is to maintain unconditional love throughout the entire cosmos and to bring peace to all.

As previously stated, I feel I am in an endless expansive journey into infinity. Have I reached my goal to actualize the characteristics of the African violet? In some ways *yes*, and in some ways *no*. However, I am still focused on the actualization of all its qualities, which I have the intention to accomplish within this life. Perhaps, someday, you, too, may want to join me in this timeless experience of spiritual expansion.

## Dr. Gretta Chamberlain

Dr. Gretta Chamberlain, DN, is a lecturer, a remote energy transformational specialist, and an educator, who channels the non-physical beings known as *The Realm of Beings*. Because of this, some have given her the title of "mystic" as she has worked internationally with individuals throughout the world and off world.

Since her childhood, she has been exposed to psychic phenomenon and now embraces the teachings and guidance from *The Realm*, who have been with her throughout her life. As a remote energy worker, she has facilitated for hundreds of people and animals of Earth, as she continues to teach the various aspects of existence and the creation of reality. Her work continues to expand beyond this dimension into other worlds that are contained within this universe. Consequently, she has a myriad of out-of-world experiences, as she facilitates for non-humanoid individuals, who reside outside of this planet. Her spiritual work is in a constant state of expansion, as she works to elevate the spirit of humankind, the Earth and the universe.

⊕ www.therealmofbeings.com
Scan QR code to learn more about Dr. Gretta Chamberlain.

chapter

# 22

# Connecting the Spiritual Dots

*by Sandi Duverneuil*

Struggling to keep up with Mom as we ran down the street to the beach, I felt the cold air piercing my lungs. My mom had just hung up the phone and bundled me and my baby sister into our winter coats. Hoisting my sister onto her left hip, my mom moved as if in slow motion. I grasped my sister's foot tightly and sensed my mom's horror.

When we reached the frozen Centerport Harbor, my four-year-old brain scanned the beach. Ambulance lights. I instantly understood my brother, Billy, was gone, before my mom had a chance to identify his lifeless body.

When I asked my mom, "Where's Billy?" she answered, "In heaven," to which my response was, "But I didn't see Jesus on the beach." Thanks to my Virgo tendency for precision, my younger self often interpreted life too literally.

Losing my seven-year-old brother, Billy, after he fell through the icy harbor, had a lifelong impact on my spiritual and emotional being. I was only four. Billy was no longer there to guide me through life – or so I thought. Over time, connecting the various signs and spiritual "dots", I realized my path to spiritual awakening started the day Billy died.

In the aftermath of his accidental drowning, I secretly looked for signs that my older brother was watching over me. One morning, while playing outside, the neighbor's daughter asked if I saw *the magical fairies,* as we gazed at sunlight flowing through dew drops on grass blades. Mesmerized by the mystical prism-like dew drops, my five-year old self remained skeptical. In my debut role of people-pleaser, I played along with her charade, wondering if this nine-year old girl next door was trying to trick me?

Despite my skepticism, from that moment, I often looked up at the trees that climbed high up towards the sky. I wondered if my brother could still see me beyond that blue patch of sky. Was Billy still watching over me and my baby sister, protecting us from afar?

It felt like a dark cloud was hanging over our family. My parents swiftly split. My sister and I, uprooted like young trees, were transplanted to Southampton, New York.

For some, "The Hamptons" conjure up visions of mansions hiding behind privet hedges or celebrity sightings. For those living there year-round, it was a bastion of creative freedom, an artists' haven tucked away in endless acres of farmland with corn and potato fields on eastern Long Island. But for an elementary school girl, the rude realization that cliques formed as early as kindergarten was as heartbreaking as losing a sibling.

*Throughout childhood, I felt like an outsider.*

When I was six years old, I had a bizarre – and yet again – traumatic experience. Sitting in the back seat of my mom's car, next to my three-year-old sister, I waited patiently for our mom. She had stopped at "The Country Store" to pick up a gallon of milk and some groceries.

Suddenly, our parked car started rolling backwards down the moderately steep incline. My six-year-old brain sensed that my sister and I were in clear and imminent danger.

*Have you ever felt frozen from fright yet by some miracle, an invisible force pushes you into action?*

Reaching over from the back seat of the car, I instinctively grabbed the steering wheel, clinging to it as tightly as I had held onto my baby sister's foot on the beach the day Billy died.

I had no idea how to drive a car, much less steer it, but adrenaline kicked in as I wildly turned the steering wheel with no rhyme or reason. Panicked, because a busy road and beyond that, a telephone pole, were at the bottom of the incline, I worried we would hit oncoming traffic, or if we escaped that, might hit the phone pole.

A few minutes later, I looked up and saw that, by some miracle, I had managed to back the car back up the hill. Instead of facing the store, the car was facing the road. As the car finally came to a full stop, I felt a brief sense of calm. My mind was quiet, as if all sound was absorbed, like going outside after a snowfall. Grabbing my sister's hand, together we raced into the store, both of us crying. We found mom immediately in the tiny convenience store, and through my tears, I told her what happened.

Expecting praise or recognition for my heroic intervention and quick thinking, I was shocked by mom's dismissive reaction when she said, "But you're okay now."

Years later, thinking back to that day, I am certain that even though Billy was no longer physically with us, he found a way to guide me and ensure my sister and I were out of harm's way. Years later, when I was a teenager unpacking the "bathroom" box and stumbled upon an empty Rx container from the early 1970s, I finally understood. My mom's nonchalant reaction was probably due to her still raw grief, numbed by Valium.

Throughout my childhood, my subconscious processed my grief at night. A friend's older sister, tasked with babysitting us, saw me wake up in the middle of the night. The next day, she described how I had gone to the dresser drawer and started pulling out all of the clothes, as if I was searching for something. She said it was as if I were in a trance.

My sleepwalking and sleeptalking continued well into my early teens. My stepmother worried when I woke up one night roaming the halls and asked the next day if I remembered anything.

*No, I did not.*

Losing a sibling at such an early age left me emotionally scarred and afraid of getting too attached to anyone. So nobody knew about my out-of-body experiences when I was ten years old, which left me more puzzled than frightened. Sometimes I felt an electrical jolt before drifting off to sleep, and at some point in the night, I was floating several feet above my body. Detached from my physical body,

I would look at myself lying in bed asleep. A common thought that would race through my mind was, *Why didn't "God" take me instead of Billy? Why did I have to be left behind?* I missed my brother, whose pleasant disposition was like a ray of sunshine, so much that I didn't want to live – but I never shared my morbid thoughts with anyone.

Sometimes in my dream state, that sense of weightlessness and floating was palpable; it felt like I was flying. I couldn't figure out why this was happening but never shared those experiences with my mom or my sister. My sister was born prematurely and was hospitalized for a month. My mom was often worried about my sister's fragile health. The night before Billy died, our parents argued about my sister's medical bills. I didn't want to add more to mom's plate. Intuitively, I felt if I shared my out-of-body experience with anyone, they would think I was strange... or wouldn't believe me.

*Fast-forward: Thirty years after my brother died.*

I moved to Fukuoka, Japan, with my young family and taught English as a foreign language (EFL) through the Japan Exchange Teaching (JET) program. Two weeks after our arrival, I received a phone call from my sister that our dad was in the hospital, in a coma, but that he was expected to pull through after being treated for an acute kidney infection.

*Have you ever received news and been told one thing, but your gut reaction and intuition told you the opposite?*

That night I had a vivid dream. I could see my deceased brother, Billy, somewhere "beyond the veil." His hand was outstretched, reaching down from "above" to pull our father up from Earth, from his physical body, to join him (wherever that was). In my dream, I suddenly felt a deep sense of panic. I begged my brother to let go of Dad, to let him stay with us.

What upset me the most within my dream though, was my brother's response when I implored him to let dad stay with us. In his little seven-year-old boy voice, he told me he really missed dad because he hadn't seen him for so long.

I was still working on healing my rocky father-daughter relationship with my dad. We had started to make progress after I became a parent (and he, a grandparent). Selfishly, I hoped to continue my conversations with him and was glad he knew I was expecting my second child.

Before moving to Japan, I encouraged my sister to work on her relationship with him too. I just wasn't ready for my brother to pull our dad "up" from Earth. But hearing Billy's voice and realizing how much he missed dad, tugged at my heartstrings.

Abruptly I woke up, sobbing uncontrollably. Immediately, I felt my dad was not going to make it. I inexplicably knew it.

I pulled my pregnant, still jet-lagged self together and headed off to City Hall where the Board of Education was housed. Just as I was about to leave City Hall for prefectural orientation, a Board of Education staff member called out my name. Holding up the landline receiver, *giggling*, he motioned for me to take the call.

My hand gripped the handset. My children's dad was the messenger: my sister had called him with the news that my dad had died. It was the strangest feeling. I don't remember what I said, but in my head, I thought, *Yes, I know already*.

I regretted that I couldn't call my sister. I had no privacy and was about to be sequestered for eight hours in a dreadfully mind-numbing orientation, so I couldn't share my premonitory dream or dial up my sister for more details. I went to the orientation in a daze; Dad would have expected me to soldier on and fulfill my work responsibilities.

What signs did Dad send from beyond? Whenever I least expected needing my dad's presence, his favorite Dire Straits song, *Sultans of Swing*, would appear on the radio or randomly on my playlist. I associated that song with my dad driving us to our grandmother's in Shenorock, a sleepy hamlet in Westchester County. Or a song that magically appeared and soothed me after dad's sudden and unexpected death, *Drift Away,* the Dobie Gray version. My dad spoke to me through music.

*Fast forward: Twenty years after Dad died.*

My mom lost her four-year battle with cancer while I was living overseas, in Nice, France. I had visited my mom a few weeks prior in Asheville, North Carolina and at some point, delicately asked her, "In the eventuality of you no longer physically being here, what will be your sign to show me you are watching over us?" My mom was too tired to think about it and said she didn't know.

Despite my mom not knowing how she would stay in touch after her death, I would find out after she passed when I returned to Asheville to clear out her house with my sister.

After a difficult morning of sorting through her belongings with my sister, I decided to pick up lunch for our family. Waiting at a stoplight, on my way back to mom's house, I noticed a beautiful dragonfly hovering over my windshield. It was persistent; it wouldn't leave me. I instantly felt my mom's presence. Everything would be okay, *Mom was still with me.* The dragonfly followed me to the next stoplight and hovered, flitting cheerfully over the windshield. It was the first time a dragonfly had shown up, so I knew it was mom reassuring me.

I ate lunch with my family and went upstairs to continue the emotionally draining task of clearing out mom's closet. The very first item of clothing I pulled out of her closet was a long sleeve t-shirt I had NEVER seen before... with a dragonfly on the front! I was in disbelief and said out loud, "Okay, Mom, I see you."

In the weeks that followed, dragonflies (actual or symbolic) randomly appeared, and sometimes I saw numbers that only made sense to me and my mom. My younger son, who was close to my mom (they had entertained each other throughout the pandemic with daily video chats and throughout her cancer journey), also stumbled upon signs from Mom. She turned up whenever he needed his cherished *mamie* (grandmother).

After my sons moved into their own place, I received a text message from my younger son. It was over a year after my mom died, so I was still deeply immersed in a fog of grief that took forever to lift. I didn't notice at first that the dragonfly he sent was sitting outside of his front door. Only then did I realize my sons' house had a purple front door – just like their grandmother's house in Asheville.

During my last conversation with my mom on her hospital bed, I shared how I had so many books inside of me but never had time to write them. Mom replied, with a twinkle in her eyes, "So just do it." After experiencing signs that my mom was still with me in spirit, I focused on writing my first book, a collection of poems, *Dragonfly Dances: Poetic Musings on Life*. The symbolic dragonfly is a nod to the sign my mom still sends to encourage me.

Interestingly, in many cultures, the dragonfly is a symbol of transformation, personal growth and change. Some believe that the dragonfly is a connection to a loved one in the spirit world. Looking back and connecting the spiritual dots, I realized that I lost each of my parents during a time of great transformation and change, shortly after moving overseas.

Thirty years after my brother's death, he was reunited with our dad; fifty years after dying, Billy was reunited with our mom. When I miss my parents, I remember they are still watching over us and have been reunited with my brother, Billy.

Grief never fully disappears, but it changes. Receiving signs or messages from our loved ones can be comforting; a reminder that love never dies, it simply transforms. The signs we receive do not bring those we lost back, but remind us they are still there, guiding and loving us from beyond as we experience spiritual growth.

My mother found a way to answer the question she was too tired to entertain in her hospital bed. She chose dragonflies. She chose numbers. She reached out in ways that we couldn't miss. The next time you notice something that feels like more than just a coincidence, stop. Listen to your intuition. Sometimes our loved ones send a gentle nudge or whisper, waiting for us to listen.

 ## Sandi Duverneuil

Sandi Duverneuil is an author and poetry healing guide who helps others process grief and loss through creative expression. Her spiritual awakening began with the loss of her brother at age four, deepening with her parents' passing, affirming her connection to the spirit world and her purpose of guiding others through the healing power of poetry.

With over twenty-five years in publishing and a global perspective from living in France, Japan and Canada, Sandi blends storytelling, intuition and soul work to create safe spaces where emotions are released, and the heart finds its voice.

⊕ www.peoniesandprose.com
◉ @peonies_prose
Scan QR code to learn more about Sandi Duverneuil.

# chapter 23

## A Rainbow Rises Beyond the Darkest Wave of Grief

*by Ellie Epstein-White*

I felt I was carrying the weight of merging oceans of grief. Grief filled every crevice of my existence, pressing in from all sides, heavy and unrelenting. After five years, I was still mourning the loss of my mother, who died after suffering complications from a stroke. Since losing my mother, I have carried this invisible ocean within me – its tides rising and falling without warning, threatening to pull me under. Some days, I managed to stay afloat, while other days, I sank beneath its depths.

Grief had seeped into every part of my life, but I didn't realize how deeply it was affecting my work. No matter how hard I tried to focus, I felt scattered, struggling to process information and retain new tasks. I worked in a busy office, conducting criminal background checks. This job required being able to transcribe personal data collected over the phone. Eventually, my supervisor advised me I had been transcribing the information incorrectly. With time, it became evident my mistakes were becoming more frequent, and visible. Supervisor Zebra felt I was "unfocused" and "distracted." She was fishing for answers, not understanding why I was making so many errors all of a sudden. At the time, I didn't know how to explain what was wrong because I didn't fully understand it myself.

I was newly appointed to the position, having transferred from another unit, but I was not new to working at the agency. This job felt like a test I was failing. I had handled customer service calls in my last position, yet now, the ringing phone sent my nerves into overdrive. Every mistake became magnified, and every correction from my co-workers was a constant reminder that I wasn't measuring up. My confidence was unraveling like a ball of yarn.

I was taken aside, behind closed doors. In this meeting, I sat across from my supervisors as they laid out my performance issues. I was labeled as "distracted", and reminded to keep "focus" on the job. Supervisor Zebra's superior, the Lieutenant, advised me that I wasn't meeting the unit's expectations. I was under probation and in basic training. "You need to exude more confidence," the Lieutenant's voice was firm, and steady. Supervisor Zebra and Trainer Giraffe nodded in agreement, their faces set with expectation, as they emphasized, "We value you." The words were meant to reassure and encourage me, however, they stung like bullets, stirring something deep inside. I was placed on a training corrective action plan and informed I couldn't move on with my training until I could be "rock solid" on the phones.

I didn't understand why I appeared to be floundering at my job. I didn't know how to meet their expectations while I carried the weight of my grief.

I was confused with my work situation. Before I'd transferred to my current position, I had consulted with a reader at a psychic fair, looking for clarity. Overall, I received a positive message to accept the job offer as it would give me financial stability, however, "it wouldn't come without challenges." The reader added, *Your biggest obstacle will be your mother.* However, it was grief, not my mother, that would be my greatest challenge. I didn't realize how her death was shaping my life.

Work was a constant stream of phone calls, and I was overwhelmed with learning new information, while being bombarded with an overload of work. The customers walked all over me, pushing boundaries, questioning my ability, assuming I was incompetent because I was new and didn't understand the intricacies of the job.

My calls were passive; I needed to take control and exude more confidence. No matter what I tried, nothing seemed to work. Every attempt to sound more assertive felt forced and unnatural.

The entire unit watched, waiting for an explanation I couldn't give because I didn't understand what was wrong myself. I had transitioned to this unit to help "save" them from drowning in a sea of work, only to need saving myself. I felt I was dragging everyone down instead of miraculously being the lifeboat I intended to be.

Frustration simmered beneath my numbness. I felt unseen and misjudged. *If they valued me, why did I feel so misunderstood?* Why did their encouragement feel more like a demand I wasn't capable of meeting?

I sat at my desk and tried to proceed with work like nothing happened. The hum of voices and the clicking of keyboards around me dissolved into a blur. I was present, yet I was absent. When Trainer Giraffe spoke, her words slipped past me, unprocessed, like water dripping through my fingers. My thoughts tangled and my chest tightened into knots. My hands trembled over the keyboard. Then, a moment of stillness came over me. Tears slipped down my cheek, landing on my desk.

The worst part was that my humiliation was fully on display. I was instructed to take calls on speakerphone so my trainer and supervisor could hear my interactions with the customers and review the conversations. Every phone call echoed through the small noisy room, airing every struggle I endured. At my desk, my trainer and supervisor would stand behind me, critiquing my every word and reaction. Once, when Supervisor Zebra asked my trainer if I was making any progress, I overheard the answer: "She's loud and boisterous."

However, loud didn't mean confident or firm. It amounted to noise without strength, and volume without conviction. I was desperately attempting to be what they wanted but missing the mark entirely.

Everyone tried to reassure me that I was still learning and just needed time. When customers called in to complain, they appeared to play it off – "She's new and she's still adjusting." I felt exposed and vulnerable, as if I was being set up to fail.

They expected me to be confident yet undermined me in the same breath. They told me I was improving yet held me back from "training up." I was trapped in a contradiction – one I didn't know how to navigate. I felt lost, as if I didn't have the right tools and no one was helping me. Yet, somehow, I was told I was "valuable" to the unit.

To make sense of my predicament, I set out on a healer's journey to try and figure out what I was missing. I realized, in order to resolve my problem, I needed to reach the solution from a different, higher perspective.

I did not realize that grief had rooted itself so deeply inside me, hidden in the spaces I couldn't reach. Yoga, meditation, breath work, and mantra cracked me open, letting light into the places grief had darkened. Movement became my medicine. Kundalini yoga, in particular, awakened something within me – like a current pulsing through my veins, reminding me I was still alive. A mantra echoed in my mind: *If you keep moving, you'll be kept up.*

Yoga helped me learn to sit with discomfort, and to trust stillness as much as movement. What once felt unbearable became a doorway to transformation. Yoga was no longer just an exercise, it was a lifeline, anchoring me when I felt lost.

I was introduced to the world of sound at a local yoga studio offering sound during Kundalini, restorative or yin yoga classes. I had always been soothed by music, but I never realized its medicinal power until I immersed myself in sound healing. Sound washed through me like a river, dislodging grief from the hidden corners of my body. The more I immersed myself in sound healing, the more I transformed; like my internal radio had been stuck on static, tuned to the wrong station, and now I was adjusting to the right frequency. The vibrations of crystal bowls, gongs and chimes washed over me, loosening the knots of grief, dissolving layers of pain.

Each note was a prayer, each soundwave a message I didn't need words to understand. The more I let sound move through me, the lighter I felt. Sound broke apart the stagnant energy trapped inside me, peeling away layers of pain and sorrow, like a snake shedding its skin. Every vibration from the crystal bowls, every resonance from the gong, moved something deep within me – something words had failed to reach. I wasn't just hearing sound – I was feeling it, absorbing it and becoming it.

One evening, I was drawn to attend an intuition circle at a local yoga studio. At the circle, we played with curiosity and wonder of our inner knowing. The leader of the circle spoke of "intuition" as being like a "muscle." The more you learn to use your inner GPS, the more guidance and information you receive and can "trust" to carry you forward. We played with words and what they felt like in our body, how our bodies, hands, breath and energy tell stories about words and want to teach us about the meaning of words.

The word "confidence" came up in the circle. The leader of the circle broke the word apart and gave me a whole new meaning of the word *confidence*:

"Confidence comes from the Latin *confidere* – to go with faith."

The phrase "exude confidence" had followed me everywhere since that meeting at work, but I wondered what it really meant. These words struck something deep inside me, and I suddenly understood. *Confidence was going with faith*. This is the part of the definition I was missing and needed to embody. I realized I had tried to force and mold confidence based on someone else's definition, and it didn't work for me. For me, confidence wasn't about being fearless or knowing the next step, *confidence* was about trusting myself and trusting in the universe. I needed to trust in the unseen path unfolding before me.

I made a choice to stop looking back and trust that *I was enough*, and flow with the river of life. Some days this was not easy, as the old doubts whispered their familiar tune. Each time I reminded myself, *I am growing*, even when I could not see it. I was worthy, even when I didn't feel it. *I just need to trust in the journey.*

One day, I discovered a life-changing story called, *The Bamboo and the Fern*. This story cracked me open, shining a whole new light on my life. I didn't realize at the time how my silent struggle shaped how I moved through life. My grief prevented me from seeing my growth happening underneath the pain. I only saw the uncertainty and the fear of stepping forward into something new without the presence of Mom in my life.

For years, the bamboo appears to do nothing, showing no signs of growth above ground or any signs of progress, but beneath the surface, its roots stretch deep, preparing for the moment it will finally rise and reach higher ground. I was like the bamboo in the parable – growing roots beneath the surface, even when nothing seemed to be happening above ground. Though I couldn't see it at the time, I was laying the foundation for growth. I was learning resilience, patience and trust. My struggles at work weren't proof of failure – but they were part of the process. My obstacles weren't meant to stop me, but to teach me. When I push through and finally break the soil, I will have climbed to higher ground.

The moment I stopped fighting the discomfort and started flowing with it, everything shifted. I focused my attention and my mind found a sense of clarity. The more I listened – to my breath, to my intuition, to the lessons buried within the challenges – the more capable I became. I had been planted exactly where I needed to be, and I was finally learning how to grow. I was called to practice yoga off the mat, breathing into everything I did, especially while I was at work.

Then, the universe sent me a "wake-up" call. Slowly, I began to listen to the whispers of the universe. One afternoon, I was looking out of my living room window, while I was lost in thought, and noticed a gust of wind set the branches of my forsythia into a wild dance. Amidst the branches, a cardinal appeared, perching gracefully on a swaying branch. I watched, transfixed, as the cardinal surfed the waves of wind, its crimson feathers brilliant against the newly budding blooms. At that instant, I learned I should let go and flow with the river of life. The cardinal wasn't fighting the movement but going with the flow.

In that moment, I felt my mother. She was there woven in the wind, whispering through the trees, shining in the golden light. I felt her in the warmth of the sun on my skin, the sound of the rustling leaves and the space between breaths. I had been waiting for my mother to come back, as if somehow, she would return in human form. Now, I feel she was never truly gone: she was the wind that kissed my face, the golden glow of the sun, and the quiet reassurance in the night sky. She was stitched into the fabric of my life, guiding me forward with the same love she had always given.

After a while, I noticed the importance of numbers: three, four and seven. I saw these numbers appear on license plates, digital clocks, receipts and exit signs. Every time I glanced at something random, these numbers showed up. Interestingly, these numbers speak of aligning mind, body and spirit, building a lasting foundation and being on a spiritual path. Later, I realized these same numbers were associated with one of the documents at work.

At first, I brushed off the whispers, not closely paying attention to the everyday wonders the universe tried to show me. But these encounters continued, trying to crack me open to my becoming. The universe kept whispering: *Trust. Keep going. I have your back and you are supported.*

During a meditation, I had a prolific vision. I saw a wolf standing at the edge of a clearing, a string of pearls glistening in its mouth. Behind the wolf, there was a lush forest and above, a rainbow arched across the sky – not just stretching but smiling. The wolf's golden eyes met mine, and an understanding passed between us, silent and profound.

At night, I came home to my guardian angel, Robin, my cat. Robin had a knowing gaze, one that seemed to see straight through me, past the grief and past the weight I carried. She jumped onto the couch beside me, curling up against me, purring with the steady rhythm of the earth itself. Her warmth pressed into my heart, her soft rumble vibrating through my bones like a healing mantra. Robin purred me back to life. She curled up close enough to let me know I wasn't alone. She didn't try to fix me, didn't expect me to move on, she just sat with me in the stillness, a quiet guardian in the storm of my grief.

It was in those small moments – her steady presence, the rhythmic rise and fall of her breath, the warmth of her fur against my side – that

I learned healing wasn't about forgetting. Healing was about being here and now. It was about trusting that life would carry me forward, just as it always had.

I returned to work and was determined to concentrate on taking the phone calls. I spoke with conviction, and I set boundaries. I didn't let customers talk or walk over me. This was no longer about meeting my supervisor's expectations but rising to my own. I wore my labradorite necklace; a stone that flickers with hidden rainbows, flaws and all. This stone reminded me that even in my darkest hour, light exists; we shine no matter what phase we are in.

Then, at work, ladybugs began to appear. I saw them crawl along my keyboard and try to fly around the office. The presence of the ladybugs felt intentional, as if they were tiny messengers reminding me that transformation was taking place, even if I couldn't see it yet.

Grief was no longer drowning me but instead shaping me into something new. I had spent the longest time resisting, waiting for life to feel normal again. I discovered that grief is like a quiet passenger, one that doesn't disappear. It transforms and carves me into different versions of myself, forcing me to grow in ways I never expected or imagined. All the signs were markers and guideposts, appearing almost like they were waiting for me: *All things are possible for one who believes.* Each one reminding me I was never truly lost and I was exactly where I needed to be.

# Ellie Epstein-White

Ellie Epstein-White is an international bestselling author and energy practitioner who draws upon her personal story to help others claim their Hero's path. As a co-author in the life-changing energy anthologies, *The Call Within* and *Whispers of the Soul*, she blends personal experience with healing wisdom. Certified in reiki and sound healing, Ellie studied crystals and Usui reiki Ryoho with Nicholas Pearson and continues to deepen her practice through yoga, meditation, and sound. She is a member of the Good Energy Healing Club, facilitated by natural health intuitive and author, Hilary Crowley. Ellie serves with the New Hampshire Department of Safety, living by the philosophy of "off-the-mat yoga" and leading others within her "field of light." Outside her professional life, she finds joy in yoga, sound healing and time spent with family, friends and her beloved cat, Robin. Through her writing and healing practice, Ellie helps empower others to build resilience, awaken joy and create meaningful change.

www.facebook.com/ellie.epstein.white
Scan QR code to learn more about Ellie Epstein-White.

# chapter 24

## Divine Whispers

*by Julie Wasmer*

The room was eerily quiet yet filled with angst. I was alone with my thoughts, praying for my son who, for the past three days, had lain intubated and drugged in the ICU following a massive epileptic seizure. Desperately looking for something to distract my mind, I curled up with my son's cat, Kitty, and turned on the television.

As I scrolled through the TV guide, I was drawn to a movie I'd already seen, *The Descendants*. I remembered enjoying the movie with the lush beauty of Hawaii, imagining the intoxicating scent and bright hues of the tropical foliage and the sound of a ukulele playing in the warm island breeze. It took me back to the seventies, when I spent two carefree weeks camping on an empty, white sand beach in Kauai.

Something was pushing me to watch it, I felt I was being guided by the spirit realm... then I realized why. The story is about coming to terms with death, forgiveness and letting go of a loved one. I cried as I sat through the movie, feeling a deep despair in the pit of my being.

In my heart, I knew I was being prepared for what was coming. It was the beginning of my heart opening, or should I say my deepest grieving, on my journey into my Spiritual Awakening.

It had been twenty-three years since I, myself, had lain in a hospital bed, receiving round three of a six-day continuous toxic-chemotherapy drip. That was when I heard my first whisper that, in the future, I would *help people heal from cancer and other diseases with alternative methods other than chemotherapy and radiation.* I had birthed a new idea that coincided with the birth of my daughter, Laura, along with a 15lb malignant tumor.

It wasn't until much later, 2018, when synchronicities and signs began to reveal themselves. I was working full-time in retail, while also completing part-time studies in the financial industry.

I had just read *Think and Grow Rich* and watched the movie *The Secret* when I had a vivid dream that woke me up: *I was driving on a freeway and had forgotten to take my exit. I turned onto a different offramp when I had to stop suddenly because a baby was being lowered from the sky by some type of aircraft.* Then I received a message that *I needed to course-correct to help save lives*, and that *I was in the driver's seat*. I changed course and quit the financial business. Looking back, something had birthed and needed to grow.

The same year, I attended a holistic fundraiser for Children's Hospital Los Angeles, at The Four Seasons. One of my dearest friends chaired the event and booked Deepak Chopra's daughter, Mallika, as a speaker. She guided us through an *I AM* meditation, which was profound. At the end, we were to write down, without thinking, the first word that came to us. After *I AM,* I wrote... *a healer.* In the fall of 2019, I stumbled upon a social media quiz from Jennifer McLean – *What Kind of a Healer Are You?* I immediately took the quiz and eagerly awaited my results. Although I had traits of five types of healers, my dominance was *frequency.*

Earlier that year, we had celebrated a double milestone – my father's ninetieth and my sixtieth birthdays. I threw a lively party filled with music and dancing, a night of pure joy, but the high faded quickly. The very next day, our beloved greyhound, Yosemite, the emotional rock of our family, had to be put down. Stunning, with a white coat and a spirited heart, he had helped our other greyhound, Sequoia, overcome fears from her racing days. They had been inseparable. Three months later, Sequoia fell ill and passed as well.

It was the beginning of a significant season of grief.

I had been managing a *Papyrus* store for just shy of fourteen years; paper had sort of been in my DNA since growing up third generation in a family stationery and office supply business. I would joke that paper was in my blood.

Then, during the holiday rush, everything changed. I was blindsided and humiliated when an unhappy employee falsely accused me of harassment. It felt like a set-up, as interrogations were taking place behind my back. I had poured my heart into my work, only to feel unappreciated and unseen.

That was when the universe began to speak to me – louder. Whenever I looked at the clock, it seemed to be 11:11. There were many spiritual interpretations, but one message stood out: *A door is closing, but another is opening.*

By the first of the year, I had been transferred to a new location. One morning a large box arrived. Inside were *Store Closing* signs. To my surprise, and to the shock of all the other managers, the entire *Papyrus* chain was shutting down.

The store closed for good on February 28th, 2020. Two weeks later, the world went into lockdown. Panic and fear broke out. People were afraid to get close to one another and were told to keep a six-foot distance. The world changed almost overnight. People were dying as Covid-19 came in waves and crept into the ether.

Sitting at my desk, peering out the window of my home office on a crisp March day, a ray of light peaked through the grey sky. It seemed utterly beautiful as the greenery lit up and became vibrant with light, yet it was different. There was a feeling in the air that day. This was not just a virus. There was something bigger at play. I couldn't put my finger on it but I could sense something was shifting. It wasn't only outside – something was shifting within me.

I was glad to be out of retail and the new-found freedom gave me a chance to spend more time with my ailing father. His once towering six-foot frame had withered and contorted with age. His inability to walk landed him in a nursing home, where he sensed he wasn't coming home. When they went into lockdown, we resorted to sneaking through bushes to talk to him through the window.

Then came the day when they wouldn't allow us to do that. The pandemic took away what he loved most of all – his family. Losing his connection with the family was akin to losing his lifeline. He was hospitalized for a hernia and when he came back, he caught pneumonia... which turned into Covid-19.

The night before his passing, the nurse held up a FaceTime screen so I could talk to him, not knowing it would be for the last time. I reminded him how much he was loved and assured him I would take care of mom. I guess that soothed his heart because the next morning he was gone.

It was May 9th, 2020.

Six months later, my twenty-six-year-old son, Gavin, lay unconscious in the ICU. Due to Covid-19 restrictions, we could not be with him and were on pins and needles all weekend. He had a pool service business and his buddies wanted to help him with his route. His paperwork was in the truck, but we couldn't get the door to open. AAA couldn't open it either, so we had it towed to a shop.

I was following in my car when the phone rang. The hospital needed permission to run a test. My hands trembled and I nervously drove around, not knowing what to do with myself. As I parked my car, I began to scream at the top of my lungs: "God help him, please help him!"

When the call came, it was the social worker and the neurologist on the line. "I'm sorry... your son has passed." The neurologist began to cry, "This wasn't supposed to happen."

In shock, I drove home shaking and screaming "NO!"... from the very depths of my womb. My husband and I collapsed into each other's arms – except we couldn't fully hold each other. His recent shoulder (rotator cuff) operation made it impossible. The pain of our grief was unbearable.

I had lost both my father and son, exactly six months apart.

It was November 9th, 2020.

That night as we lay in bed, we heard running across the roof of our house. Back and forth, back and forth. We went outside and somehow Gavin's cat, Kitty, had gotten outside. She was on the roof, darting and leaping as if playing with something unseen.

We knew. Gavin was there.

Two days later, on 11:11, I had what I would describe as an out-of-body experience. Gavin came to me while I was in bed. At first, I was flying with him in his mind's eye. We came in through the front door. I could see everything he could see; the seven-foot heart-shaped wreath covered in white roses, his surfboard lying below with photographs, memorabilia and flower arrangements. Then we flew through the wall into the family room where he was able to see who had been able to visit with us so far. It was as if he was showing me everything he'd seen.

Suddenly, I was standing next to the kitchen sink when Gavin walked in. It was our usual spot, me at the windowsill and him waiting for his bagel to toast. He had a full beard and his surfer blond hair was darker, like when he was born. It was long, down to his shoulders. He looked happy and peaceful, wearing a golden tan, colored jacket and pants.

I exclaimed, "Oh my God, you came!" After all, I knew he was dead. Then I asked him if he could give me a hug. That was when the most extraordinary thing happened. He started to reach his arms out towards me, then another set of arms, and finally a third set of arms began to approach me like floating ribbons. If you've ever seen the Goddess Tara[1], this is how he appeared.

As I stood there, so happy to see him again, I saw what looked like energetic ribbons coming towards me. I could feel and sense that I was receiving frequencies of love; an unconditional love of the highest order. It was so beautiful and comforting. I woke up wanting to share this feeling with my husband, but it was mine to experience. This was the catalyst for my spiritual awakening.

Gavin began to send me songs that I'd hear in my head, during the night and upon awakening. I'd look up the lyrics to find the messages

---

[1] Tara is a female deity in both Hinduism and Buddhism who personifies compassion and offers salvation from the suffering of rebirth and death. Tara is the Embodiment of Perfected Wisdom, the Goddess of Universal Compassion, and the Mother of all Buddhas.

he was trying to convey. He was using music and sound to reach me, again frequency. I kept a journal next to the bed and would ask questions at night and receive insights in my dream state. I wanted so badly to connect with him more.

My grief was deep, and I felt a heavy density in my body. I began to work on healing myself. I read books by Derek Rydall and Christy Whitman. I started to journal regularly and did meditations and gratitude rituals. Then, I stumbled upon an online summit of alternative healers.

I watched in amazement the different modalities being shared. One really stood out to me because it seemed so easy, and I knew I could learn it. Dr. Bradley Nelson was demonstrating *The Emotion Code*. He used muscle testing and showed how easy it was to release trapped emotional pain from the heart and the body. I wanted to learn this to help heal my grief and pain. I immediately ordered *The Emotion Code* book. I read through it and began practicing on myself. I practiced on family members and friends... it was so much fun!

Inspired, I went through *The Emotion Code* certification process and saw an opportunity to help people release their emotional burdens. One day, I decided I would try to connect with Gavin in the spirit world. As I conducted a healing session for him, I could feel his emotions. I was embodying them and releasing his pain, as a channel for the healing of his soul. It was a profound experience. I shed tears for him.

On the first anniversary of his passing, I visited a clairvoyant psychic at a healing arts fair. Without giving any details, I was elated when I realized he'd brought Gavin through. At the end of the reading, he told me Gavin would send me three songs; one to thank me, one to express his takeaway from our relationship and one to share what he wanted to do for me.

The next morning, I awoke with *Your Song* by Elton John playing loudly in my head. The lyrics resonated deeply, as I knew this song was his gift. Gavin knew that my favorite concert was seeing Elton John from the second row at the Hollywood Bowl in 1973. I broke down in tears.

The following morning, I heard *Hello, It's Me* by Todd Rundgren – a song I hadn't listened to in years. Its lyrics revealed insights, reflecting our relationship, filling my heart with joy.

Four days later, the third song came in a different way. First, I heard the words *incubator* and *trachea*. I sensed that Gavin was trying to tell me something about his death. During my psychic reading, he had shaken papers and said, "Correct diagnosis.' I had ordered an autopsy, but the grief of his death was too painful for me to pursue it further.

Then I began hearing tones, reminiscent of *Close Encounters of the Third Kind*. I tried to hum what I was tuning into. At first, I couldn't decipher them. Slowly, they formed into words. It was the song, *It's All I Can Do* by The Cars. The main lyric was a message of our connection beyond this lifetime.

My vibration was so high that morning I couldn't sleep. I went to the kitchen and my Apple Watch flew off the counter smashing onto the floor. I decided to do some yoga to calm down but was drawn to a sound bath meditation. I laid down in Gavin's room and listened. About two-thirds into the sound bath, his cat, Kitty, walked in. I opened my eyes and looked out the window. There, perched on the power line, was a white hawk watching over me.

The name *Gavin* means white hawk and Godsend. I knew then what I had to do. I created an energy healing business, naming it *White Hawk Wisdom* in his honor.

As I continued to heal myself and others, I felt called to learn *The Body Code* healing modality. It was so exciting to see the transformations in people. The more I worked with others, the more attuned I became. I began feeling where energy was stuck and intuitively started channeling breathwork to release it. I learned how to identify limiting beliefs, clearing outdated programming that holds people back from experiencing their divine potential through *The Belief Code*.

These codes and the knowledge I've gained from spiritual luminaries have been the answers to the whispers. They have germinated the seed planted in my soul from long ago. Like a tree, my roots keep growing deeper into the soil, and my branches expand into the cosmos with no limits. I embrace knowledge with my latest endeavor, learning hypnosis techniques.

Everything is frequency and unresolved emotions manifest as physical pain and disease. Releasing these lower vibrations expands our capacity to handle the things we cannot control. Let go and trust that the universe is always working for us.

*Awakening* is heart-centered living and the soul's realization of what it came to do in this lifetime. As we align with purpose, we begin to receive signs and synchronicities.

It is shining your brilliance and being a guiding light for others to follow. It is a journey and one that expands exponentially. It is the butterfly emerging from the chrysalis.

*Awakened* isn't a destination, it is a way of being. It's the ripple of the ocean currents, the colors of a brilliant sunset, the motion of a flock of birds or changing patterns of sand dunes. It is the ability to see yourself and all living things as part of the same oneness. It is being in harmony with nature and the animal kingdom.

Awakening is knowing that we are not alone in this universe and being able to connect with higher consciousness. It is understanding the universal spiritual laws and applying them. It is connecting to God, spirit, source the quantum field – beyond what we can see with our physical eyes.

My grief, once an unbearable weight, became a gift for my spiritual awakening.

I hope that by sharing my story, it will help you to understand that the suffering we go through in life is for our own spiritual growth. It is in the polarity of contrast, in the darkness, that we can hear the whispers, find the light, and perhaps, even our calling.

## Julie Wasmer

Julie Wasmer is an intuitive energy healer, a nutrition and lifestyle coach and offers emotional and spiritual wellness through a whole body approach. With certifications as an Emotion, Body and Belief Code practitioner, a Food Matters nutrition coach, group energy facilitator and Rockstar speaker award, she integrates her natural gift of frequency healing using breathwork and wisdom to guide clients into wellbeing and purpose.

Divinely inspired to launch her business *White Hawk Wisdom* in honor of her son, she has helped hundreds of people through her one-on-one sessions and group healings both in person and online – fulfilling her mission to heal past wounds and physical ailments through the heart; empowering better relationships and a life filled with joy and peace.

Julie enjoys cooking nutritious meals, spending time outdoors hiking in the nearby Santa Monica mountains, playing pickleball, biking and working out. She lives in Woodland Hills, California, with her husband, two cats, three chickens and four lizards – a legacy from her late son.

She believes the time is now to heal with grace during this chaotic shift in consciousness. When we heal ourselves, we begin to heal the world.

⊕ www.whitehawkwisdom.com
ⓕ Facebook – Julie Wasmer – White Hawk Wisdom
Scan QR code to learn more about Julie Wasmer.

## Section IV:
# Embodying the Light

- How are you embodying the person you came here to be?

- What becomes possible when you choose to live your truth, instead of trying to prove yourself?

- How are you being called to serve from an awakened heart?

chapter

# 25

# A Visitor Among Us! – Journal of an ET Being

*by Viviane Chauvet*

"You are one of us," my Arcturian father keeps reminding me. Despite my human look and demeanor, I represent an ancient interstellar civilization that ascended thousands of years ago. We originate from the Boötes Constellation, between 36,000 and 40,000 light years from the Earth's Quadrant (solar system). I am an Arcturian sentient being and have been exploring many quadrants throughout the multiverse.

In our realm, I am known as an oracle and member of the Arcturus Delegation. There are twelve members of the High Priestesses of Light, and I am one of them. What does my intergalactic origin have to do with awakening? I am here to explore human holographic consciousness in a construct known as the "3D Matrix Reality." It is my understanding that souls have experienced multiple lifetimes on Earth, which are encoded into the matrix of the quantum DNA memory. Before each incarnation through the Earth's evolving magnetic field, souls were coded with the core knowledge of the unity of all creation. Each soul's journey through space and time manifests core teaching elements from the physical reality (incarnation). Without the greater awareness of the truth of this structure held in the soul, those experiences lay dormant in the quantum DNA field. The good news is that the soul carried the seeds of universal understanding before the earthly journey even began.

Based on my perspective and observation, I attribute awakening to a series of responses that activate ancient memories – an inner knowingness, in the quantum structure of the body template and the heart center. Seeds of genetic information printed in the DNA's intelligent structure begin to resurface, thus influencing the behavioral attributes of an individual, thought patterns, emotional response, life decisions, perspective of self and the world and an intuitive connection to the stars. You would say the spark ignites the conscious realization of one's divine origin. When I came to this world, as a galactic/human hybrid, I knew who I was and how much my presence would greatly influence the fabric of the 3D physical reality. As a child, I often communed with the elementals, the animals and the planet's consciousness. It was, and still is, challenging for me to comprehend why human beings seem to find comfort and temporary refuge in the dualistic material world, thus feeding an inner sense of isolation from infinite source. Such a diversity of life and sentient beauty surrounds us all the time!

For one thing, I understand, perceive and acknowledge animals as conscious beings, whose souls have chosen to experience an Earth's incarnation. Many of them serve as teachers and guardians to the human race, and yet, they can be so easily disregarded by those who have agreed to walk with them as equals. It saddens me to see people living their lives controlled by fear, disconnected from their heart centers and source of true power. This gap needs to be healed and reconciled to accept and awaken to a higher reality. What does higher reality mean? It means choosing benevolence, inner balance, self-love, self-worth and freedom from limited mental belief systems. Then, the universal door to infinite potential truly opens!

Over the years, I have communicated with many nonphysical, celestial and intergalactic beings, including my star delegation. Although some were dark beings (meaning they have chosen the path of service to self), they all recognize me as an advanced Arcturian ambassador. Many reptilian and draconian groups have attempted to block my work and deviate my lifepath from fulfilling my Earth's mission. Being "boots on the ground", my presence accelerates the higher timeline for the planet's *re-ascension (*term used by the Arcturians as part of our spiritual teachings). In 1997, I received an unexpected invitation to travel to Tucson, Arizona, with a small group of people. Arizona seemed like a distant and unknown "country" at the time. A friend, who recently joined a team of "experts" in sales and marketing, convinced me to sign up for a conference hosted at the company's headquarters. I had zero interest in marketing... and even less in sales! Those concepts were part of the 3D matrix reality and felt counterintuitive to my mission. Nonetheless, something infinitely bigger guided my decision to travel to Tucson. Upon our arrival, I immediately understood why I was on the land. The ancient grid network of Arizona connects souls to Ancient Atlantis and Egypt. I saw my etheric light body being transported to an era of peace and ancient galactic cooperation on the planet. Many star beings, like sirians, pleiadians, lyrans, andromedans, aquatic beings, antares and others, have significantly contributed to humanity's advancement in various areas of life (agriculture, healing, organic technology, knowledge, etc.).

My holographic vision provides a deeper perception of images, geometric patterns, languages, light structures and messages. It is my innate ability to access memories, receive communication from my star delegation, and decode complex forms of transmissions, like frequencies, into verbal language. One night, as I stood outside my hotel room to gaze at the stars, I could hear the consciousness of the mountains and surrounding canyons. They welcomed me to my "new home" and expressed gratitude for my imminent arrival. As always, my Arcturian Father stepped in and said, "Arizona will be your new home. You must move here to fulfill your planetary's mission." In my heart, I knew that this ancient land would significantly accelerate my awakening journey. Several years later, I finally settled my roots in the Phoenix area, in a small town near the Superstition Mountains. What took so long before I moved? Remember that to nonphysical and interstellar beings co-existing beyond the linear time construct, everything exists in the now. To my Arcturian self, my imminent move from Canada to Arizona was a manifested reality.

If we accept the concept that every soul co-creates the blueprint of an incarnation beforehand, it is logical to declare that we are here by soul design! This soul design is the map that aligns, in divine synchronicity, all the lessons, experiences and opportunities that guide an individual to achieve the soul's purpose. Therefore, my arrival in Arizona was in perfect synchronicity with my subsequent upgrades and reconnection with the ancient grid network of the desert. As mentioned, there is a strong connection to Atlantis and ancient Egypt in this sector. Within the first two years, I underwent profound vibrational shifts in all aspects: body systems, higher mind, heart and soul. My multidimensional vision expanded to the next level, and I started to perceive (with eyes wide open), walls shifting into dimensional portals. I would wake in the morning to find light language written on the walls, while telepathically communing with my interstellar group. I was brought aboard our advanced mothership more frequently to upgrade my holographic template, nervous system (cosmic gateways), and brain function. In other words, I was stepping into the early stage of my role as an interstellar ambassador. I studied various healing modalities from many sources and teachers, including reiki, QHHT and theta healing, to explore the human relationship to the universe. I aimed to gain a deeper understanding and appreciation of the human holographic consciousness. What is humanity's perspective on holistic ways to heal and restore themselves to their original divine state? My greatest challenge has been integrating my Arcturian holographic self into the human holographic consciousness field. How I perceive the world, think, speak about reality, and radiate energy reflects my galactic nature; I am a "visitor" among humankind.

To adjust to my new life in Arizona, I found a job as a full-time French interpreter and professional voiceover artist for an international language company. In addition to working forty hours a week, I would devote my free time and weekends to teaching spiritual classes and offering meditation at a local metaphysical store in Phoenix. Over the next thirteen years, I built an engaged clientele and provided thousands of private healing sessions worldwide. I became a predominant figure in the spiritual and UFO communities overnight. From in-person classes to private healing sessions, I expanded beyond the local community and started to travel internationally. From 2021 to 2024, I explored many countries and sacred sites on five continents. My attuned empathic ability allows me to communicate with many ancient guardians and interdimensional beings around the globe, like the Stonehenge guardians in England, interdimensional aquatic beings in South Africa, and the gatekeepers in Uluru, Australia. On a human level, I would experience doubt and sadness emanating from the heart of Gaia and the collective consciousness. My doubt stemmed from my challenges to physically and energetically adapt to the dualistic dynamics of the 3D matrix-reality and heaviness of the Earth's gravity. Since my body is designed to hold higher-dimensional light frequencies naturally, I oftentimes experience pain and tension in my muscular system because of the contrast in dimensional shifts. Again, I have learned to be compassionate with my unique vessel (body) in connection to the planet.

On a bright note, I also discovered the joy of "sweets", including delicious cakes and chocolate. Oh, my! Take me to your chocolate factory! It is a joyful balm for the soul, which helps me to recenter my energy and breathe deeper. I often witnessed people and "spiritual teachers" approaching me for potential collaboration and new ventures, only to back away out of fear, feeling somehow intimidated by my presence. Whenever someone connects to my quantum signature (vibrational signature), that individual will respond based on their receptivity and inner filter systems. Of course, I have been privileged to forge genuine friendships and positive partnerships, most likely old souls and star seeds. Those experiences are all part of a powerful transformation of the heart – what I call stepping into universal heart awareness. As part of my continued awakening journey, I discovered how unconditional love and self-worth elevate the mind-heart interface above fear and lower instinctual living. My soul synchronicity would find a way to align the necessary connections and opportunities to expand my spiritual work at the perfect time. From an Arcturian perspective, perfect timing refers to precise moments in the Earth's time lines when the global consciousness has reached peaks of receptive awakening. Those peaks of awakening allow my star delegation to introduce the next set of light frequencies encoded in the planet's magnetic field for recalibration and global balance. Whether people are conscious or unconscious of the fact that we all are interconnected to one another, your thoughts and emotions affect the symbiotic eco-systems of the entire planet. In my heart, I have always known I was sent to this world in direct response to the planet's call for assistance. In my few Earthly incarnations, I recall my fondness for this "blue pearl" and her artistic ability to host such beauty in many impressive natural designs. The diversity of sentient life on Gaia is a wonder many admire in the multiverse!

Beyond my human experiences and sensitivity, I am a galactic being who has evolved on another plane of reality, in a more unified dimensional space. Since my human-hybrid form is a prototype designed explicitly for this lifetime, I have experienced the synergy of being isolated from others and this 3D construct. My soul originates from a place where all beings cultivate harmonic resonance with each other and all aspects of creation. No matter how slowly everything progressed in this dualistic and polarized world, I had to learn to be patient with myself and others. My profound awakening has helped me release doubt about my capacity to fulfill my heart's mission, live in parallel with this matrix-reality and remain true to my authentic self. Therefore, I realized it is about vibrational resonance and activating our capacity to manifest higher realities as divine co-creators. We are returning to the essentials of living, participating in life in kindness, empathy and connection to all sentient life forms.

For example, we all have the power and authority to recognize how our vibrations and belief systems affect the movement of global consciousness on the planet and even beyond the Earth (and the solar system). We can realign the direction of ascension by cleansing distortions and miscreations from our auric field and the Earth's crystalline grid network. It is about taking a leap of faith and trusting that every gesture of kindness and energy invested in others has multi-directional ripple effects in space and time. The awakening of the heart transforms our existence into a higher purpose, and this transformation supports old souls in reconciling their cosmic self with their unique human experience. It is the sacred remembrance that this incarnation, this unique blueprint, will only exist once and will be recorded in the Earth's crystal memory field, your soul Akashic field and the universe hall of records.

My question for you is, *what blueprint (or footprints) do you wish to leave as your soul's legacy in this lifetime?*

# Viviane Chauvet

Viviane Chauvet is an Arcturian ambassador, international speaker, cosmic teacher, published author and multidimensional holographic healer. Her commitment to advanced healing services is evident in the tens of thousands of private sessions she has conducted globally. As an intergalactic oracle, she navigates star systems, assisting civilizations on the verge of evolutionary ascension.

For more than a decade, Viviane has been a prominent spiritual and extraterrestrial community leader. She has spoken at conferences worldwide and featured on radio shows, online summits, and award-winning documentaries. Viviane created the Arcturian Energy Matrix Healing and the Arcturian Healing Arts Program for self-mastery, ascendancy and metamorphosis evolution.

Founder of Arcturian University and the Universal Consciousness Community, Viviane Chauvet offers unique memberships and transformative master events, including holographic group healing, meditation series, the *Infinite Star Connections* podcast, programs, intuitive workshops, high-quality classes, community gatherings and in-person retreats for members. Her passion is to support life thriving beyond fear and illusions!

⊕ www.infinitehealingfromthestars.com
⊕ www.infinite-healing.mykajabi.com
Scan QR code to learn more about Viviane Chauvet.

chapter

# 26

# Called Upon by Heaven: My 'Miraculous Awakening Experience'

*by Oracle Maureen*

Before they came for me, my life revolved around carpools and laundry. As a stay-at-home mom, I had set aside my journalism degree from St Thomas University. I dedicated myself fully to raising two young daughters in idyllic, suburban Woodbury, Minnesota. I enjoyed a comfortable life with my (then) husband and taking care of my family.

If you met me back then, you might believe me to be just another mom, running errands and making dinner. Nothing would hint at the *other* part of me. You wouldn't suspect wings would often appear before my eyes, as the angel they belonged to entered my body. You wouldn't guess that, right after, I would serve as a channeler, delivering the angel's messages. You would, however, be surprised by how often I predicted the future – that beginning as a little girl, I bridged the heavenly world to the physical dimension, delivering messages from Heaven to friends, family and whoever was in front of me.

I kept that part of myself hidden.

By my mid-thirties, I enjoyed a typical lifestyle – but one that masked a truth I had always known within me. The face I presented to the world concealed a lifelong *divine* connection. For as long as I can remember, I saw angels and guides and knew I was their channeler. I heard their voices, felt their presence and saw them when they entered me, using me to deliver their messages.

There are dangers for people blessed with such extraordinary gifts. In ages past, they were tortured in ghastly ways should their secrets be revealed. Being burnt at the stake or crucified were but a few punishments. Beyond physical harm, people like me were often mistreated in other ways; shunning, ridicule, slander.

To avoid that fate, I lived a double life beginning from childhood. Throughout my youth, I would experience extraordinary events – heavenly spirit guides and angels would envelop me with their blissful vibrations. I would *shift* and feel the most incredible state of euphoria as their souls merged with mine. Profound words, filled with guidance or warnings wise beyond my young years, would spill from my lips – giving the person before me much-needed advice as solutions to their problems. I had little to no control of what was flowing out of my mouth as I was immediately rendered into a trance.

These divine encounters, through me, produced incredible effects on people. I would see them *shift*. The peace they sought would wash over them. Clarity emerged as they now knew just what to do next, or nervousness if they were given a warning.

Always, just as mysteriously as they came, the guides and angels would leave me once their messages were delivered. Then the ordinary would spring back to life for me. My soul would drop back into my body, dazed and unaware of exactly what I said in those in-between spaces. All the channeling I did for others eluded me, as I was left with little to no idea what occurred while in a trance state. The one thing I could count on, however, was feeling drained and hungry afterward.

This part of me I hid from the world *because* God told me to.

God spoke to me when I was a child. I can still recall seeing *God* written out in white, cloudy words over a huge, blue sky when He would say: *"Do not tell anyone you are one of My helpers."* Regularly, He commanded, *"No one is to know you are an advanced channeler until the day I require you to reveal this truth."*

Feeling His strictness, I obeyed for fear of getting disciplined by Him or hurt by the humans, even when I was tempted as a teenager.

The message was clear: *Do not speak yet of this unique part of myself and how I work for heaven as their channeler.* God warned me in no uncertain terms: *"If you reveal yourself too soon, you will be persecuted and hurt and you cannot protect yourself as a child."*

Out of fear of disobeying God and the desire to protect myself from human's harmful words, I obeyed. This brings us back to my mom days in Woodbury. As I said, I was happy and content with life.

Then, one night, everything changed.

I was doing the usual things required of caring for a family. Then, one night, I opened my eyes and saw him.

The towering form was so vast he dominated my bedroom's double doors. Panic gripped me. Before I could react, the phrase *Spirit Guide* thundered into my head, along with seeing it spelled out in glowing letters.

I froze. But tranquility quickly flowed into me. A beatific halo of energy surrounded me, hugging me. My anxiety started to dissipate. It was *very* overwhelming and yet it couldn't vanquish all my fear.

Dumbfounded, I wondered in my head, *What was this very large man wearing a robe who appeared, floating, before me by my bedroom doors?* I couldn't understand why the apparition didn't go away. Finally, I had to walk past him to go to the bathroom.

Still, he stayed. Back in my Bed, I started seeing perfectly shaped pink and red hearts and red roses appear in my mind's eye. I was staring at him as they bloomed in my vision. They came with the strongest sensations of love. Every time nervousness seized me, I received more hearts, roses and more vibrations of love. After several hours, I recognized that *he* was sending these to alleviate my fears.

This continued throughout the night.

The next evening, it happened again. This time, my dad appeared in the moonlight at the door.

*"Mouse, it's Dad."* He called me by his nickname.

Dad stood as real as the day he passed more than ten years ago. More hearts and loving waves flowed into me, diminishing my anxiety. He stayed there too, all night. The experiences continued. The next night there was another guide. Then another. And another.

This continued every night. Like clockwork, each evening the guides appeared, sending me their love and messages, urging me to remember who I was. But I was in amnesia and afraid. I couldn't remember what I knew as a child. They put me through their divine intervention. Removing my amnesia, they spent two months showing me visions of myself channeling. They started with memories of when they used me as their channeler, going back to my childhood. And when I did remember, they gave me more clarity, showing me visions of how I continued to do this for them all throughout the rest of my life, up, even, until now. I never stopped, I just became used to doing it and suppressed it. They showed me countless times of predicting someone's future and being confused as to how I knew what I knew before it happened. They showed me how I would see an angel or guide appear right before they entered me and delivered their messages through me.

*I remember. I remember this*, I thought as truth dawned on me.

*"You have always been a master channeler,"* they said. *"You work for high-level guides. You are one of us, living on Earth."*

Overwhelmed, I resisted.

They became stronger with me when I tried to turn away. They said, *"We have come to wake you up to your spiritual gifts. We are calling upon you to use them and work for us."*

Fear paralyzed me. I feared leaving my "normal" existence, knowing that my life would change. *People will fear me, probably mock me.*

But they weren't taking "no" for an answer.

While their divine intervention went on, I learned that I was telepathic with them, which made it easy for them to communicate to me and try to enlighten me.

That floored me.

Fearful of moving forward, I was stunned when, toward the end of this *"miraculous awakening experience"* – as they called it – I received a visitation that truly amazed me. I opened my eyes one night to see brilliant white light flowing over my nightstand and up the side of my face. Shocked, I looked up to see a large angel with huge wings standing close to me.

Immediately, I heard: *Guardian angel*

*Now what do I do?*

Of course, I knew what to do, but I still stalled to accept my mission, even when my last visitor, none other than Ascended Master Kuan Yin[1], came to me. She tried to help me embrace my path. *You belong to our group. Right now, you work on Earth, the time has come for you to serve us. You have passed your tests, lessons, initiations. You are ready to serve. We are calling on you now.*

I didn't just receive telepathic messages from seven spirit guides, a guardian angel and my departed father – I saw them with my physical eyes and heard them. It was *the* most transformative experience of my life. At least, up until that moment – more would follow.

And yet, my fears held me back.

The visits stopped. A few months after, I met the opposite of heaven's loving visitations. Darkness replaced the light. Negative entities invaded my home. The haunting began, small at first. Unexplained noises jarred my daughters and me. Objects moved on their own, scaring us. They touched me inappropriately, and they harassed us.

My fear deepened to terror.

Desperate, I called a spiritual helper.

---

[1] A bodhisattva revered as the deity of compassion and mercy.

Arriving at my home, she said: "This happened because you turned away from your guides and calling."

After she validated the entities and events using her psychic gifts, I knew she was a "qualified" helper I could trust. She said I was sent this experience to motivate me to accept my soul's mission of working for Heaven, because I didn't. It was also to teach me about the reality of negative spirits. She emphasized that if I hadn't turned away from my guides, this nightmare would not have been as intense. She encouraged me to attend a psychic development class to learn how to manage my spiritual abilities more quickly.

At last, I agreed.

With reluctance, I drove to my first class that night. I saw angel wings beside me. Hearts and roses filled my mind's eye. Loving vibrations hugged me. When I tried to take my foot off the gas, my guides and angels put it back on and pressed my foot.

I heard, *Go. Go. Go.*

Hearts and roses followed me to class. Sitting in my chair, wanting to leave, I felt their hands on my shoulders, holding me down.

Then the teacher announced, "It's time for mediumship readings."

*No.*

Again, I wanted to leave. Again, my guides held me in place. We were to do a reading with someone.

Turning to my partner I immediately saw his deceased mother behind him. Instantly, I knew details about her, such as her passing, her appearance, and other information, impossible for me to know about a complete stranger. I rattled it all off, including a personal message.

My partner was floored.

Afterwards, when the teacher called for feedback, he was still in shock. He raised his hand. "Maureen is already at a professional level."

The floodgates opened after that. I graduated from student to expert almost overnight. My classmates requested readings, refining my latent abilities. As the guides worked through me, my reputation spread. More people came to me, seeking readings. Yet despite finally accepting my path and true identity, there was one final test – I had to break from my old life at a significant level.

With much trepidation, I honored my guides and angels' wishes to work for them. I made the shift, embracing my calling... finally. This didn't mean it was always easy. My guides were strict. They trained me by requiring me to do a lot of work and make many sacrifices. Within two years, they had me working full-time doing readings, hands-on healing, ghost clearings and psychic detective work. All along, I obeyed their orders dutifully, even when difficult, and was given further psychic activation as a reward.

Still, stepping into my mission was no simple feat. As I dreaded, stiff resistance came from the outside world, at times. People did turn on me, when they didn't like their guidance or realized how easy it was for me to get information. People slandered me, just as I had suspected, due to their fears or jealousies. Though my guides warned me this would happen, it didn't diminish the pain.

When it was time to create a business card, they insisted I lean in even further, no matter the blowback: *We wish for you to list yourself as you are – a Master Channeler.*

I froze again.

That's when God appeared and responded to my fears.

While I struggled to put this title on my business card, I received an even more powerful experience than my first *awakening*. Lying in bed, asking my guides *again* about the title they gave me, I was astounded to be answered... by God.

All of a sudden, I felt the most heart-stopping, Earth-shattering vibration fill my stomach. My third eye activated. I saw a massive globe of pure white light surrounded in a vast blue sky.

He said: *Source of life. All knowing. All forgiving. All loving. God.* Then, as the vibration in my stomach increased and expanded, I saw a large ray of white light come up out of my stomach and travel to God's sphere of white light. God said: *Master Channeler. Created and borne by Me to be a Master Channeler of communications for the higher realms and Me. This is what you are. Print it.*

I then saw *many* luminous globes of white light descend from the bottom of His white radiating source of energy, falling down into a gigantic ocean of blue water – each traveling down their own unique path. God said: *All souls are created for their own unique purpose.* I witnessed God's creations, our souls, formed directly from His *essence*, each with our own divine purpose.

As God said this, He filled me with the strongest electrical energy. It expanded inside me until I could no longer feel my bed or my physical body. I felt my soul rise up out of my body until I merged with His energy and became one with God's light. I couldn't speak. I lay there, floating in His vibration, and thought, *I cannot feel where I begin or end.* I had never been so overwhelmed or have been since. A large rainbow appeared around God's globe of white light, and I was filled with even more blissful waves of love. I was held in a state of ecstasy until He slowly lowered my soul back into my body.

All I could do was say... *As you wish.*

Let my *"miraculous awakening experience"* serve as a revelation: There *is* a higher power. God *does* exist. Heaven *is* real. God has given the world the gift of help through His spirit guides, angels and His divine grace, which you have access to. My story is but one testimony to the truth, that we were all created from source of life, God. We are divine souls, each created with a purpose as unique as the stars. My hope is to awaken you to these truths so that you live connected to Heaven, and you receive the gifts they are looking to give.

# Oracle Maureen

Oracle Maureen is a Master Channeler and spiritual teacher who assists those seeking spiritual enlightenment and guidance. She is the Chief Principal Oracle for Jesus, Kuan Yin, Mary, Buddha and God – a rare and coveted position that God anointed her with after she completed a challenging initiation, as well as a role she first achieved many lifetimes ago.

God said Oracle Maureen is a *rainbow child of the highest ranking, to the level of a saint meant for the mainstream world.* She has been granted the extraordinary revelation that she is the reincarnation of Mary of Bethany, further affirming her high ranking.

Using her spiritual gifts, Oracle Maureen provides clarity and direction to those seeking guidance while also connecting them with their departed loved ones. Additionally, she has been bestowed with the gift of protection, allowing her to rescue individuals from harmful and negative spirits.

In her classes, Oracle Maureen helps students awaken their psychic abilities and advance their spiritual growth. As a Master Channeler she serves as a vehicle for the Ascended Masters to share their wisdom at the highest level possible, helping others evolve so they can reach Nirvana more quickly.

⊕ www.oraclemaureen.com
◉ @oraclemaureen
Scan QR code to learn more about Oracle Maureen.

chapter
# 27

# Bahamas: A Journey of Healing and Awakening

*by Cristina Valle-Parke*

I am an old voyager on the healing path. Many years and battles have shaped me, and I know the journey still has a way to go. Some say you must first remove the rocks to see the pebbles, and later, the dust. In the healing space, rocks and pebbles represent blockages and traumas. Yet, after so much work, I encountered what I call "fumes" – subtle, almost imperceptible patterns still lingering, needing to be fully liberated from my earthly karma.

I write this from a plane, returning from the Sivananda Ashram in the Bahamas. I arrived by faith and innocence, unaware at the time that I was flying to this ancient site which holds such wonderful energy, though also some darkness. A woman went missing from here in June 2024. I learned this from a customs officer on my way out of the island. I am incredibly grateful I hadn't heard this before; it may have deterred me from this life-changing experience.

My journey to the ashram began with a whisper during meditation. While guiding a group in Fontana, California, the word *Bahamas* dropped in. I invited the group to visualize themselves there, blue waters, family and plenty of joy. The message repeated several times, coinciding with emails about a seminar given by a couple named Matt and Joy Kahn. I knew nothing about them, though after several emails I had to trust the invitation was coming from the higher realms and I decided to research further. After consuming a couple hours of Matt on YouTube, I ended up in Sedona, in one of their live seminars. I like them. The Bahamas was now a real possibility. Checking the ashram website, I found that some of my favorite spiritual singers were frequent visitors, Snatam Kaur and Krishna Das, with sold-out shows. Divine timing orchestrated the ashram's calendar, Krishna Das and Matt and Joy would present in the same week, so I made the arrangements. I confirmed day passes for Krishna Das as the stay at the ashram was completely booked during those days; I would be able to check in to one of their casitas just before Matt and Joy.

My husband and I arrived in The Bahamas as *seekers*, between 14 and 23 February, and left as *finders*, never even thinking that this old Atlantis energy would contribute for an amplified healing experience. It is believed the ashram sits on top of an old Atlantis temple. A lot has been speculated about this civilization, but the founder of the Sivananda Ashram said, "There's an old temple under this rock." During my Bahamas stay I embarked on what I call "baby journeys" – smaller life revelations without the aid of plant medicine. Journeys are ceremonies assisted by shamans and *allucinogenos*. My "baby journeys" were smaller, bite-size, possible due to the influx of energy in this place, the teachings, the chants, the prayers – plus Krishna Das' and Matt and Joy's magic.

I picked our seats for our first evening with Krishna Das and upon closing my eyes, I saw a purple storm of energy floating before me. I prayed to God, *Save me, purify me.* By save me, I meant from the ego and the programs that run our lives, with consent and without it. The first night was incredible. Krishna Das' wisdom and charisma spoke straight to my soul. Our way back to the hotel consisted of a walk in the white sand, with the backdrop of the moon and the Atlantic Ocean.

The ashram is a very secluded place in, literally, "Paradise Island." There are only two ways to arrive at the ashram; by foot through the white sand and by boat through the ashram's private dock. The boat runs from Nassau to Paradise, crossing people from these two islands; from its decks you can see the entire ocean that merges with the open sky. Looking to the south, you see Nassau, an old plantation island where pirates used to stop. Today it offers plenty of entertainment for tourists. And to the west, you find the famous Atlantis compound, making an elegant skyline in the horizon, resembling a treasure island from Vegas.

That night, after our short walk to our rooms, next to the Sivananda Ashram, my husband and I recapped the night before falling asleep, though I stayed lingering with what was given to me to digest; memories from my childhood. I remembered I used to cry myself to sleep, yearning for love and understanding from my parents, full of resentment and pain. Feeling misunderstood and under-loved, though this time, I saw myself differently. My younger self was no longer crying, she was sitting in peace. She absolved her parents from any wrongdoing, understood them, recognizing their innocence. She realized their love was as infinite as God's love for her, in fact, it was unlimited. In her new-found peace, I still felt I needed to recap with her, with guidance. I told her, *You are a dreamer; your job is to dream. You are the dream of God. Your dreams build. You are a healer and a builder. And your parents have unlimited love for you. It is okay to share this love with your sisters...* Now my younger self dreams herself to sleep. Her small body no longer holds pain, now it's full of positive possibilities.

The following day, after our second Krishna Das experience, another wave of realizations came, another "baby journey" indeed. I saw how an unintentional, unspoken understanding that something was *wrong* with my sister, or my grandma or my mom, lingered in our home, informing everyone's behavior. As children, all we want is our parents' validation, and these spoken and unspoken criticisms of one another led me to believe that none of us were perfect and therefore not valuable. I grew up believing that lie, taking the value from them and myself. Though in this "baby journey" (life review) I told myself: *Your sisters are perfect. Your mother, your cousin, everyone is made perfect by God. You are perfect too. My father is perfect, and so everyone around him.* Today I have my real heavenly 20/20 vision, recognizing God's creation for what is, perfect. We are all perfectly made in his image and now my thoughts align with God's essence.

My younger sister, who had joined us on the trip a day later, came with her fiancé, and shared a similar experience. "I was on a journey [baby journey]," she said, "I cried rivers after getting back to the hotel. I went back to the past and released..." (the rest is for her to share). I was so happy for her; she is a voyager of healing also. My happiness amplified through her story. I am a happy, healthy and curious detective of my non-empowering patterns. This trip gave me everything I would have wished for and more.

Then came Matt and Joy Kahn's teachings. By this time, we had checked in at the ashram and we no longer had to commute under the silver night, next to the ocean. Sleeping at the ashram, we were able to immerse ourselves in the temple's routine; 6am chanting, teachings and meditation, yoga, amazing food provided and more. The ashram is like a jungle, filled with tropical vegetation, tall trees, orchids, palms with beautiful Bahamas-style casitas. They sit overlooking the beach and its surroundings, from where you can often see enormous ships cruising through the open ocean. There's also accommodation for all budgets; tents that are usually for the yoga programs and helpers at the ashram, shared rooms and awesome affordable suites that, in any other hotel, would be priced $3,000 per night, as the rooms face the turquoise ocean just feet away from its waters.

My spirit is high, always ready to mingle with people, though also happy to hide behind the sweet silence. I am a loving detective of my old vices, and by now "baby journeys" are an expectation in the Bahamas! Ready for the next unfolding, Matt and Joy Kahn shared that some insights come with age and maturity. Patterns cannot be revealed all at once, they come when the person is ready, *so be patient*. It requires certain life experiences for them to be revealed. I am ready for more. Rocks, pebbles, or fumes, I want to keep healing.

"Stillness brings back memories and makes us face unsettled emotions."

My husband and I decided to skip dinner on our third night at the ashram. Lying in bed before our night meditation I confessed to him, "I am feeling unrested." A small amount of anxiety with an underlying fear is telling me, *What if I get hungry later?* Travis, my husband, says he is feeling the same. Again, this conversation with yourself is only perceptible in a silent mind, that is why I called them fumes; they have no weight and almost no density, almost imperceptible, though they can't hide when there's no masks nor attitudes. He asked if I had ever gone hungry as a child. "No," I replied, but the fear was there. I asked him the same. His answer was yes.

While my husband was often hungry as a young child, when he was eight years old, the court sided with his father in a custody battle. Both he and his brother moved to a new and more nurturing environment. For myself as a child, I was never officially considered poor, and I don't recall being hungry, though my parents often reminded me of starving children in Africa when I didn't eat my food. They also reminded me of my father's own struggles with poverty, and my grandma's fate; raising her five children in a ten-by-ten room with mother earth right underneath their feet in the cold highlands of Ecuador. My father had lived through extreme poverty and those tales have penetrated my psyche. Forty-six years later, I was still afraid to go hungry, even though my life now has no resemblance to my abuelita's struggles.

All these fears and beliefs were still real, whispering behind the lids... It made a lot more sense when Matt and Joy shared about stillness. "Humans make themselves busy to escape their past. Stillness reminds us of overwhelming experiences in childhood – especially when we were powerless and frozen in silence." Stillness unlocks these feelings and memories, so it's safer to scroll our phones or create unnecessary noise in our lives than face stillness. *Stillness* is necessary to see what's really behind the veil and is one of the ways to self-knowledge... and self-knowledge is the way to liberation.

In preparation for our last day at the ashram, my husband and I decided to treat the kitchen staff to some acclaimed smoothies that the store only sells during one hour every day. Everyone at the ashram works for free; from landscapers, office, cooks, cashiers, handymen and people in reservations. They do what is called karma yoga; people deliver their work in exchange for karmic liberation. These karmic yogis come from different zip codes across the planet for the same reasons I did. So, we wanted to thank these volunteers for the amazing food the kitchen had prepared during our stay, by giving them these treats. As I stepped out of my room to deliver these smoothie tickets, an old insecurity crept in, in an almost imperceptible way: *What if they're too busy and they disregard me with passive-aggressiveness?* I kept walking toward the kitchen... and in all honesty, I was excited to be able to see one more fume, with the possibility of reframing it for good.

We delivered the tickets to a girl who, a day earlier, had made some amazing grits. I asked her who made them – she said she did, "They are from home, the south." Our karmic yogi was so happy to receive the tickets on behalf of the kitchen team, she told us, "They were such a great idea!" She was incredibly grateful and made us feel well-received with her generous words, helping me reframe my old belief and insecurity.

Back in the room, I was ready to share this new insight with my husband and explore this gem further. I discovered that as a child I often had these *incredible ideas* that only made sense to me; a free-minded kid with an incredible imagination. As a kid I had an urge to give my parents gifts I made and share my *genius* ideas with them, though my spontaneous offerings often appeared to inconvenience my parents due to their multiple occupations, and I was put to the side. My gifts and ideas seemed to be out of place. *They must not be good ideas and giving is not good.* I wonder if these non-empowering perceptions about life would bring hesitation to my life as a woman and businesswoman? Obviously they did. "They must not be good ideas' is the seed, and hesitation the fruit. I just imagine a more empowering life with my new opposite belief; "people are dying to hear my awesome ideas, thank you, world!"

All healing revelations make me so excited in my passion for liberation. I know that no one intentionally did anything to me, though my young mind wanted to learn quickly and concluded, *don't give, it could hurt. Don't share ideas, they are not good.* Do nothing instead, better freeze or it can hurt, and that's not a healthy way to live.

On our way to the Bahamas, I was also guided to rewatch a Amrit Sandhu episode – an interview with Robert Schwartz about life lessons, where Robert suggests that all lessons we learn are preplanned by our souls before our incarnation. We planned all our difficulties, shortcomings and misunderstandings... way in advance. So, all the players in our story are innocent, they have been recruited to play their part in our life's curriculum. Our shortcomings are perfectly normal, they are part of our human-soul evolution. And one of the keys in our progress is to take personal responsibility, to not only understand, but to overcome each of our wounds and uncover the disempowering stories.

We all suffered from the same childhood misunderstandings and assumptions. We hide them behind our business, alcohol, anger, habitual reactions and stories that include everyone else as the responsible party except ourselves. We can only liberate ourselves through awareness and personal responsibility. Though I narrated using candid words "the way my parents made me feel", "the way some love I was missing", it's only to show my point of view and interpretation at the time that wound was created. Because my life is my responsibility and so it's the meaning I give to it.

Thank you, ashram, thank you, Atlantis, Matt and Joy and Krishna Das, karmi yogis, monks and attendees for contributing to this elevated energy that allowed for these behind the lids, "fumes", to come out safely and to be handled in The Bahamas. Thank you, higher-self and angels for whispering in my ear where I needed to go next to continue healing and learning. I learned a lot in Paradise. I learned about myself, I learned about God and I learned about life. An even more generous heart emerged out of this trip with an even more perfect image of myself.

At the ashram in the Bahamas, I reclaimed my right to dream, plan, act and share without fear of rejection. And on the 3pm Delta flight going back home, I reflect with gratitude that the divine guided me to undo the doing and to be free once more.

# Cristina Valle-Parke

Cristina Valle-Parke was born in Ecuador and now resides in the United States. She has been married for nineteen years to her incredible life partner and fellow spiritual seeker, Travis Parke.

Cristina's journey into metaphysics and self-development began at a young age, sparked by her father's deep curiosity for these fields. Later, she found a true mentor in Tony Robbins, whose teachings ignited her passion for uncovering universal truths and mastering the art of co-creating reality. Through his generosity, she was introduced to a wealth of spiritual teachers who expanded her understanding of both the metaphysical, aka spiritual, and material worlds.

Currently, Cristina is deeply committed to planetary healing through her purpose-driven company, California Recyclers. Since its inception, the company has successfully recycled hundreds of thousands of pounds of plastic and fiber, contributing to environmental sustainability on a large scale.

However, Cristina believes that to truly heal the world, we must go beyond physical pollution and address the deeper crisis – mental and emotional pollution. She is passionate about helping humanity break free from limiting beliefs and destructive patterns, knowing that true transformation begins within. Through her work, she continues to bridge the gap between external action and inner evolution.

◎ @cvalleparke
Scan QR code to learn more about Cristina Valle-Parke.

chapter

# 28

# Death: A Doorway to Love

*by Nina Palmieri*

I was quite fortunate to grow up in a close Italian family. My grandmother used to say, "We may not be rich in money, but we are rich in family and love." We were as tight as it gets. I never could imagine not being close together forever, nor could I ever have imagined that it would be possible to love each other more deeply.

Until that one fateful day...

Normally I was excited to go to work. I was like a child in a candy shop going to my job. I loved working at the eccentric, popular natural foods market in downtown New Haven. It opened me up to an array of new realms of possibility in my life.

But today was different. I had a major headache which increasingly worsened as the day went on. *How am I going to get through this day?* I thought. The surrounding stimuli irritated my sensitive nature. Each noise felt like an invasive personal attack on my being. My usual charismatic self withdrew with each encounter.

As a woman innocently laughed with her friends, my head throbbed with irritation. I looked up and caught a glance of the next customer in line. *Argh, it's him – the local who comes into the market wearing rubber gloves, careful to not touch anything with his hands and doesn't let anyone in the store touch his food.* His shoulders scrunched inwards as he reached down into his wallet and meticulously grabbed the bills to prepare to pay for his groceries. Today, I was especially annoyed by his demeanor. *He only comes in on the days I work so he can come through my register. Maybe it's because I am nice. Today I do not feel nice.*

The overwhelm of the noise of the customers, the commotion of the people walking in wanting to engage me in conversation, the smells of the bakery and hot bar food, were all too difficult to deal with.

*Ahh the clock finally struck, I am done with my shift.* I ran upstairs and punched out. I couldn't get out of there fast enough. I jumped in my car and headed north towards my parents' house. I had plans with my cousin to go to a concert, but I didn't know how I would pull it off with that headache. I just wanted to get home and lay on the couch.

I drove through the usual traffic, eager to get to my right turn in order to escape the congested area and reach the rural, woody back road towards home. Relieved, I finally turned right and continued a few miles down the road when I heard loud sirens approaching from a distance. I followed the cars in front of me and pulled over to the right, when an ambulance sped by me, passing on the opposite side of the road.

The jolt of the flashing sirens was sobering and alerted me of the seriousness of an emergency. I paused and thought to myself, *Someone's family member is in that vehicle.*

My heart fluttered and I was compelled to offer a silent prayer for whoever was hurt, as well as for the family who would be impacted. As I continued to drive down the road a little way, I approached a roadblock that detoured me in another direction away from what appeared to be a serious accident in the distance.

I felt like I was entering into a slow-motion movie, where everything in my consciousness slowed down. Disoriented, I became aware of the apparent two parts of me. The one that wanted to get home as fast as possible and not have to deal with the inconvenience of a roadblock, and the other that was quiet and open-hearted, in recognition that someone had had a serious enough accident that detoured my regular route.

I humbly drove the rest of the way home in a state of silence.

As I walked in the front door, eager to collapse, my mom sat in her usual spot at the end of the couch and greeted me excitedly, "Hi, honey, how was your day?"

"Oh gosh, you don't even want to know. I couldn't wait to get out of there. It was terrible. I have such a headache, and everyone and everything annoyed me."

"Well, come sit down then and rest," she said.

"I will... but I have plans with Matteo, so I need to figure out what I'm doing first."

The luring of her motherly love pulled me onto the couch before I could even possibly pick up the phone to call my cousin.

"Come, lay on my lap," she said.

Although I was twenty-one, I never felt too old to lay on my mom's lap and let her stroke my hair; it was one of my favorite things in the world. She gently ran her fingers through my long curls. My whole body relaxed into her soft loving touch as I surrendered into her.

The phone rang, and my dad answered, "It's for you, Maria! It's Cindy!"

My mom took the phone, listened, and responded, "No, I'm not sure if Anthony is home yet. He should be... No, I haven't talked to my mom this evening... Well, I'm on the couch with Nina, but I can go up there... Okay, thanks, Cindy."

She hung up. "Well, that was Cindy. She wants to know if Anthony is home from work and said we should go check. Do you want to go for a walk up the street with me?"

I was just getting comfortable. "As long as you promise when we come back, you will still play with my hair." I smiled.

"It's a deal," she said.

Together we walked up the street, where we were met in the middle of the road by a neighbor from up the hill. She and her husband pulled up in their car alongside us.

"Maria, have you heard?" her voice was detached, monotone.

"Heard what?" Mom said.

"Maria, your brother Anthony is dead. It was just announced on the news. You better get to your mother's house quickly before she finds out."

Both mom and I stood there, paralyzed with the unexpected blow. Time came to an abrupt standstill as the fabric of our reality completely disintegrated. I looked at my precious mom. She screamed in terror and took off running down the street "Vinny, Vinny!" Her desperate cries for my father echoed in the summer night.

I stood there alone as they drove away. Could this be true? My beloved uncle, my mom's brother, my cousin's father? The shocking narrative ran through my mind, *Maria, your brother was in a head-on collision with a drunk driver driving home from work and died.*

It suddenly registered. It was him in the ambulance that passed by just a couple hours earlier! And that roadblock that deterred me from driving by the accident scene is where my uncle took his last breath.

I began to shake, the noise of my surroundings faded into the distance, while everything disintegrated. All of the thought forms I was plugged into earlier and prior to that moment became a distant dream, no longer worthy of my attention. I was struck with the reality that life as I once knew had changed in an instant.

It was no longer significant to consider a concert tonight, or to focus on my headache, or wonder if I should leave the state to go to grad school? The chatter from the cynical judgment in my mind, towards the blessed man who walked through my line, no longer held value. In fact, I was humbled, and felt remorse that I could ever have had judgmental thoughts towards him... now all I could feel for him was love.

Everything became surreal. Our family members began to trickle into my uncle's house. My precious aunt spoke out loud the details of her beloved husband's death with such a strength that I thought for a moment, *This must be a dream and we will all wake up soon.* We all floated around the house, dispersing in whichever direction and in whatever way we each needed to cope with the circumstances.

It was getting late. My brother, cousin and I walked home in silence, to try to get some sleep. We laid down in my bed nestled close together, with an unspoken desire to find comfort in each other's company.

I awoke to the sweet melody of enchanting birds luring me into a trance. The warmth of the morning sun peered through my window and caressed me with an outstretched embrace. Absent of thought, with a soft-hearted smile, I peacefully opened my eyes and noticed my cousin laying quietly to my right, and my dear brother sleeping to the left. In a fraction of a second, it registered what had happened last night. A loud noise came crashing through my head as I restructured into the awful reality that my uncle was gone, never to be seen again. Thoughts came shooting in like a cannon blaze disrupting the enchanting melody. I broke down in tears as the pain returned. As I remembered my uncle's death, the peaceful fabric and interconnectedness disintegrated. Yet, I could not help but notice a lingering mystical presence.

The days following the sudden news were filled with countless moments of disbelief, as I watched my family deeply grieve. Every family member coped with this tragic loss differently, and I witnessed how the impact blasted us all open, into deeper love for each other.

I stood in the kitchen amidst the grief of my loved ones who gathered together at my parents' house. The field of collective pain was palatable. I tried to escape what I was feeling, as the side door invited me to slip outside onto the deck where I could be alone amongst the canopy of the woods in our backyard. I felt angry and defeated as I pounded my hand on the wooden deck. "Why? How?" I yelled.

In that very moment, I was met with a loving response to my inquiry, touched by a generous wave of grace that catapulted me into unity consciousness. The silence was deafening as I was overtaken into a trancelike feeling of *d*éjà vu. I stood in awe, with an understanding that my uncle was going to die, like I'd experienced it already. I became expanded into the eternal moment where the akashic records and eternal love exists, and where I had a knowing that this was *supposed* to happen.

My uncle was a very kind and respectable man of service and was celebrated for weeks following his death. We gathered at the final ceremony held at the state capital, where he was honored for his exemplary service as a state representative.

We were all exhausted and drove home in silence, where I was finally able to let down in the back seat of my parents' car. Flooded with a plethora of memories, I recapitulated my life with my uncle and was struck with the reality that we would not see him again in this world. I somberly gazed out the window as we drove up the hill to get back to our familiar neighborhood. The sun was shining, children were joyfully playing in their yards, a middle-aged man was mowing the lawn, birds were soaring on the currents of the soft wind. I noticed how everything was alive and still moving, even though my uncle was gone. Suddenly, I sensed something sacred and felt my uncle's presence. A soft voice accompanied by a deep knowing dropped into my consciousness, *Nothing ever dies, life is eternal.* My uncle's presence was undeniable and became part of everything; his spirit was everywhere. My heart opened and I was swept into the arms and unity of eternal love, where I recognized that I, too, am part of this sacred symphony of love. I became one with all of creation and felt euphoria in knowing my uncle was alive.

Throughout my life, I yearned to know more than what we were being taught. The divine hears us when we are sincere in our asking. My earnest, consistent inquiry led me towards the grace and faithfulness of life's generous reflections, where I received infinite whispers of truth and experiences that led me home to my heart's infinite love.

This experience forever changed my life and guided me to new heights of awareness. In the duality of my personal experience, as I was impacted with the pain and grief at the loss of my dear uncle, I was simultaneously caressed and enveloped into a vortex of love, where I experienced undeniable truths beyond the pain body. I learned I could live my life with an open heart and focus on what is real, from moment to moment, and not wait for someone to die in order to love.

Death is a great teacher and a sacred domain that opens a portal into hidden mysteries. One thing that is undeniable is that our bodies and the dream we presently inhabit, will at some point disintegrate and transform. As we encounter sudden loss, most everything we once deemed important becomes insignificant and we are given direct access to the divine, where we can awaken to our capacity to love and to what is most true.

We do not have to wait until a loved one dies, or the abrupt loss of a relationship or job, or have an encounter with a natural disaster, in order for us to share our love. Every moment is an opportunity to let go and open to compassionate love and allow grace to flow in and out without restriction.

As I faced the death of my uncle, so many people came forth and expressed their heartfelt love and acts of kindness. After his death, the love and appreciation we had for each other as a family reached new, unexpected heights. My uncle continued to make his presence known to me with ongoing communication, which was a constant gracious reinforcement that we never die.

It was a difficult passage for our family to lose my uncle so early in life, and yet what he taught me through that experience was priceless. It set the stage towards a trajectory of communion with God, to discover how to love and open my heart, and ultimately led me to the realization of our inherent divinity. My uncle's death brought me here to deliver this message to you today; to remember the truth that we never die, we are eternal love and we are divine. I am eternally grateful.

# Nina Palmieri

Nina Palmieri, MS, BS, the founder and leader of *A New Earth Movement*, is an initiated Nagual Woman, ceremonial leader, teacher, spiritual counselor and healing facilitator. She has spent the last twenty-five years educating and empowering individuals and groups to gain self-awareness and transformational tools in order to help them achieve personal freedom.

Through extensive apprenticeships with Don Miguel Ruiz, Doña Barbara Emrys and other respected Elders and Indigenous wisdom keepers, Nina has gained the gift of perception into all living things, along with the ability to deeply penetrate the illusions of the psyche. Through aligning herself with the plane of divine wisdom she has become an impeccable channel for the highest light and truth as well as a seer, a gift that she expresses and transmits to her students and the world.

Nina brings these profound gifts together with a Toltec approach in her deeply life-changing individual and group alchemical healing and spiritual counseling sessions, wisdom teachings, programs, rituals and retreats created to heal, restore and reveal our highest innate soul's purpose.

⊕ www.anewearthmovement.org
◎ @anewearthmovement
Scan QR code to learn more about Nina Palmieri.

# chapter 29

## Hotel Bedouin

*by Guru Matthew John*

Youssef and I had restarted the *Eagles* cassette for probably the twentieth time in a row.

We were traveling down a desert highway, though not in the dark – and without paying any heed to the speed limit signage the locals treated as mere suggestions.

Never in my wildest dreams did I think I'd be speeding through the untouched Middle Eastern desert in a manual transmission taxicab from the 1980s, jamming to *Hotel California* with a native Arab-speaking man who, though married, was madly in love with an American woman who rode in his cab, once, a decade ago.

But here I was, gleefully singing one of the greatest rock hits of all time for the twenty-first time in a row, with one of the only men I'd ever met who could sing as loudly – and certainly as out-of-tune – as me.

Outside the cab window, radiation from the sun's heat rose up through the air from the asphalt road. The landscape was about as far removed from the green summer paradise of my home in Western New York as one could get.

Youssef, a height (but not voice) challenged Jordanian man in his fifties, had a nice picture of him and his family on the dash, placed ornamentally among religious paraphernalia. But in the "secret" cubby-hole above the rearview mirror was his most prized possession – a passport-sized photo of an American woman, probably thirty-five-ish, to whom he had given a tour around Jordan a decade prior.

Having me, a young American buck, in the front of his cab excited him about the possibility of reuniting with his long-lost love from the other side of the globe.

On my way to Jordan, I had experienced, firsthand, Middle Easterners' fascination with anything American.

I had boarded a ferry that was as gigantic and plodding as the container ship my eBay-purchased, winch-less twenty-six-foot 1979 Ranger sailboat nearly collided with in dense fog, on another wild adventure I had undertaken a few years prior.

The ferryboat was packed to the gills with Egyptian and Jordanian families. My Caucasian face, cargo shorts, and New York Mets cap, stood out like a *Where's Waldo* cartoon. Standing in the lengthy passport control line, which felt longer than a summer Sunday afternoon at *Disney World*, two smiling civilian men approached me and inquired where I was from.

When I told them I was American, they just sort of chuckled –as if I'd said I was a wizard. I sheepishly pulled out my passport, and one of the men said excitedly, "C'mon, you don't wait."

I heard whispers and felt the excitement of the families behind me as they realized I wasn't just appearing to be American. The two men shuffled me right to the front of the line, and just as if I was holding a FastPass at *Magic Mountain*, I was instantly through passport control.

Since I was a kid, I'd always been fascinated with exploring places and cultures far from home. I always wanted to do anything that your average tourist wouldn't dare to do.

Leveraging the perks of being an only child, somehow I talked my parents into undertaking some wild adventures across North America – seeing wild horses rumble past in the Magdalen Islands of the North Atlantic; hiking in summer snow to 10,000 feet in the Canadian Rockies, joined in the rear by a pack of rams; surviving a freak windstorm in a rickety French Canadian canoe in the mountains of the Gaspé Peninsula of Québec; and seeing the Northern Lights after relieving oneself in what was purported to be North America's most famous (and celebrity-frequented) authentic Alaskan outhouse, in the bizarre town of Tok.

Now an adult, I was enthralled with traveling and exploring. But this visit to Jordan was a step up from any adventure I'd embarked on prior. I was also spiritually in uncharted territory, ever since my heart was shattered into a million pieces the summer prior.

I called her from the ferry, using ten international minutes for what, to me, was the most important purpose in the world.

She didn't always pick up, but tonight she did. It was afternoon for her back in Buffalo. I was wedged between a metal wall and a rack of life preservers on the top deck of the massive vessel. Bathing in the bright moonlight on the Gulf of Aqaba, I attempted, for the hundredth time, to get her back.

Hearing her voice was both comforting and gut-wrenching at the same time – like watching a tragic movie where you know how it ends but feel a strange sense of comfort seeing the tragedy unfold anyway.

Here I was halfway across the globe, but due to the magic – or curse – of a cell phone, I could desperately hang on by a thread to a life I had energetically outgrown. If she had said, "Matt, I want you back," I would have, without a second thought, found my way via Expedia back to Buffalo, and ran breathlessly to her door.

After I had used enough international minutes to fulfill my addiction, we ended the call. I let the tears flow freely under the full moon. *We always did this on a full moon.*

As Youssef gushed about how the American woman was the most beautiful lady he'd ever seen, I chuckled inside at how delusional he was. I was saddened to think he had put this fantastical pipe dream on a pedestal, way above his actual wife and kids.

But was it really that much more delusional than me obsessively trying to coax my ex-partner to come back? Despite our frequent communication – filled with *what-ifs* – she was with another guy... and I was alone.

Every cool accomplishment and experience felt incomplete because she wasn't there with me. When she picked up the phone or read my texts, I got to experience a glimpse of that feeling of completion – but it was a bastardized version, like traveling to Paris in virtual reality versus cramping your neck to marvel at the majesty of the Eiffel Tower scraping the clouds in real life.

When the ferry arrived in Aqaba at sunrise, I walked about the beach, riding that adrenaline high you get when foregoing a night's sleep. I passed by several women, covered head-to-toe in black *jilbaab*, walking with their young children on the rocky beach.

I smiled and waved. The looks they gave me back were a mix of awe and fear. I realized, not only was I not in Kansas anymore, *but Kansas wasn't even on the map*. I felt alone, but freer than I'd felt in a while.

The next morning, I checked out of the small beachside hotel in Aqaba and approached the first yellow cab I saw. The almighty universe had arranged a meeting between Matthew and Youssef.

This grand meeting between two humble unknowns was seemingly insignificant in the grand scheme of things – but in a very real way, was just as significant as any synchronous meeting of souls disguised in human form. It was no more or less important than Reagan meeting Gorbachev just a few weeks before I left the warmth and safety of my mother's womb in October 1986.

Youssef was thrilled at the prospect of spending the whole day with me. The plan was to reach Petra by early afternoon, then return to Aqaba in the evening.

On the way to Petra, Youssef enthusiastically insisted that I eat lunch. Of course, my gifted-of-gab cabbie knew everyone at the restaurant. The Kingdom of Jordan encompasses over 34,000 square miles – about the size of Maine – but my American-loving driver seemed to know everyone in the country.

Back on the road, Youssef excitedly informed me that we were just about a half hour from Petra, as he pointed to the cassette deck and rhetorically asked, "Again?" We giggled like children as the iconic opening guitar riff rang out from the aged speakers.

Of course I made *besties* with a cabbie. It was in my blood.

My father put himself through college driving a New York City yellow, surviving long nights and occasional gunpoint robberies. His father drove a cab for six decades in New York, retiring only when he hit his ninth decade of life. In the evenings he would fight in illegal street boxing matches in Brooklyn, strengthening his muscles to ward off the frequent thefts he would face in his day job.

Youssef certainly was much more amicable than your average harried NYC cabbie. I wondered if my grandfather would have enjoyed driving a cab on open highways, winding through red rock skyscrapers, rather than gridlocked streets under concrete ones.

We had arrived at Petra.

Petra is an ancient city carved into rock in the middle of the Arabian Desert. The city was first settled at least nine thousand years ago, making it one of the most ancient archaeological sites on the planet. One historian[1] has even suggested that Petra – not Mecca – was the original holy city of Islam.

Not only are the pillared buildings built entirely into massive rock faces visually exhilarating, but from the moment you enter the sacred city through a rock tunnel called *Siq* that seems more suited for Mars than Earth, you palpably feel like you are in an energetically significant – and powerful – place.

My afternoon was extraordinary; I felt like Aladdin riding the magic carpet. After drinking my fourth delicious tea of the day, served to me by a bright-eyed youngster who wanted to know everything about

---

[1] Noted from the work of Dan Gibson – *Early Islamic Qiblas: A survey of mosques built between 1AH/622 CE and 263 AH/876 CE.*

life in America, I found myself wandering solo through a narrow rock passageway, feeling like I was traversing a higher-dimensional plane.

I'd had inklings of extra-sensory perception, especially after the break-up. It was as if the heartbreak was so severe, it had ripped my third eye open too. I had seen and heard spirits and ghosts. I had begun to feel what others were thinking before the words came out of their mouth.

But as I stood in front of an ancient doorway carved into the rock wall that any sane person (at least as deemed by societal consensus) would say is nothing more than a carved rock face, I felt something more. *Much more.*

As I pressed my right hand into the rock face, *I felt my hand go through the rock.* In my third eye, I saw my arm go through, all the way up to my bicep. Astonished, I pulled my arm out and tried again. *My arm went through the rock once more.*

I pressed my face up against the rock. In my third eye, I saw a mysterious realm inside, where everything was hued with blue.

Back in the cab, I shared my experience with my new, best Jordanian friend. He laughed it off but told me he did believe there were supernatural things happening at Petra.

We were having so much fun together, and I was feeling so expanded after my contact with an alternate dimension. Not wanting the party to end, Youssef suggested I explore another popular site among Western tourists – Wadi Rum, or the *Valley of the Moon.*

Wadi Rum is a breathtaking valley carved into the red sandstone. Nomadic tribes have occupied the area since prehistoric times, leaving their marks via petroglyphs on the valley walls. It was the filming site of *Lawrence of Arabia* in 1962, pretty much making it the entire initial basis for Jordan's fledgling tourism industry. Later on, in the years after my visit, it served as the filming location for a pair of *Star Wars* films. It really does look like the surface of Mars.

After yapping with the Bedouin camp folks for a good hour, Youssef departed. As he drove away, I wondered if his fantasy of the American Dream was his *Hotel California.*

I ventured out into the desert once again, with the sun getting low in the sky. Sweaty but curious, I trudged through the sun-beaten *sandscape,* my Walmart-purchased New Balance sneakers making the only discernible footprints. About as far away from a Walmart as one could get, I passed a small village where men, women, and children of the Zalabieh tribe lived peacefully and humbly in the company of the red rocks.

A group of children waved to me. I waved back and smiled. In my ears were Apple earbuds connected via cord to an iPhone. I was jamming to the comforting sounds of Berkeley, California's *Green Day*.

I felt really, really *free*.

Yet, in my head, I looked forward to telling her all about my interaction with the nomadic tribe. *Does technology bind us to our past?*

As I smiled and studied the carefree children, I envied their relative disconnection from the technological world. I coveted the slow-moving Arab culture. In my travels through Egypt and Jordan, I learned that things always happened on their own time – usually after tea and hookah.

The next day, I ventured out into the desert again, my Mets cap my version of an explorer's hat. This time, I allowed the subtle rustle of the wind rearranging the sand to tickle my auditory fancy.

I was determined to make it deep into the desert, much farther than any other tourist would have been.

I never wanted to do what tourists did. My dad and I were the only two adventurous enough to summit Mount Wilcox on that snowy late summer day when I was a teenager. We watched the heated tour buses parking in the paved lot at the Columbia Icefield from ten thousand feet in the air, as we battled icy gusts at the summit.

I wandered for hours, utilizing the outline of Wadi Rum Village in the rear distance as a compass. Deep in the untouched desert, my inner child had me summit a 200-foot-tall red rock vista, accompanied by a very friendly and curious tan-furred dog.

No matter where the universe has led me on this wonderful planet, animals have always found me. *Animals always know my heart.*

From atop the vista, I saw where the dog had come from. There seemed to be someone living alone in a hut beneath the shadow cast by the towering geological feature! I had to find out more.

As I circled the rock formation and came within a few hundred yards of her, it's as if I stepped into a wormhole that brought me back in time. *Way back.*

There she was: a Bedouin woman, a woman of the Earth. Dressed in a traditional white cotton *thawb,* she washed her clothing by hand on a wooden washboard. She lived in a tiny solo hut made simply from clay – accompanied by animals who knew her heart; sheep, dogs, goats and camels.

I waved to her. She gave me a look very similar to the one I received on the beach back in Aqaba, *sans* the fear. It was a look of shock to see someone dressed as I was – but it was wrapped up in a peaceful openness.

As I stared at this scene from thousands of years ago, I felt a mix of awe and jealousy creep up from deep within. *This woman couldn't possibly have a worry in the world,* I thought, *other than the scorpions perhaps.*

All the entertaining pieces of the modern world that I was accustomed to indulging in, ran through my mind. This woman lived without any of them – not even a television or a radio. I didn't want to give up my *Green Day* or Mets games. *Would you?*

As the new and old worlds met, a mutual acknowledgment was felt. *She was me. I was her.* We were the same, just wearing different outfits that the almighty costume designer lovingly created for us.

I had left home to escape the shadow of the woman I couldn't let go of. I found a woman on the other side of the world who, in an instant, showed me that I didn't need anything I thought I needed.

I trekked back with my cell phone turned off, *feeling more Bedouin than American.*

I remembered that the adventurous, funny, exuberant, optimistic self I adored when I was with my ex-lover never actually went away. *He was here now.* And he didn't actually need the reflection of a woman to shine in all his glory.

The last line of *Hotel California* is so ominous and defeating, like the final pages of *1984*. We all have our beasts, but as we become wiser, we become free of self-defeating prophecies. In reality, whenever we choose on a deep level to check out of the hotel, *the night man opens the door right up for us.*

I thought I was chasing a person, but I was really just desperately searching for myself. And I realized that self was always there, just waiting for me to believe in him.

In the years to follow, I went on to traverse the most profound spiritual journey. Through the internal and external twists and turns, it has always led me back to where it started – myself. Every trial and tribulation has been carefully crafted to lead me back to me.

*And I love what I've found.*

# Guru Matthew John

Guru Matthew John – *The Guru from the Stars*™ – is an internationally recognized modern Spiritual Guru for the New Age. He teaches Ascension, self-knowledge, self-mastery, and humanity's connection with Star Beings to his global audience. As the founder of the *You Are A Divine Human*™ movement, Guru Matthew John is on a mission to assist people in stepping into their highest Divinity, power, and purpose by knowing and healing themselves deeply on every level.

Guru Matthew John is a renowned Spiritual Teacher, Intuitive, Psychic, Astrologer, Medium, Energy Healer, Medical Intuitive, Trance Channeler, and Spiritual Life Coach—as well as a celebrated Speaker, Author, Filmmaker, and Podcast Host.

Guru Matthew John is a spiritual leader for the Golden Age. He has a unique ability to see the big picture and connect the dots. He makes spiritual and occult knowledge understandable and relatable to people at all stages of their spiritual journey.

Guru Matthew John makes his teachings accessible and affordable to a global audience via his monthly *Ascending as One*™ *Academy*. He also offers the opportunity to connect intimately with his wisdom and guidance at multiple in-person retreats per year.

Guru Matthew John resides with his beloved Ascension Dog Sebastian in beautiful Western New York, U.S.A. In his free time, he enjoys exploring nature, sports, music, and photography.

⊕ www.youareadivinehuman.org
◎ @gurumatthewjohn
Scan QR code to learn more about Guru Matthew John.

## chapter 30

# Invited to Remember

*by Christina L. Woods*

By then, I was stretched thin. The kind of tired no sleep could fix.

I did it because I had to. The job, the benefits, the stability – it all mattered. But I hated how it pulled me from the people I loved. I hated missing bedtime stories and not being there to read my kids' body language, trying to understand what they needed, how they were feeling.

Even with help from a partner who said *it was handled*, I still lined everything up before I left: appointments, homework, groceries, errands. But while I was gone, the calls came in. The energy was clear, *they didn't want me gone. They needed me.*

I was trying to give them stability. But nothing felt stable. Deep down, I didn't feel seen. My mind kept scanning, my body braced – and I was tired of holding it all.

That Saturday morning, jet-lagged and tired, I stepped into the backyard. My home looked forgotten. The planter beds were overgrown, the weeds curling through the cracks. The patio tiles were dusty, the yard unwatered. Even the dog mess hadn't been picked up. It didn't feel like neglect – it felt like no one had noticed. Like no one had cared. And in that moment, I felt forgotten too.

The dirt was dry and crumbly. I pulled at the weeds with no plan, just trying to do something. I didn't know what I needed. I just knew I couldn't keep standing still. I crouched low and kept pulling. I wasn't gardening. I was grasping, trying to ground myself. Trying to feel something.

I was in my mismatched pajamas, no bra, sweaty under the morning sun. Not a moment you'd post on Instagram. I needed something to hold onto. Something simple. Something that was mine.

As I was bent down, trying to keep it together, my husband slid open the door and said, "I'm going to the beach," closing it behind him.

It wasn't about him. He didn't know what I was carrying. But something cracked in the quiet, like the ache had finally outgrown its hiding place.

Is it possible to feel completely lost inside a life you have built? To wonder, if maybe, it's not the life that's broken, but the part of you that's still hiding in it.

That's how it felt. Like I was performing a version of myself so well, even I couldn't find the real me underneath. From the outside, I had it all together. But inside, a quiet war. No matter how much I gave, it never soothed what felt off.

My boys were teenagers, growing, busy, becoming their own people. They weren't supposed to carry the weight of what I was feeling. But I loved them fiercely. I wanted to give them something truer, something softer. I just didn't know how.

I had no idea what I needed, only that I couldn't keep holding it all in. Something in me was unraveling and I was too tired to stop it.

I just stood there, the heat pressing against my face, staring at the sliding door that had just been closed.

Then came the stillness. Quiet. Heavy.

Something in me stirred. I didn't have answers yet, but I felt the ache of them rising.

Then I heard it.

A voice – not in my head, not a thought. It came from just above and to the right of me; calm, clear, almost amused, like a best friend who'd had enough of my BS:

*Why are you complaining about what doesn't make you happy, instead of doing what does?*

Time stopped. It was like lightning moved through me; clarity, truth, power and something else – remembering. The air felt different. Brighter. My skin buzzed, like it had heard something my ears hadn't caught.

In that moment, I knew, without logic, without planning, without resistance, that it wasn't just burnout. It was my soul saying: *Enough. It's time.*

I couldn't keep living like this.

I couldn't keep abandoning myself.

I didn't want to feel this way anymore.

Or keep proving my worth, like it was something I had to earn.

I wanted my kids to see and know love – true, honest, connected love.

I didn't know what would come next. I just knew I was done with everything that wasn't real.

I was done feeling small, buried under the weight of trying to prove my worth to everyone, including me. I just wanted to be... Me. Fully.

That voice, whether it was my soul, God or the universe, it was the wake-up call I hadn't known I was waiting for.

And I smiled. Just slightly. Because I realized I was being lovingly, divinely called out. Not punished, but invited; invited to remember myself.

Maybe in sharing this, I'm inviting you to remember the voice inside you, the one that's been whispering: *You don't have to live this way anymore.*

If no one's ever said it before, let me be the first: *You're allowed to begin again.*

I entered a world already bracing for impact – everyone was just trying to survive.

I was born to teen parents, kids themselves, doing the best they could, but overwhelmed. What I remember most is how it felt in my body:

fear, confusion, instability. I absorbed the tension in the room, the bracing-for-impact energy that shaped my nervous system before I even had words.

I remember being two years old watching my parents fight. I felt their chaos, their disconnection. And I remember thinking: *Who's going to take care of me?*

That question didn't come with tears. It came with silence. A knowing. A decision.

Something in me knew, *this is how it is. Be quiet. Be good. Make it easier. That's how you stay safe.*

It was just me and my little brother back then. I adored him. He was my joy, my anchor. And even though I was just a kid, I took on the job of protecting him. I didn't know how – I just knew I had to.

I used to whisper, "Come into my room... It's going to be okay."

Even in the chaos, I was attuned. I didn't think I was magical, but I was wide open. I absorbed everything; seen and unseen. I could read a room like a map. My sensitivity was survival. I was energetically porous, hyperaware of everything – except how to protect myself.

There wasn't room for emotions. Everyone was trying to keep it together. My big feelings didn't have a place, so I tucked them away and stopped expecting anyone to notice.

The babysitters we had were both loving and terrifying. Raised voices, slammed doors, hot and cold energy. That push-pull wired itself into my nervous system. Love could turn on a dime – warm one minute, explosive the next. I never knew what version I'd get.

It became too much to stay in my body. So I left – not physically, but energetically. That was the beginning of my disconnection.

Looking back, I see it now; part of my soul's curriculum. The forgetting before the remembering.

I became hypervigilant. A chameleon. I tracked moods, adapted constantly, read the room before anyone said a word. It was how I stayed safe.

In high school, that survival turned into performance. I was the straight-A student, class vice president, homecoming queen. Always doing, always achieving, always making sure no one saw how unsure I felt inside. Pleasing people gave me control. It looked like confidence but it wasn't – it was a mask.

And no amount of praise could reach the part of me that still felt invisible.

That belief was reinforced over and over. Maybe you know what that's like. Maybe you've lived it or maybe you're still in it.

And if you are... I want you to know something:

*You're not broken.*

*You're not alone.*

*There's another way through.*

I didn't know it yet, but my soul was gathering the wisdom it would one day use to help others remember their worth too.

From the outside, I had it all; a successful career, a beautiful family, a home, vacations. And I did love those things. But I had built them from a place inside me that believed I needed them to feel safe, to feel worthy, to feel enough.

I lived in survival mode and called it achievement. I was the first in my mother's family to go to college. That milestone wasn't just about education, it felt like redemption. I believed success would protect us from shame, from struggle. That I could rescue us, *make it okay.*

I built a multi-six-figure career, led national teams. I wanted my kids to have more safety, stability and love. That was always my heart's intention. If you've ever looked back and realized you were parenting through pain – you know. I didn't always have the tools but the love and desire to protect them was fierce.

The pressure to be everything never stopped. And I still felt like I was failing.

No matter how much I achieved, it was never enough to silence the voice inside that said, *You're not enough.*

Somewhere along the way, the space between us grew quiet. There was love and pain. A growing distance we didn't know how to name.

I'd pour myself into planning birthdays, organizing before trips, doing most of the invisible labor to keep things running. And still, my husband would say, "Why can't you just relax?" The more I tried to create order, the more misunderstood I felt. I wasn't trying to be controlling, I was trying to create peace. To offer love. To build the kind of safety I never had. I didn't know I was doing it through survival.

Some days I sat at my desk – lipstick, heels, awards – feeling like I was disappearing. Watching my life from far away. I had built a beautiful life but I wasn't really living it. I'd been living behind a mask I didn't even know I was wearing; a mask I'd worn before I could even speak. It was never safe to be me, so I became who I thought I needed to be.

I used to think panic attacks happened to *other people*. Until one day, mid-sentence in a meeting, I had to excuse myself, race home and ask my kids' babysitter to drive me to the ER. I thought I was dying. I remember the nurse shouting, *"Breathe! You're having a panic attack!"*

That moment cracked something open in me – shame, confusion and something else I couldn't name; a flicker of truth.

And then came the moment, the one I now call *the garden moment* – where it all caught up to me.

I came home from yet another business trip tired and aching to feel something like peace. And in the quiet of my backyard, something shifted. It wasn't dramatic. It wasn't loud. It was subtle, but seismic.

A voice – clear, calm, not mine, asked:

*Why are you complaining about what doesn't make you happy, instead of doing what does?*

Time froze. Something in me cracked open. And in that stillness, I heard the truth I had been running from:

I couldn't keep doing this. I couldn't keep abandoning myself. I didn't want to feel this way anymore.

It wasn't about a plan. It was a choice to stop becoming who I thought I had to be and remember who I was.

It wasn't just exhaustion, it was my soul speaking. Time to come home. Time to walk back to myself.

I didn't change everything overnight. But something in me knew, a line had been drawn. And from that moment forward, I couldn't unknow it. I had opened the door to something more.

Possibility.

Grace.

A new way of being.

I finally listened to the part I had silenced.

Maybe you've had a moment like that too. Not a breakdown – a breakthrough. The kind of moment that whispers, *You don't have to keep living like this.*

That was the breaking point.

Not when it all fell apart... But when I stopped pretending it was working.

And in that quiet, I chose to begin again.

After the garden moment, I dove into the inner work like my life depended on it – because it did. Therapy. Hypnotherapy. Spiritual retreats. I needed to understand why I felt broken when nothing on the outside looked that way.

In therapy, a memory I had buried for decades began to rise, something I'd once tucked away so far I convinced myself it never happened. I was eight. A neighbor's relative. A moment that split my childhood into before and after.

I remember sitting on their couch, frozen. His body pressing against mine.

Then the voice inside: **Get out.**

I ran. I stood behind the bush, shaking and made a decision no eight-year-old should ever have to make – to carry it alone.

I told no one. I buried it so deep I forgot it was real. But secrets like that don't stay buried, they echo in every part of you. It shaped how I loved, how I worked, how I saw myself. Shame wrapped itself around everything; my success, my motherhood, my sense of self.

For years, I believed the lie that it was my fault; my silence, my shorts, my shame. But the truth came slowly. And one day, sitting across from my therapist, the words came through me like a prayer: *I am not bad.*

Whether or not your story looks like mine, we all carry parts of ourselves we're afraid to face. But those are the very places our healing begins.

What we bury doesn't disappear... it waits. And when we finally turn toward it, it becomes the very path home.

I used to think healing meant *fixing*. That if I just worked hard enough, cleared enough energy, read enough books, I'd be whole. But healing, it turns out, is remembering. It's not becoming someone new. It's returning to who you always were.

For me, that meant leaving a career that no longer fit, building a business rooted in service, and stepping fully into the woman I was always becoming. It meant listening to my intuition, opening to divine guidance, and walking in deep partnership with something greater. But the most unexpected gift? *Compassion.*

It's not always a voice in the garden that changes your life. Sometimes it's a whisper that rises quietly from within. And the moment you choose to listen... everything shifts. The more I gave compassion to myself – the messy parts, shadow parts – the more I had for the world.

And isn't that how we change things? Not by fixing or forcing. But by softening. By being.

If I could whisper to the part of you that's still afraid, still hiding, I'd say this:

*There is nothing wrong with you. You are not broken. The world just taught you to forget who you are.*

*Your essence is good. Your voice matters. Your timing is divine.*

And when you begin to trust that, when you stop abandoning yourself to belong, that's when life begins to feel like yours again.

That's when your heart remembers its way home.

And from that place, barefoot and awake, you begin to walk toward the life that's been waiting for you all along.

Not because someone told you how.
But because you finally turned inward.
And listened.

**The answers were always there.**

**Waiting to be remembered.**

# Christina L. Woods

Christina L. Woods is an internationally recognized clinical hypnotherapist, Advanced Medical Intuitive Technique® Practitioner, ThetaHealing® Practitioner, empowerment coach and energy healer trained in multiple modalities. She is the CEO and founder of Wise Woods Hypnotherapy, Inc., where she helps capable women stop proving and start receiving, guiding them to break free from the patterns that keep them second-guessing, people-pleasing or proving their worth.

After three decades in corporate leadership, Christina experienced a profound awakening that led her to leave behind what no longer fit and step fully into her purpose. Today, she combines neuroscience, energy healing and spiritual insight to help clients remember the truth of who they are – and reclaim their power from the inside out.

Christina has been featured in Brainz Magazine and on over one hundred US and international podcasts and radio shows.

🌐 www.christinalwoods.com
📷 @christina.lwoods
Scan QR code to learn more about Christina L. Woods.

chapter

# 31

# Inner Rebirth: How I Rediscovered My Strength and Life's Purpose

*by Victoria Basil*

Who am I? What is my purpose in this life? Why am I going through so many hardships? Why does everything happen so painfully? Can I still go on? Why am I not like everyone else? Why can't I enjoy life the way others do? Why don't I feel "at home"? Where is that place where I will feel happy? Will I ever be happy, even if everything seems perfect on the surface? Does happiness come from the outside? These questions, and many others, have guided me to seek more, and to begin opening myself up to something greater!

One of the cornerstones of my belief system, the faith that there is something more than these mere human bodies, was religion. I come from a simple family of devout people, who carved their own path in life as they deemed most fitting for themselves. Religion was, for them, the foundation that kept them connected to this higher power, giving them the confidence that there exists something more powerful than we can imagine. From a young age, I was taught to go to church, to pray, to stay in touch with this divine force, even though, back then, I saw and attributed this force as something outside of myself. Connecting with God through the church and religion helped me believe in this majestic force, full of wisdom and love.

God, or *the source*, as I call it, is within us all. There is no good or evil, no bad or good people – everything is part of an experience our soul chooses to live. Though Orthodox Christianity was laid as my foundation (both of my grandparents, now deceased, were monastics at the Căpriana and Răciula Monasteries in the Republic of Moldova), I always felt that the soul cannot be confined to just this one life. It didn't seem logical to me that millions of people would go to heaven or hell after death. Could it be that you live just one life, mess it up, or fail to learn or fulfill your mission? I felt that God and His creation were limitless, and this conviction pushed me to seek answers, to understand how it could be possible for heaven to have enough space for millions upon millions of souls.

Deep within my soul, I found it hard to believe that our planet was God's only creation. I felt intensely, in every fiber of my being, that science has a close connection to religion and the divine force. I always saw a bridge between these two paths, though certain aspects were taboo to discuss or imagine, even considered sinful.

This desire to seek answers deeper than what society or my childhood had shown me – when I felt that religion alone didn't provide all the answers my soul craved – led me on a profound journey. Through both pleasant and painful experiences, I opened myself to spirituality, to techniques and tools that helped me energetically release all the pain, emotions and suffering I thought defined me.

In my darkest moments, I sought the inner voice to guide me and say, *Breathe, Victoria. Just breathe.* I was afraid to breathe deeply because my defense mechanism had taught me to express anger more often, to fight life rather than accept it, to acknowledge my emotions and give them space to exist.

I always felt that life had been harsh with me, even from a young age, but only now have I understood why all the experiences I went through were necessary for my soul's evolution.

My spiritual path began dramatically in adolescence, with periods or experiences one might call exorcisms, followed shortly by deep soul-level healings and the permanent release of those situations. Another, even deeper wave of awakening began abruptly after two painful events.

For years, my desire to become a mother overwhelmed me. There were times when every step I took toward motherhood failed. I thought I was defective, that I needed to be fixed, that I had too much pain, blockages, and unprocessed emotions from childhood – all of which made me blame myself, believing I didn't deserve it, that God was punishing me. My entire mindset and way of acting were built on this programming.

I needed to connect with myself, to do inner work and to have the support of my galactic family to realize that what I felt didn't define me, that I could, and was allowed to, become a mother, but at the right time and with the right partner. My soul had chosen certain circumstances, before coming here into the physical plane, and this was part of those choices it knew were for the best. No matter how much I tried to force or control this desire, it only led me to profound despair.

Running from myself and the inner pain drove me to a temporary solution, which, at the time, I saw as a way to cope: alcohol. At every event or party I attended, I drowned my sorrow and numbed my senses, and all those emotions, so I wouldn't feel the inner void, pretending I was happy like everyone else. When I drank more, my channels of perception opened even wider. I began seeing more of the unseen world and receiving information about people, without intending to. I remember moments when I could connect to people's energy through a simple photo, clearly sensing whether someone was deceased or not.

Soon after, a second event followed, where I felt my entire inner being had literally died. When you stray further and further from your path, God allows you to realize it, giving you a final wake-up call. For me, this wake-up call came in the form of betrayal, a heartbreak from the romantic relationship I was in. Being disconnected and hiding in that "perfect" bubble, where no one knew or saw what I felt or experienced, sank me deeper into an inner hell.

I began to question my faith in God or the divine plan, and for a while, I completely disconnected from that profound connection. Then came a cascade of situations; a car accident, degenerative bone issues, various illnesses, weight gain, excessive eating, all intensely showing me that the path I'd chosen was no longer aligned with who and what I'd decided to experience next. And here, even more questions arose: *How can God be so harsh? Did I really come here to suffer endlessly? What did I do wrong to deserve this life? Why, when you love and are loved unconditionally and mutually by that soul, does everything turn upside down?* Endless "whys" flooded my mind, leading me to a period of intense overthinking.

I was in a deep state of victimhood, believing all these circumstances came from outside me, not from within. Every particle of my soul was fragmented into tiny pieces, preventing me from finding meaning in this existence or wanting to continue my journey in this plane.

Over the years, an inner voice guided me to various therapists and psychologists, both in the Republic of Moldova and the United States, but every effort I made to give life another chance, to understand and know myself better, seemed in vain. I distanced myself from family, friends, acquaintances, and loved ones because being around people felt uncomfortable. Hiding the inner pain that screamed to be heard, felt impossible.

This was just the beginning of a wonderful awakening process.

I started doing various research; reading became my only friend and help back then, even though it was never my favorite thing. I began with self-help books, psychology, near-death experiences, numerology, energetics and spirituality, books about the Akashic records, and so on. I started delving deeper into this side of spirituality. That's when I stumbled upon a book completely different for me, about the Arcturians – a benevolent extraterrestrial civilization supporting humanity in this planetary ascension. Every piece of information I learned about various ET races and civilizations, beings from higher planes of Creation, reignited that inner spark waiting to be reactivated. Drawn to such complex information and directions, my family began saying I was "with the cosmos", though I'd always been considered the black sheep of the family.

Even as a young child, I could connect with advanced ET civilizations and races. I could see the world with both my physical eyes and my third eye – that invisible world imperceptible to the human eye. But back then, there were no logical explanations for what I saw or experienced. Society didn't fully accept that there could be "life" beyond this planet. Deep within, the ability to see what the human eye couldn't made me feel limitless, both physically and spiritually, but I didn't know how to explain what I saw or felt. During one connection with a race of beings from higher planes, fear set in; fear of the unknown, of the darkness. My spiritual guides and higher self decided then to erase those memories of encountering those civilizations because, otherwise, the flood of information would have been too overwhelming for me to handle at that moment, and I might have veered onto a much steeper path of self-destruction.

I began studying astronomy, quantum physics, neuroscience, epigenetics and nanophysics on my own – time line jumps – always noticing a link between religion and science. Now, I call this link metaphysics; a blend of spirituality and quantum physics. Back then, spirituality was the space where "miracles" happened, where the limits of my mind ended.

I then discovered reiki therapy, and through energetic sessions, I began integrating and releasing various blockages, which helped me slowly rediscover this joy. The abilities I'd had since arriving in this plane, clairvoyance and clairsentience, started making sense and gaining intensity. Then I came across Akashic record readings, and in 2022, I decided to deepen my knowledge of this technique alongside reiki therapy and quantum regression, taking courses with mentors specialized in these three healing tools and techniques.

These three tools helped me heal more deeply, pulling me out of the chronic depression, prolonged anxiety and daily panic attacks that had accompanied me. At the end of 2023, my higher self guided me to a new school of energetic healing and another course on studying the Akashic field using a different technique. There, I discovered souls who shared stories similar to mine, each with their own path to spiritual awakening. Within this group, I connected with wonderful souls, feeling understood and accepted as I am, without judgment or criticism for not being *like everyone else*. Here, the definitive breaking of the "chains" that held me in self-doubt and fear of accepting myself as I am took place. I realized I'm a normal human being, perfect just as I am, and I don't need to try to fit into society's accepted standards anymore.

With many souls in this group, I had deep connections; ties from other existences and past lives, from other planes and existences as ET civilizations. Here, within this "family", I experienced a stronger evolution, managing to release traumatic experiences from other lives and close karmic cycles, through lessons and experiences that taught me to see and accept my inner power.

Today, in the present, I've fully embraced my power as a creator. I've understood that all the dynamics and experiences I've lived through were created and built by me, helping me gain a deeper understanding of life. I realized that only I can save myself, from within, and that no one and nothing outside me is to blame for what I was experiencing.

The lessons and insights gained from this profound awakening are as follows:

- Self-knowledge brought me clarity.
  Exploring my own identity and life's meaning led me to live authentically.
  Reflection: *How well do I truly know myself?*

- Suffering led me to growth.
  Difficult moments are opportunities I've learned from.
  Reflection: *How would I transform suffering into growth?*

- Spirituality and science can coexist offering me different perspectives.
  Reflection: *What's my relationship with spirituality and science?*

- Authenticity is liberating.
  Accepting myself, as I am truly balanced with my inner peace.
  Reflection: *How authentically do I live?*

- I am responsible for my own life.
  I choose to be aware of my thoughts and actions that shape my reality.
  Reflection: *Do I fully take responsibility for my life?*

- Community and support are essential.
  Authentic connections helped me heal.
  Reflection: *Do I have a supportive community?*

- Darkness taught me to appreciate the light.
  Every tough experience was a valuable lesson.
  Reflection: *How do I perceive my own moments of darkness?*

- Inner power is the key to change.
  True transformation comes from embracing my own strength and capacity for self-healing.
  Reflection: *Do I believe in my inner power?*

How many times have you fallen into the same trap, believing someone is punishing you instead of taking responsibility for your own creation?

Every obstacle or difficulty you encounter in this life is a blessing, no matter how unfair or painful it may seem. In the beginning, there was darkness, but if I hadn't perceived the darkness, I couldn't have accepted the presence of light, just as light cannot understand darkness without crossing through it. These situations are opportunities for moral and spiritual growth, all lessons chosen by our soul before we were born. You just need to accept that everything is part of a higher plan and allow yourself to rediscover yourself; to understand your purpose, mission and the lessons you chose to learn.

Life shouldn't be taken too seriously because it's all a game. When you truly find yourself and realize that the only love and savior is you, then you can live a happier, more harmonious and prosperous life.

*Where am I now?*

I'm not lost but in a continuous process of becoming. Every fall has strengthened me, every wound has taught me something, and every separation has brought me closer to myself.

Happiness doesn't come from the outside, but from living in your truth. And if you feel lost, misunderstood, and adrift, remember – nothing is by chance. Until then, breathe. Live. Trust. Everything falls into place exactly as it should. Everything makes sense. And one day, you'll look back and realize nothing was random, and that you are more than you were ever taught to believe.

What have you learned from your own struggles? If you knew that every obstacle is, in fact, a gift, how differently would you start looking at life?

This was the story of a traveler through space and time, living a simple human life with ups and downs in the USA. To you, the reader who resonated with my story, thank you for making it to the end. I embrace you infinitely with much love and light, and I want you to always remember that YOU ARE PERFECT just as you are. Don't let thoughts or fears define you. Within you lies that divine light waiting to be discovered. Never give up. You are enough, worthy and loved – ALWAYS!

# Victoria Basil

Victoria Basil is a channeler for higher multidimensional beings—affectionately called star people—and an energetic healer mentoring heart-centered souls on their spiritual path. Certified in the Akashic Records and Dolores Cannon's Quantum Healing Hypnosis Technique (QHHT), she is also a quantum reader. Her unique Body Scan & Healing Technique draws on her extrasensory ability to perceive and energetically heal organs, neurons, DNA, and more through consciousness.

She also developed Megaquantic Reading, a groundbreaking method distinct from quantum reading and unknown to science. As founder of Infinity Triangle, Victoria has supported hundreds through channeling, daily mentoring, and guidance from star people. She helps clients activate their abilities, uncover purpose, and step into their power.

Victoria collaborates with a master artist to bring through channeled images from light beings. She has proposed two original theories in quantum physics and is an experienced earth grid worker with the ability to shift timelines. An avid hiker, she's explored all 50 U.S. states and most national parks. Her first book, *Infinity Triangle: Star People's Wisdom Channeled*, will launch internationally in five languages in September 2025.

⊕ www.infinitytriangle.net
◎ @infinitytrianglestar
Scan QR code to learn more about Victoria Basil.

chapter

# 32

# Rising From Hell and the Infinite Power in Our Bodies

*By Desi Dimitrova*

## *A New Vision: Seeing the World Through Fresh Eyes*

I don't know what *hell* is but in our physical world and bodies we live in – we *feel*.

We can feel all kinds of pain; physical, emotional or in our minds. In fact, as strange as it may sound to many of you, most pain will start in our mind first, and I have experienced it myself. Before getting my real diagnosis, one pain specialist presumed that *my mind* was the root of my back and neck pain. She suggested I read some books and they were all about *the illusion of pain we create in our minds*. Well, she basically undermined my experiences, thinking I was making up the story of my pain!

But after the MRIs, she completely let me go, saying, "You are not my specialty, you need to see a neurosurgeon." They had found a very rare tumor in my spinal cord, neck area (an ependymoma), obviously causing the unexplainable symptoms I'd been experiencing; inability to sleep from neck pain, chest and back tightness, even heart function abnormalities, lack of energy to even walk. My PCP was amazed because I was only thirty-eight at the time.

My mind though was, and still is, a very strong creator of reality. However, even though we were a very fortunate, happy family on the outside – blessed with a new house in a good neighborhood, cars, a successful business – my soul was not happy. In fact, my soul was screaming to get out of the cage and enjoy each precious moment of life. My life was all about serving my family, and I did nothing to feed my soul. Though I did take a small step towards my desires by taking yoga teacher training in 2016; I found these practices were very helpful for me. I wanted to help others by teaching these gems of wisdom too.

In fact, my whole life here in America was due to the spiritual voice I had heard in 2006. That year, I met my first yoga teacher, and after applying breathing practices, I connected to my inner voice and started asking myself the big questions of life. *What is life really about? There must be something more than sitting behind a desk and a computer all day long, five days a week.* My soul was starting to awaken... slowly.

My son was only three years old and my daughter was seven when I became a student to train as a yoga teacher. And so, I would only train on the weekends, when my husband was at home taking care of the kids.

This was the first time I was aligned with what I was going to do for others and myself, moving me spiritually in the right direction. I had so many deep realizations during that year of yoga teacher training. It was brought to my mind that my daughter and I should do something together. I imagined we would sing a song together. (This is still in my dreams – perhaps when she outgrows her teen years.) God places people in our lives so we can help each other grow. We can see ourselves in our closest ones as they are our mirrors, sometimes showing us aspects about ourselves we don't like to see or even accept.

My yoga training has helped me tremendously with my recovery. I will intuitively move into poses I know and my body will slowly be able to do all the things it was able to do before. After my surgery, I wasn't sure I would ever be in downward-dog again without feeling pain somewhere in my back or neck. But I realized one thing; *our bodies are self-sustainable machines!*

They know how to heal, if only we get out of the way and allow time. One thing I started doing every morning, after my experience where I lost my body temporarily, is to express gratitude for my body. I thank every cell for working hard for me every day. I talk to my body. One morning, as I did my breathing practice, laying down on the floor – as I often was after surgery, being in pain, suffering with low energy – I passionately said to my body, with all my heart: *Come on, we can do this together,* my voice screaming inside, *Let's rise, let's move, we've got this, we can do it, we can move on!*

Five years later, and to this day, as I write, I never fail to express gratitude to my body first thing every morning.

Your body is your temple. Before you thank something else, honor your body, as divine God and the infinite energy of creation resides in every cell in your body. From here, the question arises; *How do I take care of this temple of mine that carries me through my life, from place to place, every day?* We often look for external advice to "fix" our bodies, as we allow our negligence over many years, and our lost connection to nature, to lead to imbalances of all sorts. I have studied the ancient wisdom for a balanced lifestyle and am passionate to share this with others. For everyone who is serious about taking the step of getting their life in the direction they say they want to go – be it physical, mental or emotional – please know it's all possible... and I am a living proof of that.

There is unstoppable force within us and once we decide to harness it, we become unstoppable, or as the great Tony Robbins says, "unshakable."

When I was diagnosed with my spinal cord tumor, my shift to empowerment and fearlessness began. I've gained so much *fearlessness,* that nowadays my kids sometimes tell me they feel embarrassed if I have too much fun and joke too much, when we are out and about. I try to turn every moment into a good experience by adding lightness and effortless energy into all I do. Interestingly, that sometimes can make other people jealous or even angry, as I have fun like a child. I have learned not to hold on to bad moments that inevitably happen sometimes. I just live life, without stressing myself too much... about anything. I have adopted the teenagers" mindset of "I don't care" and find it very helpful because it counterbalances my nature. *I care about everything, and I can fix and help everyone* – that is my natural state – helping. So, I have learned to say "no." With that said, have in mind that it takes hundreds of hours of meditation and breathing practice to live this way. As with everything else, consistency and dedication are the key.

When my body went through ten hours of surgery, I was put to sleep, so as not to feel anything, and remember all the drilling, cutting and digging in my neck, muscles, tissues and bones. To allow more flexibility to my neck, they even took facia (tissue) from my lower back and added it to my neck. It feels unreal to say this now, that a body can actually recover after something like that. Honestly, it's hard to believe I have a functioning, normal-looking human body knowing what it went through. (Chronic issues my neck and back are now my new normal and numbness from my neck down.) After I woke up from the anesthesia, I could hardly move any part of my mostly numb body! I was so weak, as I had also lost muscle strength for the months prior to surgery, as I did not walk or move much. I would spend my days in bed, though I was not able to sleep from the pain.

With all this in mind, I have to say I was so happy to open my eyes when the anesthetic started to release my body. But before even opening my eyes, my conscious mind awakened. When that happened, I had a profound feeling of *immense gratitude*. It is hard to express with words how strong this feeling was. It was gratitude and infinite joy to be alive. I called for my mom and husband, and when I did not hear them in the room, I felt irritated that they were not there, although I knew they were in the hospital.

My path from victimhood to living a victorious life I call *a path to greatness*. I realized the greatness, the power I was looking to find from outside was actually within me. My proof for that is the moment I started to use my own hands to heal my neck. Nothing, I mean nothing else I tried, was giving me positive results. For years, MRIs kept showing a slight increase in the size of my cyst. This was a cyst that appeared three to four months after the complete removal of the tumor. I was given orders to have a scan every eight months, though the scans were bad for my kidneys and I wanted to avoid them as much as I could.

Regardless of years of trying different diets, energy healings of all sorts, even magical chanellers of celestial beings, there still showed a slight increase in the size of the cyst. Nothing seemed to work. I was often going through ups and downs in my mind, replaying fearful thoughts of the worst-case scenarios. When I was not meditating, negative thoughts would creep in, so I meditated a lot.

I have no idea what to do to stop or reverse the regrowth, but I have trained my mind with meditation, over time, to settle and move into a state of expanded consciousness, joy and peace. It has become my natural state. The most important thing here for you to understand is that after countless hours of meditation, I experienced a beautiful feeling when I was in a very deep, relaxed, meditative state. I felt warm waves all over my body. It felt amazing. I think I felt pure love of the creator: divine love. It's like a warm hug from a good friend but multiplied by a thousand. Imagine that kind of warm energy flowing through your entire being. Something was happening, and yet I didn't know what or why. I craved to have this feeling again. I was enlightened. I didn't know it at the time but realized it months later, in my Chopra meditation teacher training.

With this training, I dove deep into the roots of spirituality of all the masters of ancient vedic wisdoms and spiritual teachings, and all they gifted us; dharma, consciousness, dreams and reality, what is *really real*. Those topics, often hard to digest, expanded my awareness and understanding of my experiences.

My biggest lesson and takeaway from this is what I want to teach others: *Enlightenment means being light*. This is so profound! *How can anyone be light about all the suffering they are going through in life?* Is it even possible? Yes, it is! Knowing we can decrease our human sufferings, the things we all tend to attach to and to believe are true, is liberating... don't you think? We tend to believe our negative thoughts (conditioned mind), and we live in fear instead of in love.

Love is our natural birth state. A newborn baby's mind is like a blank piece of paper... and then the stories and experiences begin the conditioning and we start to forget who we are in our essence.

I realize now it is all the experiences we wanted to experience, no matter how hard they may seem. Our soul, who we really are, never dies and takes steps to do what has not been experienced before. But in order to step into our powers, we truly need to learn to honor and love ourselves. And *why?* you may ask... because loving the self is loving God, who lives inside of you. Your soul is part of God. Until we tap into the liberation of the soul's desires our lives never feel fulfilled. Honoring and following your inner voice is truly the only thing that matters in our life.

Oftentimes, people on their deathbed regret that they didn't follow their dreams. "If I only had the courage to do what I wanted," they say.

So did I follow my heart? Well, after the surgery, I stated to my mom, "From now on I am going to do whatever I want. I will eat whatever I want and stop listening to others telling me what to do." I started by feeling what my body needs. If I pay attention to my body and my needs, this is when I come to a more normal, healthy state. When I started to function as most people do, I almost got back into the trap of losing my goals and prioritizing work over my own wellbeing. But I catch myself! With my awareness now expanded, I can sense when I'm stressed and take steps to correct my priorities, which is, as wise people say, all about balance. But balance is, of course, different for different people. Some people can handle more stimulus than others, who are more sensitive.

So do we teach our kids to live a life of balance? We live in an era where, from a young age, we were taught to strive for success... and success equals money. Our parents' idea was that you need to go to school to get smart, to find a good job and to be successful in life. For me, this kind of success is often the opposite of living a joyful life. It's wrong from the very core. Our motivation is based on social norms for success, or our parental view of it. But they didn't know better. My generation of people have started to realize they are not happy because money doesn't really give them the fulfillment they need. The soul feels empty.

Living a life guided by anything else but your soul is a definite path to suffering. I experienced it myself. But what would my life be if, from a young age, my family, society and our schools were nurturing my talents? What if they were not living from a scarcity mindset but teaching me to explore and find my talents and practice them daily? Imagine the power of humans living in alignment with who they came here to be. The expression of joy would shine upon everyone. What a wonderful world it will be! I believe this is the future for all of the world and humans.

I see too many people tired and depressed, all over the world, in their middle-age looking for an outlet for their stress, looking for support to change their lives, eagerly dreaming to connect with other like-minded individuals and to have meaningful conversations while forgetting their reality for a moment. Why? Because being disconnected with your true self, true guidance and true purpose for many years leads to a person whose soul can no longer take it. When we don't connect to hear our soul's voice, it will sometimes have to stop you in a harsh way, so you can hear it. For me, it was exactly like that. I will sometimes hear a quiet voice inside but the habit *to not listen* will easily disregard it. I will let my mind and software run the show of my life.

Any software that needs an upgrade can only happen through expanding awareness. My voice, the inner voice, my guiding light was shut down from childhood. I was constantly told to stay quiet. I was not accepted as I was. They found me strange and didn't approve of my ways of wanting to live. My parents praised my sister and wished I was as good as her. She cooked and wanted to help in the house, while household chores were averse to me. I had my inner child wanting but dreading to dance, to paint or to heal others. I did not realize why people did things that were not good for their bodies and why they would harm themselves by drinking or eating too much. My five-year-old brain didn't get why people hurt their own bodies. I wanted to help them! I wanted to tell them to stop. Nobody allowed a little child, a girl to give them advice; she was small but an old soul and so she was wise. I learned people change when they are ready to take the step on their own and helping them without being asked only has adverse effect.

So are you ready? Do you want to take the steps needed to create the life you deserve, live and dream about?

# Desislava Dimitrova

Desislava Dimitrova is a dedicated holistic health consultant, renowned for her intuitive and healing abilities. With a deep passion for empowering mothers, she guides them toward a lifestyle filled with joy and fulfillment. Clients often describe her as both practical and nurturing, embodying the essence of a compassionate mentor.

Desislava takes a personalized approach, addressing the mind, body and spirit with a wealth of knowledge grounded in various healing modalities, complemented by her own life experiences. She specializes in working with mid-aged professional and businesswomen grappling with overwhelm, stress and a sense of lost purpose. Through her gentle guidance, she helps them rediscover their inner peace, clear away obstacles and take inspired action with newfound confidence and clarity.

Creating a calm and safe space for transformation, Desislava offers tailored programs, insightful teachings and practical advice that resonate with each individual's unique journey. Her diverse certifications include spiritual life coach, theta healing practitioner, free mE EFT practitioner, yoga teacher, soulful card reader, chopra meditation teacher and Vedic health practitioner and coach.

If you're ready to transition from feeling stuck to living your dreams, Desislava is here to support you every step of the way. You deserve to embrace a life filled with joy, and she would be honored to help you reach your aspirations swiftly.

⊕ www.desi-divine.com
Scan QR code to learn more about Desislava Dimitrova.

# Afterword

Hello friend,

If you've made it here, something inside you has been stirred. Maybe even softened. Maybe even set free.

That was always the purpose of this book...not to tell you what awakening looks like, but to remind you that your path is sacred, your pain is valid, and your light is needed.

You've just traveled through stories of deep loss and radiant breakthrough, of courage, surrender, trust, and truth. Now it's your turn.

What story is rising in you?

What light have you dimmed that is ready to shine?

You don't need all the answers to begin again. You just need a willingness to listen to the voice inside that's always been speaking.

Let these stories be a spark...and may your awakened heart lead the way!

You are loved.

David Trotter
Curator / Publisher - Awakened Hearts
Co-founder / Publisher - Awakened Magazine

*P.S., Will you help us spread these stories of awakening around the globe? Simply post a heartfelt review on Amazon and tell a friend about the book. It's that easy!*

# David Trotter

David Trotter is the curator and publisher of the *Awakened Hearts* book series, a collection of transformational anthologies featuring stories of spiritual awakening, healing, and personal growth. He is also the co-founder and publisher of *Awakened Magazine* (alongside his partner Mandy Adams), and the creator of *Awakened Lifestyle*, an online directory connecting conscious leaders, healers, and coaches with seekers around the world.

David is the author of a dozen books—including *Empowered to Rise* and *Superconscious Conversations*—and the producer/director of four award-winning feature films on meaningful social issues including orphans in India, trafficking in the United States, and LGBTQ inclusion within faith-based communities.

Earlier in his journey, David spent over a decade as a pastor before stepping beyond traditional ministry to embrace a more expansive spiritual path. He holds a B.A. in Pastoral Ministries and an M.A. (abt) in Church Leadership from Vanguard University, along with an M.A. in Cross-Cultural Studies from Fuller Theological Seminary.

He is also a Certified Breathwork and Guided Meditation Facilitator and regularly leads sessions at Behind the Lids Healing Collective in Costa Mesa, California.

⊕ www.awakenedmagazine.com
◎ @awakenedmagazine
Scan QR code to learn more about Awakened Magazine.

If this book stirred your soul, just wait for what's next.
Awakened Hearts #2 brings even more powerful stories of
transformation to inspire your own awakening and ascension.

More Information:
www.awakenedmagazine.com/awakenedhearts

www.ingramcontent.com/pod-product-compliance
Lightning Source LLC
Chambersburg PA
CBHW070127080526
44586CB00015B/1586